ISLAM, THE PEOPLE AND THE STATE

Essays on Political Ideas and Movements in the Middle East

SAMI ZUBAIDA

I.B.Tauris & Co. Ltd
Publishers
London · New York

Published in a revised paperback
edition in 1993 by
I.B.Tauris & Co Ltd
45 Bloomsbury Square
London WC1A 2HY

175 Fifth Avenue
New York
NY 10010

In the United States of America
and Canada distributed by
St Martin's Press
175 Fifth Avenue
New York
NY 10010

First published in hardback by Routledge, London and New York

A full CIP record for this book is available from
the British Library

A full CIP record for this book is available from
the Library of Congress

ISBN 1–85043–734–3

Printed and bound in Great Britain by
WBC Ltd, Bridgend, Mid Glamorgan

Contents

Acknowledgments

Some of the papers in this volume were previously published, others presented at conferences and symposia.

'The Ideological Preconditions for Khomeini's Doctrine of Government' (Chapter 1) was published in *Economy and Society*, vol. 11, no. 2, 1982. I am grateful to the Editors and the Publishers for permission to reprint.

'The quest for the Islamic state: Islamic fundamentalism in Egypt and Iran' (Chapter 2) appeared in Lionel Caplan (ed.), *Studies in Religious Fundamentalism*, Macmillan, London, 1987. Permission from the publishers to reprint in this collection is gratefully acknowledged. The paper was first presented to a seminar on religious fundamentalisms organised by Lionel Caplan at the Department of Social Anthropology, School of Oriental and African Studies, London. The later version of the paper benefited considerably from the comments and suggestions made in the seminar discussion. Thanks are also due to Lionel Caplan for his editorial comments.

A previous version of 'Classes as political actors in the Iranian revolution' (Chapter 3) was presented at the World Congress of Political Science in Paris, July 1985. It was also presented at the Iranian history seminar at St Antony's College, Oxford in February 1986. The discussions on both occasions were helpful in identifying problems and issues. I am particularly grateful to Ali Ghayseri for reading the paper and making valuable comments.

'Class and community in urban politics' (Chapter 4) was first presented to the Franco-British Symposium on Arab and Muslim Cities: the State, Urban Crises and Social Movements, Paris, May 1986, funded by the Franco-British Programme of CNRS-ESRC. The paper benefited from the discussions at that Symposium. A version of it will be published in the Proceedings of the Symposium.

'Components of popular culture in the Middle East' (Chapter 5) first appeared in Georg Stauth and Sami Zubaida (eds), *Mass Culture, Popular Culture and Social Life in the Middle East*, Campus Verlag, Frankfurt and Westview Press, Colorado, 1987. I am grateful to Campus Verlag for permission to reprint here. I am also grateful to Georg Stauth for his editorial comments, and to the members of the seminar organised by him at the University of

Bielefeld in February 1985, where an earlier version of the paper was presented, for their contributions to the discussion.

'The nation state in the Middle East,' (Chapter 6), written specially for this book, was started in April-May 1987 at the Institute de Recherches et d'Études sur le Monde Arabe et Musulman, CNRS, Aix-en-Provence, to which I was attached for that period. It owes much to the discussions I had with many colleagues there and to the excellent facilities offered by the Library and the documentation services at the Institute. I am grateful to André Raymond, Director of the Institute, and to the many researchers, librarians and documentalists there who offered so much help and advice.

In 1981-4, I carried out a research project jointly with Abbas Vali on 'Religion and the Intelligentsia in the 1979 Iranian Revolution', funded by the Economic and Social Research Council. A considerable input from that research has entered into the essays in this book. I am grateful to Abbas Vali's contributions to that research, and for his many helpful comments on various papers in this volume. I am also grateful to ESRC for funding this research, and to their joint programme with CNRS for funding two Symposia on Arab and Muslim Cities in 1984-6 which have contributed much to my work on the subject.

In December 1982 - January 1983, I was visiting Professor at the American University of Cairo. There I benefited greatly from discussions, materials and references on the Islamic movements in Egypt. I am particularly grateful to Professor Saad Eddin Ibrahim for his generous help.

I am happy to acknowledge my debt to the many friends and colleagues in the Middle East Study Group. Some of the papers in this volume started as informal notes presented to meetings of this Group. The lively and critical discussions on these and many other topics have proved to be such a valuable stimulus over the years.

Talal Asad, Ken Brown, Paul Hirst, Terry Johnson and Roger Owen, have each read one or more of these papers and made valuable comments. I am particularly grateful to Paul Hirst for his help and advice in putting this book together.

Introduction

The prominence of Islamic politics in the Middle East in recent decades, notably the Iranian revolution and its ramifications, has raised important questions regarding society, politics and culture. This apparent retreat from modernity posed a challenge to the main theoretical positions in the social sciences, from Marxism to modernisation theory to dependency theory, and they all responded with various attempts at interpretation. The only position which appeared vindicated was that of traditional 'orientalism' which held 'Islamic' society and culture to be *essentially* distinct from Europe and impervious to the superficial grafts of European politics and culture; the 'return of Islam' would then be read as the assertion and triumph of this distinct essence. A regular theme in the essays contained in this volume is to challenge this essentialism, and to argue that the Islamic phenomenon in politics is the product of particular political and socio-economic conjunctures, and that the success of the Islamic revolution in Iran is a major (if not *the* major) factor in these conjunctures. Moreover, current Islamic movements and ideas are not the product of some essential continuity with the past, but are basically 'modern'. Even when they explicitly reject all modern political models as alien imports from a hostile West, their various political ideas, organisations and aspirations are implicitly premised upon the models and assumptions of modern nation-state politics.

The essays in this volume were written over the years since the Iranian revolution of 1979 placed Islamic politics firmly on the agenda for the study of the contemporary Middle East. It brought the term 'Islamic fundamentalism' into wide currency in the academic and political discourses of the West, and posed it as an enigma and a challenge. The first two essays were, in part, responses to this currency, attempting to problematise the term, and to show that this 'fundamentalism' is modern, and can best be understood in terms of the concepts and assumptions of modern political ideas associated with models of the nation and the nation state. The first is an attempt to situate Khomeini's doctrine of government, *velayat-e-faqih*[1] (the guardianship of the jurist), in the history of Islamic political thought and practice, and to underline its innovations and dependence on modern political assumptions, in spite of its seeming total containment within traditional Shi'i discourses. The second, originally written for a series of seminars on 'fundamentalisms', and subsequently published in a collection of papers from these seminars (see Acknowledgments), contains a survey of the development of strands of Islamic political thought and movements in the recent history of Egypt, then contrasting this picture with Islamic politics in Iran. Inevitably, there is some overlap in the arguments and examples in these two papers. For the reasons given in these two papers, the term 'fundamentalism' is then abandoned, in favour of the more general and less ambiguous 'political Islam'.

The two papers constituting Chapters 3 and 4 have a common concern with conceptions of political actors and constituencies in terms of socio-economically constituted entities of 'class' and 'community'. The first takes up this problem with respect to class explanations of the Iranian revolution, in both their Marxist and more general sociological forms. The logic of these forms of explanation is critically examined. It is argued that the political field itself plays a very important part in the constitution of political actors and forces, and that these are not given to the political level already constituted at the socio-economic. In Chapter 4 a similar argument is extended to examples of urban politics and social movements in other parts of the region.

Chapter 5, on aspects of popular culture in the Middle East, traces common themes and elements in the popular cultures of the region which cut across boundaries of nationality, ethnicity and religion. These common themes and practices are paradoxical when considered in relation to the conventional characterisations of Middle Eastern societies as fragmented into well bounded communities based on religion, ethnicity, regional, tribal and occupational affiliations. The 'purification' of this syncretistic and heterodox popular culture then becomes part of the political projects of both nationalism and of political Islam. This consideration of popular culture in relation to religion and politics has clear implications for the question of imputed religio-political consciousness and allegiance of 'the people', and, therefore, to the general question of essentialist conceptions of Middle Eastern history and politics.

These five papers were written in various contexts, mostly as contributions to seminars and conferences. Chapter 6 is a much longer paper written specifically for this book. It brings together thematic strands from the other papers and focuses them on the question of the state and the political field in the Middle East. It considers the challenge posed for the concept and model of the modern nation state by the recent salience of Islamic politics, both at the level of the Islamic political ideologies themselves, and in the revival of essentialist cultural explanations among some Western students of the region. It is argued that the model of the nation state and associated political concepts and practices, products of Western history, and widely diffused throughout the world, while they do not produce replicas of the Western states in the Middle East, or anywhere else, have nevertheless structured the institutional and ideational construction of politics in these countries. These models are based on socio-economic and cultural transformations, which are the conditions for operation of political models and processes, including the Islamic ones, however much these might explicitly oppose 'imported' models. These developments can best be understood in terms of general socio-economic processes of a generic political sociology, rather than in terms of historico-cultural essences perpetuating a historical continuity of mentalities and institutions. I wrote this paper during and soon after two months spent in France (see Acknowledgments) where I found many exciting recent works highly relevant to my current thinking and writing. This explains why the arguments of this paper are developed predominantly in relation to French material. The introduction of this material to the English reader is an added advantage.

Notes

1 *Velayat-e-faqih* is the Persian form used in all the essays except for Chapter 1 where the Arabic *wilayat al-faqih* is used. This is because the discussion in Chapter I refers to the Arabic text of Khomeini's book on Islamic government.

Introduction to the second edition

The continuing advance of the 'Islamic current' since the first publication of these essays has appeared to many observers and writers, in the Middle East and in the West, as a confirmation of the neo-orientalist accounts of 'Muslim society', that is one in which social patterns, mentalities and moralities emanate from a continuous historical essence of Islam. This has enhanced the tendency to read history backwards and to ignore or dismiss the secular and secularising forces, institutions and practices in the modern history of the Middle East and the lengthy episodes in which nationalist, liberal and leftist politics predominated. It obscures the fact that behind religious rhetoric and symbolism, social and political practice remains, for the most part, unrelated to religion, notably in the Islamic Republic of Iran.

This is not the place to present a systematic account of relevant developments in the region since the first publication of this book, nor to review the large volume of literature on the subject which has appeared since. I shall take up just a few key points of concern to the arguments in the essays that follow.

Islamic Politics

First, we have the fact of the overwhelming success of Islamic political movements in many countries in the organisation and mobilisation of mass popular support. The most spectacular case has been in Algeria, where in 1991 the Front Islamique du Salut (FIS) gained massive electoral support (though with only about half the electorate voting), a success which led to its suppression. The suppressed organisation is now waging a war of assassinations and terrorism against the regime and official targets which can only succeed with considerable popular support and complicity.

In Egypt, the Islamists have scored popular successes on many fronts. The 'respectable' branch represented by the Muslim Brotherhood has had considerable electoral and parliamentary success within the limits of Egyptian democracy. It has also succeeded in controlling the professional syndicates through elections to their executive councils (a success which the government is now attempting to reverse or control through ad hoc legislation). Also of great significance is the conversion of considerable sectors of the official religious establishment, including leading figures in al-Azhar, formerly subservient to the state (see Chapters 2 and 6), to political militancy in line with the Brotherhood. Through this conversion, the Islamic current now enjoys considerable control over the broadcasting media, as well as the power to censor books and periodicals in the interests of ethical conformity and religious orthodoxy. Add to this sympathies and collusions within the ranks of government bureaucracy, the judiciary (with notable exceptions) and the armed forces, and you have important sources of social power within the frameworks and networks of Islamic politics. The more militant and violent ('terrorist') branches of *Jihad* and the *Jama'at Islamiyya* reinforce these powers at the popular level by imposing their control and organisation on popular urban quarters.

We can continue with examples from other countries: Jordan, where the cautious experiment in democracy brought the Islamists into parliament in considerable numbers; Palestine where HAMAS and *Jihad* are enjoying increasing popular support at the expense of the PLO; and the very different case of Sudan, where a highly repressive Islamic regime has been imposed through a military coup.

This seemingly unstoppable progress of Islamic politics in so many countries in the region at the same time lends *prima facie* plausibility to the essentialist positions contested in this book. Ernest Gellner, a notable and influential exponent of a particular version of the essentialist position, has repeated his well-known arguments in a recent book.[1] The 'High Culture' of the urban ulama and bourgeoisie, of scriptural, puritanical Islam (which Gellner contends was characteristic of the urban history of the whole Islamic world) is, under modern conditions of political centralisation, urbanisation, mass education and communication, appropriated at a much wider popular level. Its egalitarian and puritanical ethos is well suited to the requirements of modernity, and reformed Islam has been at the base of modern nationalism. This High Culture Islam constitutes within its revelations and doctrines legal, political and social prescriptions, a unitary normative order which is valid for all times. Modern political Islam, then, is the demand for the realisation of this norm, and the popular support it enjoys stems from the aspiration to the High Culture by the newly urbanised masses. This, argues Gellner, is entirely congruent with the requirements of industrialisation and of political modernity, contrary to the previously dominant assumptions of social theory that modernity requires secularisation.

In Gellner's version of essentialism, Islam is affected by one historical process, *the* world historical process, of industrialisation, urbanisation and their consequences. 'Before' and 'after' we have social/normative totalities whose attributes are expressions of the Islamic essence. Otherwise they have no history, no variety, and are not subject to analysis in terms of the general concepts of sociology and politics: they write their own political sociology.

An example of an interesting explanation offered in terms of this framework is the following:

> . . . this inner intensity [of 'divine nomocracy'] can be kept alive even after independence, fed by the jealousy felt by the lower urban orders when contemplating their co-national, co-religious, but nevertheless inevitably more or less westernised rulers. These lower urban orders continue to be politically impotent even after independence, and can only console or express themselves in terms of their Islamic purity: for a nationalist expression of the *ressentiment* is no longer open to them.[2]

There is an important insight in this formulation, but are the essentialist assumptions from which they proceed necessary? *Ressentiment* against westernised compatriots is a powerful component of popular sentiments. The question, however, is why do they find their expression in Islamic politics? Gellner's answer is clear: it is part of the essential nature of 'Muslim Society', albeit under modern conditions. But this is to forget or ignore that these frustrations, aspirations and discontents had found (and continue to find in many cases) their expressions in secular nationalist and leftist forms before, during and long after independence. Nasserism, Ba'thism, communism and liberalism, as well as various Islamic trends, are features of contested political fields in independent and 'revolutionary' Egypt, Iraq, Iran, Syria and elsewhere. These are not part of some basic pattern of 'Muslim society' but differentiated social forces expressing their aspirations in terms of various political ideologies and contests. As for 'nomocracy' and ulama culture, I argue in the chapters that follow that the various modern Islamic political currents have not been continuations of historical forms. Some of the ulama in Egypt, as recounted above, are now following political Islamic currents which originated outside their culture, and often in antagonism to it. And part of the reason for their conversion is the bandwagon effect of success, of seeming government retreat, and of the vociferous calls for the application of the *shari'a*. In effect the ulama are afraid of being left behind: 'The *shari'a*,' they are saying 'that is us!'

At the root of the 'Islamic phenomenon' are the well-known economic and demographic problems and the policy dilemmas they pose for government. Continuing increase in population, especially in the younger age groups; ramshackle education systems; stagnant economies with vast debt problems, further burdened with rampant corruption and mismanagement; mounting unemployment, under-employment and dead-end low pay jobs; overburdened and corrupt social services. There is a withdrawal of the state from some of these arenas, unable to cope with the mounting burdens. This is where the Islamic economic and social sectors are moving in to provide services and aid, partly as charitable associations, but mostly making modest charges. The existence of an Islamic economic sector in the form of banks, investment companies and commercial enterprises also provides avenues for jobs, businesses and advancement for a wide range of people. This is an important avenue for building up networks of patronage, religious orthodoxy and political mobilisation. This phenomenon is widespread in Egypt, Sudan, Algeria and Tunisia, and in Gaza and the West Bank.

This area of 'social Islam' was little explored in the first edition of this book.[3] In Egypt it has emerged as a major area of activism for both the respectable Muslim Brotherhood and the militant *Jihad* and *Jama'at*. These latter were characterised in Chapter 2 as 'messianic' with little in the way of political strategy, but an affinity to the spectacular gesture. I also anticipated, however, that this could not continue if the organisations were to survive. In fact they have evolved two lines of strategy: one is communal entrenchment, by seeking to impose their authority and discipline on particular urban quarters which form the bases of their power. Providing social and communal services is part of this strategy. The other is that of armed confrontation with the security services and what they consider hostile or anti-Islamic targets.

It is important to point out that the phenomenon of social Islam does not represent a continuation or recreation of an 'authentic' Muslim community, part of the supposed essential pattern of mentalities and social forms, but, on the contrary, a response to the breakdown of traditional communities. The processes of urbanisation, population migrations, and the expansion of shanty towns and informal quarters, have all surely led to the attenuation or disappearance of many communal bonds,[4] save, perhaps, those of close kinship. Communal authorities such as shaykhs and notables have been separated from the poor as part of the social differentiations of habitat. The political patronage of ruling parties and local bosses does not reach beyond a few mostly privileged middle-class sectors. It is into this vacuum of organisation and power that the Islamic groups have stepped to impose their authority and discipline. The organisation they impose is not one of popular participation. The activists and the militants remain in charge, and the common people, to whom they provide services against modest payments, are considered as subjects of ethical reform, to be converted to orthodox conformity and mobilised in political support. This politically oriented communal authoritarianism has peculiarly modern conditions. Its leaders and agents are drawn from the proletarianised intelligentsia of students, teachers, functionaries and the many unemployed graduates who constitute the ideological class *par excellence*, the class that leads and agitates in all ideological contests. At present in Egypt and elsewhere, this class is predominantly Islamic in orientation, as much as earlier generations were Nasserist or leftist. Neither they nor the common people they attempt to control and mobilise are following historically conditioned Islamic 'nomocratic' aspirations, but reacting to great hardships, disappointments and disorientations in the one idiom which remains available and untarnished after the fall of their former idols.

The international context and the Gulf War

The social and economic problems, blockages, resentments and frustrations outlined here do not in themselves determine an Islamic response. The question 'Why Islam?' has been posed in the various chapters of this book and answers attempted in terms of the shrinkage or collapse of ideological and political alternatives, and, crucially, in terms of the international conjuncture and the exemplary effect of the Islamic Revolution in Iran in 1979. Events since the time of writing, particularly the collapse of world communism and of Western/American hegemony, as demonstrated in the Gulf War of 1991, have made these answers even more pertinent.

In the political fields of the modern Middle East the contending ideologies, as we have seen, are those of the various secular nationalisms, of varieties of socialism/communism with Marxist and Third Worldist elements, often combinations of the three as in Ba'thism and Nasserism, liberal constitutionalism (exemplified in the Egyptian Wafd) in the earlier stages, and various Islamic currents. The problem for secular nationalism and the left by the 1980s was that they had been compromised by complicity with regimes such as those of the Ba'th and of Nasser, which became identified with tyranny, corruption and mismanagement. Their leaderships and ideologies had been subordinated to and utilised by the ruling cliques, and were consequently tainted. They had become less credible as strategies and solutions. In addition, decades of nationalism, Third Worldism and socialism did not seem to have diminished the subordination of Arabs and Muslims to the Western powers, nor to have succeeded in shifting the dominance of Israel and its occupation of Arab lands. In this context, the Iranian Revolution appeared to be a fresh departure, and one which was genuinely popular. This theme is pursued in the chapters that follow.

The collapse of world communism in the late 1980s and the widely publicised exposure of the corruption, incompetence and mismanagement of its regimes rendered socialism/communism even less credible as a solution or as a slogan of identity and opposition. Furthermore, the Soviet Union as a world power against the West and Israel and a supporter of the Arab national cause also collapsed, and the US and its allies were left dominant on the world stage, as was to be demonstrated in the Gulf War.

The political ramifications of the 'new world order' is not, of course, confined to the Middle East and to Islam. We see in Europe, east and west, the collapse of the old ideological alignments and demarcations of left and right resulting in political disillusionment and cynicism which, in many places, have facilitated ethnic, regional and nationalist identifications. This scenario seems to dominate the political fields in countries as diverse as Italy, Greece and the former Soviet Union, not to mention the former Yugoslavia, and to have important effects in the politics of France and Germany. Political Islam in the Middle East *is* nationalism, and one which appears much more viable and credible than the old tainted nationalisms of the failed authoritarian regimes.

The Gulf War and its ramifications were crucial in reinforcing political Islam as the most potent form of nationalism. Saddam Hussain, despite his bloody and secular record, struck a chord with the popular masses as well as the intelligentsia throughout the region by appealing to Arabism and Islam against the Western ('crusader') invasion. These were not peculiarly Muslim religious sentiments; for Hussain appealed to many staunchly secular intellectuals on the left, and helped facilitate a convergence between secular nationalism and political Islam based on their antagonism to Western domination. Islam, however, for the reasons cited, has become the dominant idiom in this antagonism. The conflict has reinforced the communalist model of international relations, of Christians and Jews against Muslims, as described in Chapters 4 and 6. This is further strengthened by the failure of the UN and its dominant Western members to act in favour of Muslims in Israel–Palestine or Bosnia, when the Jewish Israelis or Christian Serbs failed to comply with UN resolutions, in contrast to the West's readiness to mount massive force against, say, Iraq.

The position of most Arab regimes on the Gulf conflict has further enhanced the credibility of political Islam as the most viable nationalist force. Saudi Arabia and the Gulf regimes reinforced the deep antagonism and resentment felt towards them by most Arabs. More seriously, the clear exposure of their dependence on American protection widened the deficit of legitimacy with their own people, opposition being most commonly articulated in the very Islamic idioms used by the authorities. The bounty of oil may no longer be sufficient to maintain the distributive 'rentier' state (Chapter 6).

The alignment of other leading Arab regimes with the US

and the West in the conflict is indicative of the dilemma they face. Even militant, radical Syria, deprived of its former Soviet protection, had to fall in with the US in the new uni-polar world. The 'peace process' with Israel further exposed the weakness and dependence of the Arab regimes, and this time of the PLO. It became clear that they had no strong cards to play against Israel other than American pressure, which soon slackened under the new Clinton regime. From a nationalist point of view, it would appear that the Arab regimes and the PLO capitulated to American and Israeli dominance, but without gaining any benefits or concessions. It is humiliation without a payoff. What credibility do they have left? Only Islamic Iran appeared to refuse such capitulation and to stand on principle (the Western coalition having conveniently neutralised Iran's main antagonist in the process).

It would appear, then, that the Islamic regimes and the Islamic political currents (notably HAMAS as against the PLO) are the only forces refusing to capitulate or compromise with the US and Israel, the last remaining bastion of nationalism and anti-imperialism, the heirs of Nasser. Where are the alternatives?

Islam, then, is gaining ground as the current idiom in which many social groups are expressing their identities, aspirations and frustrations. It is worth emphasising that it is an *idiom*, in terms of which different and conflicting views and aspirations are being expressed: by some conservative entrepreneurs and rentiers, beneficiaries of Saudi connections and of Sadat's *infitah* (what an Egyptian writer termed *al-infitah al-multahi*, the bearded infitah); by the salaried lower middle classes, especially women, for whom Muslim identification provides a badge of respectability on the edge of poverty and with the conflicting demands of family and work, but who are at the same time often hostile to political Islamists; by alienated youth who are the main activists in the radical and violent *Jama'at*, and some of whom are now speaking the language of 'class', about exploitation and oppression by the first group; and, no doubt, by many others. It is important for us to listen to the discourses of these different groups and to understand their social and political constructions. There is very little research at this level of social life. This is partly due to the difficulty of access, but also because of the preoccupation with other, more visible, political events and episodes.

To say that Islam is being established as a dominant idiom of political expression does not mean that it is not contested. In Iran and Sudan, the Islamic regimes have to rule with a considerable measure of repression. The examples of Algeria and Egypt show clearly that there is crucial resistance to the Islamic currents among important and prominent social sectors: intellectuals, feminists, human rights campaigners, ethnic and religious minorities and ordinary Muslims who do not want to be told how to follow their religion and who value their social liberties. These contests raise another topical question, that of democratisation and human rights.

The question of democratisation

Chapter 6 deals at length with arguments about state and society in the region. One of the central issues is the intrusive, totalitarian state, which derives its power, and in some cases its revenues, from sources outside the society it governs. The question then is: is some form of democracy and pluralism possible? And what are its possible social bases?

A number of countries have moved cautiously in the direction of greater democracy and pluralism, notably Algeria, Jordan and Yemen. Egypt maintained its measure of democracy, best summed up as elections and parliamentary debates which everyone recognises cannot lead to a change of government. The wide powers of the president and the executive are little constrained, in practice, by law or constitution, although there have been notable cases of executive decisions effectively challenged in the courts. Elections in Egypt and Jordan bring Muslim Brotherhood deputies into parliament and into the public debates. There is a feeling that if elections were really free, then Islamic candidates would win a clear majority. This, after all, did happen in Algeria.

The case of Algeria, because it is extreme, is illuminating. A bankrupt and corrupt Front de Libération Nationale (FLN) regime is under considerable strain, with mounting economic difficulties and multiplying factions. An opportunist president, Shadhli, tries a strategy of elections from which the FIS would clearly benefit, hoping to reach an understanding and a compromise with its leaders. He fails: the top brass of the armed forces with sectors of the ruling FLN realise Shadhli's game and pre-empt him and the FIS by cancelling the second round of the vote, deposing the president and imposing their rule. They clearly acted against the incipient democracy, or did they?

Is 'democracy' to be understood simply as a free popular ballot, regardless of the legal and institutional framework? That would surely make a nonsense of democracy, as was clearly happening in Algeria. It would constitute a referendum on choosing the next dictator, who is then not even bound to hold any further such referenda. A first step on the road to democracy must be the establishment of a legal and institutional framework which specifies and protects rights and procedures, which cannot be violated even by an elected government. Democracy can only make sense as part of a 'law state'. What are the prospects, then, for the establishment of some degree of the law state in any of the countries of the region? The way it looks at the time of writing, not very bright.

The threats to human rights and civil liberties in Egypt, Algeria and elsewhere do not emanate only from the state and its organs, but increasingly from the Islamic currents. In Egypt, there is now an Azhar committee which has taken on the right to censor books and publications, mostly successfully and with the acquiescence of the authorities and some publishers. Violence and threats of violence against secularist and critical writers and artists constitute a serious deterrent to free expression, especially when backed by the example of the assassination of the secularist writer and publicist Farag Fauda and the harassment of other writers. Similar threats face independent women in many urban quarters.

The authorities respond to these events with a mixture of compromise and repression. In relation to some aspects of public life in Egypt, notably the broadcasting media, the government has been playing a 'more-Islamic-than-thou' game, with manifestations of piety and censorship of items that might be found offensive to Islam. At the same time it is mounting campaigns of violent repression against the *Jama'at* and *Jihad*, against which their militants retaliate by assassinating security personnel and attacking tourist targets. In both Egypt and Algeria there is now a vicious circle of escalating repression against militant Islamists, who in turn resort to ever higher levels of terrorism. Social peace, which has been a blessing in Egypt for most of its modern history, is now being threatened.

And without social peace there can be no rule of law and no genuine democracy.

The case of Iran

Iran and its Islamic Revolution constitute a recurrent theme of analysis and discussion in the chapters that follow. What can we add now in relation to developments since they were written?

Khomeini's death in 1989 was a watershed in the history of the Revolution. The Revolution and the Islamic Republic were so closely identified with the person of Khomeini. He was the *faqih par excellence*, the one whom the doctrine of *velayet-e faqih* implicitly designated. If this doctrine can be said to have survived him at all, then it has done so in a very weak and diluted form. President Rafsanjani's clever manoeuvre was to ensure the assumption of the post by the relatively minor figure of Khamenei, who had little religious authority or political charisma.

Before his death, Khomeini proclaimed an important ruling with far-reaching constitutional consequences. Early in 1989 he ruled that the Islamic government, acting in the interests of the Islamic community, is empowered to suspend or alter any element of religious rules or worship, even prayer and fasting. *Velayet-e faqih* always contained an element of arbitrariness, in that the ruling *faqih* is the ultimate arbiter of law and practice. With this ruling, this arbitrary discretion is transferred to the executive, in effect to the president. Potentially, both constitution and *shari'a* can be set aside under the rubric of 'interests (*maslaha*) of the community'.

The *shari'a*, then, is not binding on the Islamic government in Iran. Whatever element of the 'law state' may be supposed to exist there can ultimately be abrogated by executive fiat. Can the *shari'a* provide the necessary constitutional system for a law state elsewhere? The main elements of the *shari'a* that have been codified are those of the Ottoman *majalla*, which covers personal status and civil law but not constitutional or public law. In theory, the corpus of arguments and rulings which constitute the *shari'a* can be codified with regard to state law, but is wide open to a variety of constructions, some mutually contradictory. So the codification of the *shari'a* becomes an eminently political matter. Given the authoritarian and illiberal cast of the currently dominant Islamic movements, it is not hard to guess the direction of their legal constructions. And would any conceivable Islamic government in the present conjuncture desist from allowing itself the arbitrary discretion over *any* law which the Iranian government claims? The examples of Saudi Arabia, Libya, Sudan and Zia's Pakistan are not very encouraging.

The political scene in the present world is one that encourages mutual demonisation: Arabs and Jews; the nationalities of the former Soviet Union and Yugoslavia; Islam and the West. The peoples of the Middle East in the modern period are well known for the elaborate conspiracy theories they advance and embroider to explain every event. The Islamic currents excel at this game: the bookshops of Cairo feature a wide array of books exposing Jewish demonic plotting, historically and at the present time. The US has been designated by Khomeini the Great Devil.

Demonisation, however, is not confined to one side. For some of the media and even for some scholars in the West Islam has been a potent source of menacing stereotypes, reinforced now by the paranoia regarding the supposed Muslim 'invasion' of Europe through migration. In this atmosphere it is important for scholars and commentators to break up these monolithic and totalising images of the other. It is important to point out the *diversity* of the so-called 'world of Islam', no less than the diversity of 'the West'. 'Islam' is not a closed and separate world ruled by a peculiar essence, any more than Christianity or Judaism. The current dominance of Islamic politics in the region, like the dominance of Christian politics in Europe in the sixteenth and seventeenth centuries, has to be explained in terms of social forces and political processes, not eternal essences. This is the task to which the following essays are addressed.

London, June 1993

Notes

1 Ernest Gellner, *Postmodernism, Reason and Religion*, London, Routledge 1992, pp 4–22.

2 Ernest Gellner, *Muslim Society*, Cambridge, CUP 1983, p 66.

3 I have since written on these subjects: see my 'The Politics of Islamic Investment' in *BRISMES Bulletin*, 17:2, 1990; and 'Islam, the State and Democracy: Contrasting Conceptions of Civil Society in Egypt', in MERIP *Middle East Report*, No 179, Nov/Dec 1992.

4 Gellner, in the works cited above, also considers these processes of communal dissolution as important factors in the popular spread of Islamic politics. However, he interprets the phenomenon as an emanation of historically based aspirations to the High Culture of the city, whose fulfilment is made possible by the processes of modernity which remove the communal conditions sustaining the Low Cultures.

1

The ideological preconditions for Khomeini's doctrine of government

The term 'fundamentalist Islam' has in recent years acquired wide currency. It is assumed to have a clear reference to a form of Islam which is 'orthodox', scriptural, traditional, which in its political and social applications makes no compromises with 'modern' or Western conditions and ideas. The context of the usage of this term is the success of the 1979 Iranian revolution in establishing an Islamic republic based on 'fundamentalist Islam' and the Islamic political movements in some Arab countries, like the Muslim Brotherhood in Egypt and Syria and the Shi'ite movements in Iraq, also called 'fundamentalist'. In a general sense, the term does have a clear and understandable reference: 'fundamentalist' most commonly refers to those movements and ideologies which insist that a necessary part of the Islamic religion is a form of government (*al-islamu dinun wa dawlatun* – 'Islam is a religion and a state'). An Islamic state must apply the tenets of Islamic doctrine and above all *shari'a* law to *all* aspects of social and economic life. This poses an explicit opposition to most states in Muslim countries, which for the most part operate as secular states with a nominal commitment to Islam. This position is also 'fundamentalist' as distinct from both conservative ulama who have in effect accepted the secular state, and from reformers like Muhammad Abdu (1849-1905) who sought to revitalise Islam in forms compatible with the modern state and economy to ensure 'progress' for the Islamic nations.[1]

In terms of the usage outlined here, the term 'fundamentalist' has a more or less clear meaning, although it should be emphasised that 'fundamentalism' in this sense does not necessarily entail ideological uniformities beyond the common grounds mentioned above. But the term 'fundamentalist' poses problems in so far as it has connotations of a return to some kind of original or essential

1

Islam. As we shall see, all the movements called fundamentalist base themselves on a particular construction of early Islamic history, the period of the Prophet and his immediate successors. But in this respect they do not differ from *all* recent advocates of a revitalised religion, like the already mentioned reformer Abdu and those who followed in his tradition, who also emphasised the examples and tenets of this early period of Islamic history, although they reach different conclusions regarding the organisation of state and society in our own day.

And, of course, an important part of any fundamentalism is the insistence on the centrality of the Quran and the traditions of the Prophet, again a point shared by all recent Islamic thinkers and reformers who also draw conclusions different from the 'fundamentalists'. Scriptures always allow a variety of interpretations. But there is another whole area of Islamic religion which is also 'fundamental'; the Islamic religion as it has been known and practised over the centuries drew on the Quran and the tradition and example of the Prophet (the Sunna) and of his immediate successors, to build up an elaborate body (or bodies) of law and theology. Some of these 'fundamentalists' of Islam are acknowledged and respected by modern 'fundamentalists', but feature hardly at all in the construction of their ideologies and discourses. I shall return to this point.

There is a sense in which *all* Islam is fundamentalist (perhaps with the exception of certain extreme heresies) in that its ultimate source and validity are the acknowledged canonical sources of the Quran and the Sunna of the Prophet (and in the case of the Shi'a the traditions of the twelve Imams).[2] But the doctrinal and political edifice they build from those 'fundamentals' can differ widely. Paradoxically, the insistence on the unity of state and religion which characterises modern fundamentalists is at one (theoretical) level also a common tenet of all Islam (perhaps with the exception of certain Sufi tendencies and some modern 'revisionists').[3] However, throughout the Islamic centuries after Muhammad and his immediate successors, religion and the state were united only in theory: in practice, as we shall see, there was a clear differentiation, a state of affairs accepted and rationalised by the ulama. In most of the modern states in Islamic countries, this *de facto* differentiation has become *de jure*, in that the application of *shari'a* law is explicitly confined to areas of personal and family affairs, while all affairs of state and society are regulated by secular legal codes. It is against this differentiation, whether *de facto* or *de jure*, that

2

modern 'fundamentalists' have proclaimed their struggles. In this respect, what characterises modern 'fundamentalism' is not so much a common *doctrinal* position which distinguishes them from other Muslim thinkers, but more a political stance which they take up against the governments and the rulers of their countries.

In insisting on a strict Islamisation of society and government (and it should be emphasised that it is never clear what this actually means in institutional detail), the modern fundamentalists represent a departure rather than a continuity with Islamic political traditions or precepts. This break is accentuated by the fact that modern Islamic groups are operating ideologically and politically within the context of the modern nation-state and the political concepts related to it.

Khomeini's doctrine of government, which will be the focus for this paper, is as we shall see quite distinct from other 'fundamentalisms', but it furnishes a good example of the innovatory nature of modern fundamentalism. I shall argue that Khomeini's 'fundamentalism' is problematic in that while it draws on traditional sources and forms of reasoning, it reaches very novel conclusions and that these conclusions are only possible and plausible if we add the assumption (implicit in Khomeini's work) of a modern nation-state and its peculiar form of politics. In order to make this argument effective, I shall first pursue the discussion started in the introductory paragraphs, with the aim of considering types of Islamic ideas regarding religion and the state, which will thus provide a background for distinguishing Khomeini's 'fundamentalism' both in relation to previous Islamic ideas and to other forms of contemporary 'fundamentalism'.

As we have already mentioned, the basic historical reference for four contemporary 'fundamentalists' is the Islam of Muhammad and his immediate successors *(Al Rashidun* 632-661) in their Medinan community, what may be called the charismatic period of Islam. Now *all* modern ideologies, whether 'fundamentalist' like Khomeinism and the Muslim Brothers or reformist like that of Muhammad Abdu, or even revisionists like Ali Abdulraziq (see n.3), are agreed that this is the real, original Islam, and that the way forward for Islam now is to revive the principles of righteousness and justice which it carried. But here there is a basic difference between Sunnis and Shi'is, in that the latter would identify this original purity with Muhammad and his fourth successor, Ali, while rejecting the three first caliphs preceding Ali as usurpers. Concomitant with this difference is another regarding the doctrine

3

of leadership (Imama) and its relation to the community, as we shall presently see.

Let us now turn to the question of Islamic religion and society under the dynastic states such as the Umayyads (661-750) and the Abbasids (750-1258). This included periods of expansion and consolidation of the Islamic empires and 'golden ages' of flourishing civilisation, the arts, the sciences and philosophy. They also include the periods of construction and elaboration of Islamic theology and law. There are complex sets of 'fundamentalist' attitudes to this pattern of religion and society. On the negative side, it represents the increasing reliance of the state on methods and procedures of government derived from the pre-Islamic Persian Empire. The Caliphs became for the most part worldly kings, and were only Imams and successors to the Prophet by name and title, and in that they maintained the dominance of the Islamic religion and formally enforced and protected its observances. It is precisely this differentation of religion from the state which is bemoaned by Khomeini and the other modern radicals when they proclaim Islam to be *dinun wa dawla,* religion *and* state. But the theologians and jurists of those dynamic periods for the most part accepted the state of their time as an Islamic state representing the unity and powers of the Islamic community, and the 'mainstream' of Sunni ulama to the present day think similarly. And it was indeed under the Abbasids that the authoritative formulations of Islamic theology occurred and the four main schools of law were established. That is, substantially, Islam as we know it, and must constitute part of the fundamentals of any 'fundamentalism'.[4] Yet for our contemporary radical 'fundamentalist' this is an area of ambiguity. For the Shi'a it is relatively easy, for they can reject most of this as alien Sunnism; their own Imams and legislators, notably Ja'far (d. 765) the sixth Imam, were in this period, but not of it; they developed a separate theology and law (although profoundly influenced by the intellectual ferment of the time). But the Shi'a also have *their* dynastic states, notably the Safavid (1500-1722) (more on this later), which nurtured some of their prominent theologians. In this respect, the modern non-clerical Shi'i radicals, notably Ali Shari'ati, are consistent in rejecting the Sunni *and* Shi'i dynasties (Shari'ati counterposed the Shi'ism of the martyrs and the saints to Shi'ism of the Safavids) (Shari'ati, 1979a). For the Sunni fundamentalists, it is much more difficult to adopt a clear position: denunciation of irreligious tyranny in one context, counterposed by the celebration of the great achievements of these states in the military, civilisational and cultural fields. No religious Sunni can fail to acknowledge and revere one or all of the great legal scholars and theologians, such as Al-Shafi'i (767-820), Abu Hanifa (d.798) or Al-Ghazzali (1058-1111); and yet the contributions of these figures to the legal and spiritual foundations of Islam did not include political doctrines which are relevant to the struggles of the present time. The elements of political activism of the community present in the early charismatic Islam (as it emerges in the modern accounts) had by the medieval period developed into mere formalities: *Shura* (consultation), often cited as one of the 'democratic' institutions of Islam, was only practised (if at all) in the Islamic states as a show or formality; *Ijma'*, originally consensus of the community, soon became consensus of the chief ulama, but seldom pronounced in matters of state, unless requested by the authority; and the '*amri bil ma'ruf wal nahyi'an al-munkar,*' the injunction to command the good and forbid evil, binding on every Muslim and extending to watchfulness over the actions of princes and leaders, soon became confined to the private and ceremonial sphere, its extension to matters of state lapsed, and this was realistically justified by the notion of *'ajz,* impotence. These elements and principles are precisely what are upheld by recent fundamentalists and reformers alike as constituting the democratic or popular bases of Islam. They acknowledge, more or less explicitly, that these principles had lapsed for the bulk of Islamic history. But they are mostly silent on the fact that the great founders of Islamic theology and jurisprudence acquiesced, for the most part, in this state of affairs and sometimes justified it in their doctrines. The great intellectual and doctrinal struggles of the early Abbasid period, which brought some of the ulama, notably Ahmad Ibn Hanbal (780-855), to confrontations with the state, were not over questions of legitimacy of political rule but over theological principles, mainly over the question of the 'createdness' of the Quran. The struggle was between different factions of intellectuals in which the Caliphs and their courts took part, establishing the one or other as 'orthodoxy'. It would seem that the ulama took a realistic view of the state, that is, that they and their followers were powerless to change it (that is if they wanted to do so) and that in the circumstances the supreme political objective was the maintenance of the unity and the integrity of the Islamic community. Let me elaborate a little further.

The picture of Islamic political thought which emerges from the historical record is one in which the unity of the Islamic community is accorded supreme value. To that end any subversion of this unity by heresy or rebellion is considered a great evil. The dynastic kings (whether Caliphs or Sultans), their staff and functionaries, did not generally adhere to Islamic tenets in personal conduct or in matters of government. But they did for the most part uphold the supremacy of the Islamic religion and encouraged its observances, as well as enforcing, through religious functionaries and judges, the rule of *Shari'a* law in civil and family matters and to various extents in the punishment of crime, but not always in matters of state, such as the specification of taxes. That is, *shari'a* law was in some respects binding on the subjects, but seldom on the rulers. The ulama, in so far as they acknowledged this state of affairs and had sufficient standing and power to disapprove it, nevertheless confined themselves to preaching virtue and justice to their princes, sometimes so eloquently as to drive them to tears of regret and penitence.[5] But this disapproval seldom extended to public denunciation, let alone a call to rebellion. For it was deemed that so long as a prince is Muslim and upholds and defends the unity of the community, then he is owed allegiance. Another aspect of the political attitudes of pious Muslims is that some of them tried to avoid as much as possible any dealing or association with the state and authority for fear of being drawn or forced to impious acts.

What attitudes do we find among our contemporary Sunni radicals to these aspects of the history of Islamic thought? In practice, silence. The great jurists and theologians are acknowledged as part of the Islamic heritage *(turath)*. The legal systems they constructed are for the most part accepted as Islamic law (although, both reformers like Abdu and radicals like the Muslim Brothers have sought to re-open the 'gate of *ijtihad*'[6] in order to reform and develop the law). But ideologically, both the reformers and the radicals draw very little on this 'heritage'. The main ideological springs within Islam on which they drew are the Quran and the Sunna[7] of the Prophet and the examples of the early community under *Al-Rashidun*. References to the medieval theologians and legists where they do occur in the modern writings are usually amplifications of the themes of early Islam in their writings. Or the examples are cited of the defiance of authority in favour of religious righteousness by some of these medieval figures, the most prominent being those of Ibn Hanbal and the Hanbali tradition, notably Ibn Taymiyya (1263-1328), which will be considered presently. It would seem, then, that the Sunni fundamentalists are highly selective in the elements of Islam which they use as 'fundamentals', with the result that the theological and legal foundations of Islam, constructed in the medieval period, while not rejected, are nevertheless set aside. The reason for this silence is that the modern radical Islamic struggle is one against their respective states aimed at the institutions of Islamic government, and the works of the medieval period can offer little in this struggle. For their political doctrine, in so far as it was explicitly stated, was in effect quiescent. The question of the legality of the state was not posed beyond the simple requirement of a formally Islamic state. The questions which exercised their minds were those of faith and dogma, and it was on the occasion when the state attempted to dictate on these matters that the pious ulama and their followers resisted and confronted the state, but never in rebellion. In this and many other respects, the examples of Ibn Hanbal, and the Hanbali tradition are instructive.

Ahmad Ibn Hanbal's confrontation with authority was over the proclamation by the Caliph Al-Ma'mun of the doctrine of the 'createdness' of the Quran as the official orthodoxy (the view that the Quran is an object created by God as against the view, which later prevailed, that the Quran was God's breath and direct speech. These positions have doctrinal consequences for it follows from the first positions that the Quran is open to interpretation and constructions, while the latter view would force a literalist acceptance of the scriptures, a literalism closely associated with the Hanbali school to the present day). Al-Ma'mun and his two successors attempted to enforce this orthodoxy and required all men of religion to subscribe to it. Ibn Hanbal emerged (at least in later histories) as the most prominent resister, upon which he was imprisoned and 'examined' *(al-mihna)* by the Caliph and his doctrinal supporters.[8] In this historically famous inquisition, Ibn Hanbal defended his position with great courage and tenacity. As a result, he suffered continued imprisonment and ill-treatment until the Caliph Al-Mutawakkil 'reinstated' Sunnism in 847, at which point Ibn Hanbal was released and honoured for the rest of his years.

Ibn Taymiyya also suffered imprisonment and deprivation at one point in his career through a confrontation with princely authority which supported the Sufi Shaykhs, his antagonists. For in true Hanbali tradition, Ibn Taymiyya upheld literalist orthodoxy against what he saw as lax and heterodox Sufi practices, then enjoying princely patronage. But it is not for this episode that Ibn Taymiyya is favoured by the modern radicals. Another episode, his *fatwa* (ruling) against the Mongols provides historical authority and precedent for the modern radicals' questioning the Islamic credentials of nominally Muslim rulers. Ibn Taymiyya was asked to give a *fatwa* as to whether the Islamised Mongol rulers of Mardin (now in Turkey) could be regarded as true Muslims. He ruled that they could not, because in their government practices they mixed the Islamic *shari'a* with the *yasa,* the law code of the Mongols. The implications of this ruling for modern political preoccupations are crucial: in its terms modern rulers who do not strictly follow or enforce the *shari'a* are not truly Muslims. Such a ruling is rare in Islamic history; to declare a self-proclaimed Muslim an unbeliever *(takfir)* is a grave sin. Ibn Taymiyya would only have made such a ruling because the Mongols were feared antagonists and conquerors of the Mameluke princes and territories which were his home. He certainly did not extend this denunciation to the conduct and rule of his own Mameluke princes, who were not always the most faithful followers of the straight path.

The Hanbali legal/theological school has been known at various points of its history for fierce adherence to scriptural orthodoxy, and of the four Sunni legal schools as the least likely to compromise with Sufi or Shi'i doctrines or practices (although it should be emphasised that no branch of Islam has entirely escaped some degree of involvement with Sufism, which became an important form of religious organisation from late medieval times to the turn of our present century). In recent times Hanbalism has been associated with movements to revitalise and purify Islam from popular and 'decadent' accretions. Its influence is evident in the conservative Salafi trend among establishment circles in some Arab countries in the earlier decades of this century. But its most prominent recent manifestation was the Wahhabi movement in Arabia, and the militant puritanical movement associated with the rise of the house of Sa'ud to royal power.

Because of its historical record and recent manifestation of militancy, Hanbalism has been claimed as a 'radical' trend in Sunni Islam; a Sunni counterpart to the Shi'i radicalism which culminated in the Iranian revolution. It is one object of this paper to argue that modern 'fundamentalist' Islam, and especially Khomeinism, represent radical departures from the mainstream of Islamic political thought. To that end, I have to show that the Hanbali tradition does not constitute an ancestry to modern radical Islam in challenging the legitimacy of the *de facto* separation of government from religion, and certainly does not constitute a parallel to

Khomeini's *Wilayat Al-Faqih.* Hanbalism does not make any claims for the special qualifications of the Faqih or jurist to assume governmental role.

Ahmad Ibn Hanbal features in the historical record as a pious and courageous *'alim* known for his astute collection and validation of the Prophet's traditions *(Hadith).* As we have seen, his confrontation with the successive Caliphs and the philosophers of their courts came about through his refusal to endorse their doctrine regarding the 'createdness' of the Quran. The political implication of this refusal is clear: the commander of the Faithful (the title of the Caliph) does not have the authority to pronounce on matters of faith and dogma. Every believer and especially a scholar is duty bound to adhere to the canonical sources of the Quran and the Sunna, to exert his own *ijtihad,* effort and reason in judging the compatibility of any doctrine or dogma with these sources. By these criteria, he judged, the doctrine of the createdness of the Quran was an innovation and a heresy and had to be resisted by all pious men. But it should be noted that challenge to the Caliphs in matters of faith did not extend to their authority as rulers or to the legitimacy of their rule. Quite the contrary, Ibn Hanbal maintained the general Sunni emphasis on preserving the unity of the Community and avoiding any utterances or deeds which might lead to intrigue *(fitna)* or rebellion. Allegiance is owed, he maintained, to an *amir* regardless of his moral qualities if he was Muslim and protected the institutions and conditions of Muslim observance. In his *Kitab-al-Sunna* he had this to say on allegiance to a prince:

> The *Jihad* should be pursued alongside all Imams, whether good men or evil doers; the injustice of the tyrant or the justice of the just matters little. The Friday prayers, the Pilgrimage, the two Feasts should be made with those who possess authority even if they are not good, just or pious. The legal alms, the tithe, the land taxes, the *fay'*, are due to the amirs, whether they put them to right use or not (Quoted in *Encyclopaedia of Islam,* p. 276)

The only condition under which a Muslim must resist his prince is if the latter commands him to commit a *ma'siyya,* a disobedience to God. But this resistance must stop short of rebellion.

Ibn Taymiyya was equal to his intellectual ancestor in courage and steadfastness in the defence of the faith against what he considered to be innovations and heresies, and consequently suffered persecution and banishment at the hands of the princely patrons of his theological adversaries. But his doctrine regarding allegiance to Muslim amirs is almost identical to that of Ibn Hanbal. In his book *Al Siyasa Al-Shar'iyya* (Islamic Statecraft) he devoted a chapter to the rights and duties of the Imam (the bulk of the book being devoted to punishment and taxation) as derived from the Quran and the conduct of the Prophet and his *Rashidun* successors. He tempered religious principles with a consideration of the realities of power (e.g. in appointing a military commander, an Imam faced with the choice berween a pious but weak man and one who is capable but lax in religious observance must choose the latter). But these principles and examples of the duties and desirable conduct of the Imam were almost wholly theoretical in relation to Mameluke military princes of his time; and quite realistically Ibn Taymiyya did not make any attempt to reform or oppose them as such. His concern was the purity of the faith, not of government. In relation to government, he enjoined obedience and allegiance of all believers short of committing a *ma'siyya*, almost in identical terms to those of Ibn Hanbal. As we have seen, his special place as a historical hero for the modern radicals is due entirely to the terms of his ruling against the Mongols, who were the enemies of his Mamluke princes.

It would seem that both Ibn Hanbal and Ibn Taymiyya conformed to the general Sunni pattern of emphasising the unity and integrity of the community, and the abhorrence of rebellion and fragmentation. In the light of their record of steadfastness in defence of the faith, they clearly did not hold these views opportunistically or to curry favour with the authorities, but out of genuine conviction.

Let us now turn to a more recent manifestation of Hanbali activism, that of Wahhabism in Arabia. Muhammad b. Abdulwahhab (1703-1792) was an *'alim* of Najd, who called for the purification of Islam from what he considered to be heretical and magical accretions. In this he was fighting a similar battle to that of his Hanbali predecessor Ibn Taymiyya, only now in context of fragmentation and weakness of the central power. A militant and ambitious chieftain could wield exclusive power over a territory he was prepared to defend. It was under the patronage of such a chieftain, Muhammad Ibn Sa'ud, that b. Abdulwahhab spread his message.[9] And it was a potent alliance which rallied the Shaikhdoms and tribes of Najd against the politico-religious establishment of Mecca as well as the agents and clients of the

Ottoman Empire. The Wahhabi message and its carriers were for a time defeated by Ottoman power (for most of the nineteenth century). But its influence persisted, not only in Arabia, but in many parts of the Muslim world as far as West Africa and Malaya where it was carried by learned pilgrims, concerned over the state of Islam in their countries where it had developed in highly heterodox and syncretistic modes quite remote from the Quran and Sunna. At the turn of the present century, a capable and ambitious prince of Al Sa'ud, Abdulaziz, revived the Wahhabi call and rallied the forces of the faithful under his banner. Many supported Abdulaziz not as tribal sections but as individuals, even against the allegiance to the tribe. This was known as the *Ikhwan* (brotherhood) movement.[10]

The *Ikhwan* were settled by the Abdulaziz in villages *(hujur)*, where they led an ascetic life according to the dictates of the faith, and were always prepared for *jihad* or holy war in its defence. In them, Abdulaziz had a formidable force which he used first to impose his exclusive power over Najd, and then from its centre in Riyadh to wage campaigns against the forces and clients of the Ottomans and of the Sherif of Mecca. The British, in their effort to dislodge the Turks from the Arab countries, were backing both Abdulaziz and the Sherif of Mecca, the first for his proven military and political capacity, the second for his supposed religious prestige in the Muslim world (much over-rated as it turned out). In the end, Ibn Sa'ud's forces occupied Mecca and expelled the Sherif and his retinue, much to the dismay of the British, who were paymasters and suppliers of arms to both parties. (The British acquiesced in the situation, then made the Sherif's son Faysal King of Syria, and when expelled by their French allies, they made him King of Iraq.) Ibn Sa'ud owed a considerable debt to the British in the kingdom which he established as Saudi Arabia, and remained after the end of the First World War highly dependent on British power financially and militarily. In all this, Ibn Sa'ud was reaching accommodation and making compromises with his British patrons, which was not to the liking of his ascetic warriors. It was bad enough to be allied to the infidels and to keep their company, but what stretched them to the limit of their tolerance was the imposition of a moratorium on further *jihad* (the *raison d'être* of their existence) at the borders of what were now British-protected Iraq and Kuwait. Ultimately armed conflict broke out between Ibn Sa'ud and his holy warriors, a battle which he won, leading to the dispersal and dislocation of the Ikhwan movement. But the state and society which emerged as Saudi Arabia was stamped with the strict scriptural orthodoxy of Wahhabism and remains formally so to the present day.

The Ikhwan movement is perhaps the first of the modern 'fundamentalisms' insisting on the unity of religion and the state. The state established by Ibn Sa'ud was seen in this light, but the requirements of state and of modern international relations entailed certain compromises which were unacceptable to the religious followers. Ultimately the state-religion duality was restored in the Saudi state, but one which made more concessions and allowances for religion than any other modern state in a Muslim country (until the Iranian revolution). *Shari'a* law is formally instituted, including the law of punishment, Muslim observances of prayer and fasting are formally obligatory, the rule of *hijab* — the veiling and public segregation of women — are enforced, and so on. But the application of religious law to the state, its economic policy and administration, or to the private conduct of the vast royal family and other powerful families, is but a thinly disguised pretence. For this reason the Saudi state does not escape the wrath of the modern 'fundamentalists'. Some of the 'moderate' and politically practical leaders of the Muslim Brotherhood may be friendly to the Saudi state (especially in view of its financial largesse), but that does not extend to the militant cadres who see much more cause for sympathy with Iran, and with the shadowy Islamic militants inside Saudi Arabia.

We have shown that Wahhabism, at least in its manifestation in the Ikhwan movement, can be classified with the modern 'fundamentalists' in its insistence on the unity of religion and the state in Islam. But in one crucial respect it is different from the radical ideologies which developed and thrived among the urban poor and 'traditional' middle classes of Egypt (Muslim Brothers) or the equivalent groups in connection with sectors of the clergy in Iran. Islam and Islamic authority for the Ikhwan was clearly conceived in terms of a tribal model, and Ibn Sa'ud was for them a chieftain with a religious charisma. It is a much simpler and more direct kind of politics than that of the 'nation' and the 'nation state' which I will try to show are assumed by the modern 'fundamentalist' ideologies, especially those of Khomeini and Shari'ati. One may speculate that without the impact of the 'modern' world in the form of colonial empires, the Ikhwan may have developed an Islamic state with religious charisma which is subsequently 'routinised' into another dynastic state, much like the one developed by their ancestors in eighteenth- and early nineteenth-century Najd.

Khomeini's political doctrine

We shall now turn to the task of distinguishing Khomeini's political doctrine from 'fundamentalist' ideas. The first and most striking feature of Khomeini's doctrine is that it is conducted exclusively in terms of traditional Islamic discussions with hardly any reference to Western or Western-inspired politico-ideological notions. This is in marked contrast to all recent Islamic writers, fundamentalist or reformist. For even the most 'fundamentalist' of thinkers who ultimately reject Western political thought nevertheless fight some of their ideological battles on its terrain: they incorporate the language of modern statehood and its constructs, of parliaments, constitutions, administration, policy and planning and the concepts of democracy, equality, liberty and social justice. However, these elements of modern political thought which are adopted and incorporated have to be clothed in Islamic terms. For instance, in some of the works of the Muslim Brothers, the Islamic religion is held to be a universal and inclusive outlook which encompasses in essence all the most desirable elements in political philosophies and concepts, and at the same time possesses the intellectual tools to see through and reject all that is false and vain. Witness the proclamation by the Muslim Brotherhood:

> Internationalism, nationalism, socialism, capitalism, bolshevism, war, the distribution of wealth, the relations between producer and consumer, and whatever is related to these topics ... which have occupied the leaders of nations and philosophers of society — all of these, we believe, Islam has penetrated to the core. Islam established for the world the system through which man can benefit from the good and avoid dangers and calamities. (Quoted by Mitchell, 1968 p.233)

Other Islamic writers like Ali Shari'ati make similar claims regarding both the inclusiveness and superiority of Islam in relation to Western social and political thought. This will be considered more fully at a later stage in this chapter. Khomeini as we shall see makes no claims or references to Western thought — he writes as if it does not exist.

Another basic factor which distinguishes Khomeini from other 'fundamentalists', especially the Sunni varieties, is in the conception of the leadership of the Islamic community, the question of Imama.

From the early days of Islam there have been two distinct ideals of the 'good society': one centred on the self-governing community and the other on the charismatic leader. Montgomery Watt (1973, pp. 34-7), writing on the divisions of early Islam, characterised *Khariji* doctrine in terms of its emphasis on the charismatic community, and the Shi'ite schism in terms of the pursuit of legitimate rule by a descendant from the house of Ali with a presumed charisma of descent, both being in opposition to the newly established dynastic state. A roughly parallel division can be discerned among the modern radicals which seems to coincide more or less with the Sunni-Shi'i division. The Sunni radicals such as the Muslim Brotherhood, while attaching great importance to leadership, do not specify qualifications for leadership in terms of descent or institutional rank. The leader should be learned and just, and as such attract the support of the community. These qualifications are not, however, attached to institutional standing, such as that of, say, the Azhar ulama. These are regarded, for the most part, as conservative and subservient collaborators with the government of the day, and the leaders of the radical Sunni movements have, with few exceptions, come from outside the institutional ranks of ulama, in contrast to their Shi'i counterparts. For the Sunnis, the question of leadership, while important, is not posed as a systematic doctrinal problem. In contrast, Khomeini's doctrine of *Wilayat al-Faqih,* by its very title, is centred around the question of leadership of the Islamic state, which is vested in the just *faqih,* unquestionably emerging from the higher ranks of the religious establishment. As we shall see presently, the justification of this doctrine is intimately connected to the Shi'i doctrine of *Imamat.*

For Khomeini and his followers there are no democratic or populist scruples to disturb their faith in this doctrine. But for the 'modernist' Shi'ite radicals the doctrine of the Imamate clearly poses problems: how can it be reconciled with their populist ideals and the notion of 'sovereignty' of the people? The title of one of Shari'ati's essays, *Ummat va Imamat* [11] (The Community and the Holy Leadership), labels this tension and the essay attempts to resolve it. The resolution is at best rhetorical: the religiously enlightened community will realise that the leadership of the Imam is the perfect expression of its own unity and will, and at that stage there will be no tension between sovereignty of the people and the rule of the Imam.

We should note one more ideal of leadership, that of the the the Just Prince. For the pious Muslims, Sunni or Shi'i during the centuries of Islamic history, both the Imamate and the self-governing communities were Utopias. They were governed by Caliphs or Sultans backed by military cliques and a predominantly secular bureaucracy. In this context the most that the ulama and other religious Muslims could hope for was a Just Prince who would govern in accordance with the Quran and the *shari'a*. The pursuit of the Just Prince became an important element in the political affiliations of Muslims until recent times. Wahhabism as we have seen combined the ideal of the self-governing community with rule by a Just Prince, in the form of a member of the house of Sa'ud. But this combination was ended when Abdulaziz Al Sa'ud acquired foreign allies and appeared to be compromising Islamic principles.

Perhaps the nearest that a recent Sunni thinker had come to the idea of *Wilayat al-Faqih* was Rashid Rida (d. 1935) in his doctrine of the Caliphate.[12] In this, he saw the restoration of the Caliphate as a vital condition for the organisation of Islam. Islam is a religion which requires both the state and the law as a necessary part of its functioning. Both the Islamic state and religion have declined and decayed over the previous centuries. The revival of the Islamic community will depend in part on the successful adoption of Western science and technology and the local institutions necessary for the modern world — but this can and must be done within the ambit of Islamic religion and law. To do this successfully, Islamic law must be flexible without sacrificing its fundamental principles. To do this, and to generate unity and strength, the Islamic community needs correct leadership from inspired politicians and well-trained ulama, headed by a Caliph for the whole of Islam. The talents or skills necessary for this task are lamentably lacking at present, and need to be developed through a rigorous programme for training and education of ulama. The Caliph of the future will not be concerned with directly ruling the community (especially with the multiplicity of Islamic states accepted by Rida as inevitable). But he would be the chief *'alim* and *mujtahid* whose authority will hold sway — a conception of the Caliphate very similar to that of the papacy in Catholic Europe (but also with hints of a Comtean 'philosopher-king'). But such a Caliphate is not possible at present, argued Rida, and a temporary substitute is needed, a 'caliphate of necessity' to unite the Muslims against foreign dangers. The problem thus becomes one of finding a suitable person from a suitable national and religious context to be acceptable to all the Muslims. Rida's speculation as to suitable candidates then turned to the states and the royal houses of Islam; in theory a supreme *mujtahid* with papal authority, in practice a just Islamic prince. This is clearly a very different figure from Khomeini's *faqih*, constructed from different sources and arguments and for a different purpose.

Armed with this perspective on the different types of the ideal society and government in Islamic thought, let us now turn to a consideration of Khomeini's doctrine of government, *Wilayat Al-Faqih*.

Khomeini's doctrine of *Wilayat Al-Faqih* is a radical departure in modern Islam. His 1969 lectures in Najaf, subsequently published as a book entitled *Al-Hukumah Al-Islamiya* (Islamic Government) attempted to establish this doctrine on two grounds: rational, by demonstrating the theoretical equivalence, in relation to government functions, of the just *faqih* with the Prophet and the Imams, and traditional in advancing relevant traditions from the Prophet and the Imams, which he interprets as confirming this governmental function of the *faqih*. The argument starts by insisting that Islam as a religion *must* include a governmental system. The separation of religion from government and its relegation to a system of worship and ritual is completely alien to the spirit and teaching of Islam, a perversion perpetrated and reinforced by Imperialism and US agents in order to subjugate and exploit the lands of Islam. Islam is above all a divine law, and the law is not given merely to be studied and analysed in religious schools but to be *applied* and instituted as a form of state. The Prophet clearly intended an Islamic state. That is why he appointed a Khalifa (successor). The functions which are integral to the Islamic religion require a government. For example, the collection of taxes and faithful spending of the funds for the needs of Muslims and their affairs: the Islamic laws specifying duties and punishing infringements cannot be applied without a directing and authoritative government. The people cannot be expected to punish themselves! 'It is a logical necessity that there must be a government which undertakes to put the [Islamic] rules into practice and to apply all [Islamic] measures absolutely' (p. 48).

What are the qualifications of an Islamic ruler who can undertake these responsibilities of government? There are two qualifications, answers Khomeini, on which all Muslims have agreed: total knowledge of the law and total justice in its execution. The Shi'a believe their Imams to have these qualities as part of the ontological attributes of the Imamate (they are a superior form of being and are infallible). But what should Muslims do during the period of the Great Occultation which has lasted more than 1200 years, and whose end cannot be known? The *shari'a'i* cannot remain in abeyance for all this period. Muslims cannot live in anarchy without government or continue to be subjected to alien and godless governments. The qualifications for leadership are not restricted to the Prophet and the Imams. The just *faqih* has the equivalent qualifications for government in so far as he has total knowledge of the law and is able to apply it justly. This is not to say, of course, that the *faqih* shares in the personal superiority of the Imams. He is merely their equivalent for the functions of government. For example, the Prophet and the Imams collected taxes and punished offenders and so does the *faqih* (Khomeini seems to have a limited view of the functions of government).

By these criteria, incidentally, all the Caliphs, except for Ali, and certainly all the Sultans and princes, are disqualified from legitimate governorship or *Wilaya*. Khomeini argues (on orthodox Shi'i lines) that this resulted from the usurpation of the succession to the Prophet away from Ali, and by the time Ali did succeed it was too late; matters had deteriorated too badly and the greedy and the corrupt (like Mu'awiyah) were already deeply entrenched in positions of power.

Khomeini then proceeds to support these deductions with *hadith* (tradition) of the Prophet and the Imams. We need not go into the arguments based on traditions here, except to note that the same traditions are open to completely different interpretations and constructions.[13] Now, in the terminology of the modern non-Islamic world, what kind of government will the Islamic one be? Khomeini is quite explicit that it is not comparable to any other. It is not a dictatorship: the leader must rule according to the divine law, not by his own will. By the same token, it cannot be an elected system in which representatives of the people can legislate. Nor can it be a popular republic which makes the people their own rulers. It is the rule of Divine Law as interpreted and applied by the Just Faqih. Once such a regime is established, Khomeini makes clear, the duty of the people is to obey in accordance with the Quranic verse:

O believers obey God and obey the Messenger and those in
authority among you *(awlial-amr).* (4, 63)

Two things strike us about Khomeini's political theory: its
simplicity and its novelty. Simplicity, in that its derivation is
straightforward, from first principles and does not require any
abstruse reasoning (this is not to say, of course, that it is the only
possible derivation from those principles): its support in terms of
traditions does not seek obscure sources or tortuous interpretations.
If it is so simple, why, one wonders, is it so novel, why does the idea
of *Wilayat al-Faqih* not have a more secure ancestry in Islamic
jurisprudence (that is *Wilaya* in Khomeini's sense of government,
not in the possible legal sense of 'guardianship' over minors or over
property, more properly *wisaya*)? Indeed, it is striking that
Khomeini does not cite any contemporaries or predecessors for
support, except perhaps by example, but not by legal argument. He
has to draw traditional support from primary canonical sources.

I should like to suggest here that the explanation of the novelty
of the doctrine of *Wilayat al-Faqih* is that its credibility and
'thinkability' are facilitated by the conditions of the modern state
and politics. What makes Khomeini's theory plausible is the idea of
the people as a political force which can effect revolution and
transformation. It is an idea which in Khomeini's writings is
incidental and untheorised, but nevertheless crucial. It comes in the
rhetorical plea which he makes to his audience of religious students
at the end of the fifth lecture: 'Awaken the People' *(Ayqudu
ash-sh'ab)* :

The great reformist movements in history did not possess
power at their inception. Each started by proselytising among
the people and spreading to them social consciousness. The
movement would then grow gradually in opposition to the
prevalent oppression. The cadres of the movement would
draw the attention of the people to oppression and awaken
them to the dangers of submitting to the rule of tyrants, then
the people become the active force which sweeps all the
obstacles in its way. When the people awaken from their
slumber, they will destroy the throne of the oppressor, and
then righteousness and virtue will prevail. (p. 75)

This concept of the people as 'the nation' as a political force is
distinctly modern. It is specified by modern political ideologies as

an entity with a territory and a state. And the field in which this 'people' can constitute a political force to displace the ruler is provided by the organisation of the modern nation state.

The point will emerge more clearly if we compare an ideal-typical pre-capitalist state or empire, roughly approximate in outline to forms of historical Islamic states, with an ideal-typical nation state. The first type comprises a variety of social units, tribes, villages, ethnic and religious groups, military castes, merchant and artisan guilds, etc. Many of these social forms, especially outside the main urban centres, are relatively autonomous and isolated, with their own forms of political and economic organisation. The social division of labour does not extend far beyond the main urban centres and such links as exist are rudimentary and simple, such as provisioning of towns from surrounding hinterland (if such a clear distinction can be made: in some instances, urban groups produced their own food). One is reminded of Max Weber's image of trade networks in the ancient empires being like a web of lines between the major urban centres, by-passing for the most part the vast area of subsistence communities in between. In this ideal type, political unity is only maintained by the power of the central state supported by an administration and military apparatus whose personnel may be drawn from outside (for example the Mamelukes and the Janissaries of the Ottoman Empire). The initiative for political change cannot be said to come from 'the people' in such a political unit; urban populations may riot if pushed too hard, or may side with one military faction or another, but these are hardly initiatives in political transformation, let alone social ones. The only initiative which would dislodge the ruling clique came from another potential clique: a militarily organised group, usually tribal, with a dynasty of princes or of holy men or both at their head. In this context, the concept of 'the people' as a politically active and effective entity, if it occurs at all, has rather different sociological and ideological references from that in the context of the modern nation state.[14]

To turn to the ideal-typical nation state. An essential element of this type is a fairly advanced and integrated social division of labour. The image of a 'nation' is one constituted not merely by a central state, but by deeper social and economic processes which underpin the state, perhaps as expressed in the couple 'state/civil society'. In this context, the concept of the people as a political entity, as 'nation' with resources of political initiative which can transform the state, whether by elections or by revolutions, is an appropriate and plausible notion (see Chapter 6 below).

For the purpose of the present argument, it is not necessary to raise the question of the historical accuracy of these ideal types. It is sufficient to say that the widely-held concept of the nation state is an ideological condition for the plausibility of the concept of 'people' as 'nation' with resources and potential for transformative political action. While Khomeini does not explicitly adopt this ideal-type of nation state, his use of 'the people' clearly presupposes it.

This notion of the people, while crucial to the credibility of Khomeini's theory, is brought in by him incidentally and *ad hoc*, it is not theorised or elaborated. In this respect, Ali Shari'ati's (d. 1977) Islamic populism, although greatly different in spirit from Khomeini's legalism, nevertheless complements Khomeini's theory of Islamic government. For central to Shari'ati's work is the notion of 'the people' as *masses*, the victims of oppression and exploitation and the main agent for the bringing about of social transformations into the just Islamic society.

Shari'ati's Islamic sociology

Let us turn to a consideration of Shari'ati's 'Islamic sociology',[15] which is relevant to the present discussion in two ways. First, Shari'ati represents another interesting paradox of 'fundamentalism' in that he advocated the revival of the Islamic community modelled on the precepts and examples of the Quran and the conduct of the Prophet and the Shi'i Imams. But he supports his arguments and exhortations by extensive recourse to modern European social thought while insisting that all the modern concepts and doctrines were contained in a superior form in the Quran. Second, Shari'ati in explicitly articulating the concept of 'the people' demonstrates the necessity of this concept to the idea of 'revolution' which is in turn necessary for the transition to 'Islamic government'. In this, he does not only articulate the modern ideological assumptions underlying Khomeini's doctrine, but he also gives them an Islamic ancestry, by building modern populist concepts into the Quran and the traditions.

According to Shari'ati, there are two types of historical explanations of development and change. First, there are those which see no order or structure in history but regard all change as resulting from a series of accidents. These include materialist explanations which liken historical process to the natural, following immutable laws and allowing no room for human will or responsibility. Second, there are 'great men' explanations, in which all major developments are explained as the result of the will and actions of historical personalities. The Quran, while recognising these factors, gives the greatest weight to the People *(al-nas)*. The Prophet is a great man, but it is repeatedly emphasised in the Quran that he is only the carrier of a message. Whether that message has an effect or not will depend on its reception by the people to whom it is addressed. Everything is in the hands of the people. But their reaction will depend to some extent on the nature of the society and its traditions. For every society has a life and a path of its own, and knowledge of this peculiarity is essential for understanding the course of its development. So, according to Shari'ati, the Quran gives us what is called in the text books 'multi-factorial' explanations of social change:

> In short, four factors affect the destiny of societies – personality, accident, norm and people *(al-nas)*. Among them, the two most important are *al-nas* and norm because *al-nas* represents the will of the people, and norm the scientifically demonstrable laws existent in society. *(On the Sociology of Islam,* p. 53)

'Norm' *(sunnat)* here refers to the basic traditions and laws of development of a society:

> Tradition, in the form derived from Islam and the Quran, has the sense that each society has a fixed basis, or in the words of the Quran, it has a road, a path, a particular character. All societies contain definite and immutable laws within themselves. A society is like a living being: like all organisms, it has scientifically demonstrable and immutable laws. (*Ibid.*, p. 50)

We should at this stage comment on Shari'ati's attitude to the two forms of discourse he is dealing with, the Western and the Quranic. Confronting the two discourses, he concludes that the 'discoveries' of Western sociology and social thought are indeed to be found in the Quran, but in a more profound, more universal and more balanced form. Thus, not only does the Quran combine all the otherwise partial theories of the Western thinkers, it achieves a

21

unique systhesis, giving much greater weight to the masses *(al-nas)* than even the most democratic Western theories.

It does not require any great analytical skill to show that Shari'ati's conclusions are in all respects 'modern' and 'Western' and bear only tenuous relation to the Quran or Islamic tradition. Indeed, the references to the Quran in his text are sparse and the verses referred to do not always bear the interpretation placed upon them. Let us look in particular at the word *al-nas* in the Quran and at the question of 'norm' *(sunnat)* .

'*Al-nas*' is one of the terms referring to collectivities of 'people' in the Quran (and in Arabic usage generally ancient and modern). It is the most general term with no connotations of unity or solidarity, precisely equivalent to the English 'people' as in 'people talk'. There are other, more specific designations of collectivity, such as '*qawm*' (with some connotation of common attributes and solidarity and sometimes of descent) or '*umma*' (community), with stronger connotations of solidarity and common purpose. These are used in relation to a particular sort of people:[16]

> Our Lord, do not Thou assign us with the people *(qawm)* of the evildoers. (7, 45)

or to a particular people (in the sense of tribe or ethnic or religious group), as in:

> And we sent Noah to his people *(qawm)* . (7, 59)

Al-nas is more general, as in:

> Say O people *(nas)* , I am the messenger of God to you all,

And

> Said He, 'Moses, I have chosen thee above all men' *(nas)* .(7, 144)

The modern usage of 'the masses' (Arabic *al-Jamahir,* publics) or 'the people' (Arabic *Al Sha'b*) have specific political connotations typically related to the couple 'people/government', 'mass/elite'. This is the sense in which Shari'ati is using *al-nas*. But in the Quran *al-nas* is not opposed to government, state or elite, it is either used neutrally: 'O People', 'I have chosen you of all mankind', or, together with *qawm* and *umma,* to refer to collectivity having moral/religious attributes as in 'the people of righteousness' or 'people of the evildoers'. They (people) are often the interlocutors of the Prophet (or of his predecessors, Abraham, Noah, etc.) who respond to the word of God, with faith, doubt or cynicism, and to whom the Prophet, following God's commands, presents proofs and arguments as well as threats of the consequences of God's wrath: 'Say O mankind *(nas),* I am Messenger of God to you all' (7, 158).

And we cut them up into nations *(umma)* in the earth, some of them righteous and some of them otherwise. (7, 168)

In these contexts, the collectivity, including its elite, leaders and government, are juxtaposed to the Prophet, reiterating the word of God. They either believe or doubt, or split into believers and doubters, the doers of good and the doers of evil. Quranic verses referring specifically to the conduct of affairs in the Islamic community juxtapose 'the people' to their leaders *(awlya'al-amr)* as in:

God commands you to deliver trusts back to their owners; and when you judge between the people that you judge with justice. ... O believers, obey God and obey the Messenger and those in authority among you *(awli al-amr).* (4, 62-3)

This is usually interpreted (see Ibn Taymiyya *al-Siyasa al-Shar'iyya)* as defining the complementarity of rulers and their followers in terms of right and duties: the rulers have the duty to rule justly but have the right to obedience. This is in line with the mainstream Islamic tradition, enjoining unity, solidarity and obedience. It certainly did not pose an opposition of 'people' to 'government'.

Shari'ati the political modernist is rediscovering the Quran in the image of his modernism; his 'fundamentalism' is if anything inverted.

To return to the question of 'norm' *(sunnat),* Shari'ati is using it in the sense of the nature and laws of development of particular societies. In this respect, 'society' is being used not in the sense of 'people' as a collectivity, but in the sense of an ordered field of phenomena like the 'economic machine' or like Durkheimian 'social facts' or Marxist 'laws of history'. It is doubtful if any such conception is present in the Quran, or for that matter in any such social or religious thought before Ibn Khaldun (fourteenth century), or in any elaborate form in the West before Machiavelli. Shari'ati does not refer to Quranic norms exemplifying such a concept. As has already been said, collectivities in the Quran are moral, not 'systematic'. The only laws they are subject to are those of God's will and their destiny following from it:

> God changes not what is in a People (*qawm*) until they change what is in themselves. Whensoever God desires evil for a people, there is no turning it back; apart from Him, they have no protector. (13, 11)

Shari'ati refers to this verse quite correctly to show the importance of a people's will in their destiny, but only through influencing God's will through their faith and good works:

> To every nation (*umma*) a term; when their term comes, they shall not put it back by a single hour nor put it forward. (7, 34)

Here the fixed destiny of a people is formulated in terms of predestination.

Also in the Quran is the implication that the divisions between different people is 'natural' in the sense of being original to the creation of the world:

> O mankind (*nas*), we have created you male and female and appointed you races (*sha'b*) and tribes, that you may know one another.[17] (49, 13)

The suggestion here is that the division between peoples is of a similar order to that between the sexes.

But none of these usages would justify Shari'ati's contention that there is a sociological concept of 'society' as an order of phenomena in the Quran. So why did he put this view forward? Apart from his often reiterated aim to demonstrate that all modern wisdom is contained in a superior form in the Quran, there is also an important purpose in his political theory served by this attribution. He wants to say that the People, with their faith, reason and will, can change society. This statement required a concept of 'society' (systematic order of phenomena) distinct from 'people' as a collectivity of actors.

In the Quran, 'people' in their various divisions are seen as supporters or adversaries of the faith and the object is to win them over to the faith. What they are changing by embracing the faith is their moral status and their destiny. There is no question of 'changing their society' for they and their 'society' are one.

Shari'ati on the other hand, operating within the paradigm of modern social and political thought, does want to say that people, 'the masses', will change society, partly through changing themselves. But changing themselves (that is being enlightened by their religious convictions) is only a first step towards changing society as a system of institutions and processes, through the Islamic revolution.

Now given the central status of the concept of 'the People' for Shari'ati, how did he see their relation to government and authority in a truly Islamic government? This is a crucial question in the light of debates conducted in the early days of the Iranian revolution with each contender claiming the support of Shari'ati's writings. Hamid Algar, for instance, put together in English a number of Shari'ati's essays which he (Algar) entitled *Marxism and Other Western Fallacies* (Shari'ati, 1980). In his Introduction, Algar discloses that his purpose is to show that leftist claims that Shari'ati was on their side are false. Those who have interpreted Shari'ati's thoughts as anti-clerical and therefore opposed to the present regime are not only wrong, but are hypocritical and are wreckers trying to sabotage the revolution. How should these statements be evaluated?

The most cursory reading of Shari'ati's essays in comparison with Khomeini will show him to be a profoundly different thinker. Against Khomeini's authoritative legalism Shari'ati's essays are discursive, humanistic, allegorical and sentimental. He was certainly opposed to the clergy, but a particular mould of the clergy, what he saw to be wooden and ritualistic conservatism, blindness to the basic truths of Islam, a neglect of the Quran, in favour of scholastic disputations, and above all not being awake to the political imperatives and the need for Islamic action. However, Khomeini would also denounce such clerical sins but not so explicitly and vocally. What is more, Shari'ati also shared with Khomeini a commitment to Shi'i Islam, the central tenet of which is the doctrine of the Imamate: a doctrine which gives unquestioned and absolute authority to the Imam.

But what should the community do in the period of the 'Great Occultation' or the absence of the Imam? Shari'ati did not advocate a self-governing democracy of the *umma:* authoritative leadership and direction is necessary. It is not clear what forms of leadership Shari'ati envisaged; in spite of his general distaste for the clergy, his formulations would not exclude the type of leadership envisaged in *Wilayat al-Faqih.*

I do not want to underestimate the gulf between the thought of Khomeini and Shari'ati intellectually, politically or spiritually, and it is not not necessary to do that to make the point that the modern ideological conditions unspoken but assumed by Khomeini are precisely what is elaborated and theorised by Shari'ati. He tried to give them Islamic roots and traditional ancestry. These ideological themes are of 'the People' as 'Nation' with a political will for changing society in accordance with Islamic Enlightenment.

One may speculate that the kind of government achieved by Khomeini is profoundly different from that dreamed by Shari'ati. But then, Shari'ati's ideas were neither systematic nor pragmatic: it is difficult to see how the unity of *Ummat* and *Imamat* could have been achieved outside a messianic fulfilment or be being forced through a stern disciplinary course of religious 'enlightenment' under an Islamic government, which is precisely what the clergy-dominated Islamic Republic is trying to achieve in the application of Khomeini's doctrines.

Revolutionary Shi'ism?

Both Khomeini and Shari'ati relate their respective discourses to specifically Shi'ite doctrine and symbols. There are persistent statements and arguments in the modern historical literature to the effect that the Shi'ite tradition because of the legitimist claims for the Imamate to be in the line of Ali, necessarily challenges the legitimacy of other Islamic rule and is therefore potentially revolutionary, or at least oppositional.[18] Within this line of argument, the contemporary Iranian revolutionaries follow in the mainstream of Shi'ite tradition, realising its potential for revolt. Indeed, Shari'ati in an essay entitled *Red Shi'ism* (1979a) explicitly subscribes to this line of argument, with the qualification that certain strands of Shi'ism in history had betrayed this mission by compromising with kings and dynasties. We shall argue here that 'mainstream' Shi'ism (that is, the Shi'ism of the Imams and the scholars and of the settled communities as against the 'extreme' (*ghuluww*) Shi'ism of certain sects, tribes and Sufi tendencies) was

26

for the most part quiescent and accepted the political rule of various caliphs and sultans, providing they left Shi'ites free to observe religious obligations in their own way and to have their own courts and Qadis administering their codification of Islamic law, that is, providing they could lead the life of a sectarian community.

At its inception, Shi'ism was an oppositional legitimist movement, contesting the assumption of the Caliphate by the Umayyads in favour of a designated descendant in the line of Ali. The great Shi'i rebellions and the martyrdom it engendered belong to this period. Abbasid propaganda and agitation against the Umayyads drew heavily on Shi'i ideas and sympathies: their agents and missionaries gave the impression that they were acting for a 'legitimate' member of the House (of the Prophet). When, at their success in defeating the Umayyads, the Abbasids revealed themselves as the descendants of Al-Abbas, the Prophet's uncle, there was great dismay in Shi'i circles, but any agitation or rebellions were firmly put down. The succession of designated Alid Imams and their followers for the most part acquiesced in Abbasid power and in return were respected and honoured by the Caliphs, but kept firmly under surveillance. When 'orthodox' Shi'i doctrine was systematised and codified in later times, it was primarily on the basis of the traditions of these quiescent Imams, especially Ja'far the sixth Imam. These traditions pertained primarily to the reform of worship and ritual and to the reform of law regulating communal and personal relations. In these respects, 'orthodox' Shi'ism developed into a sectarian community with its own peculiar forms of theology, law and ritual. Of course, the basis of its separateness was political in that it rested on the refusal to accept the authority and legitimacy of the state and of Sunni religious codes. But the *de facto* acquiescence in Abbasid power meant that this refusal was, at the political level, nominal:

> A decisive step of compromise with political reality by the Imamites was the granting of a *de facto* recognition to the Abbasid caliphate by accepting coexistence and ceasing to strive against it militarily. Simultaneously, though, they retained the conviction that it is incumbent upon the believer to pay obedience and loyalty to the Imam. Probably this act of compromise crystallized at the time of the Imam Ja'far-as-Sadiq. (Eliash, 1979, p.22)

Nevertheless, Shi'i legitimism always posed an implicit threat to the caliphate and for that reason the Imams and their followers, although tolerated and respected for the most part, were also kept under close surveillance and in some instances subjected to harassment and persecution. After the 'disappearance' of the Twelfth Imam (in AD 873) the orthodox (now Twelver or 'Imamite') Shi'a continued to live peacefully and there were Shi'i families like the Nawbakhtis who became prominent in the Abbasid court and in the affairs of the state. The 'disappearance' of the Imam, only to reappear at an indeterminate point in the future, removed the implicit political threat or challenge of Shi'ism and made for its easier acceptance by the state (but not always by the Sunni ulama) as a separate religio-legal community. The abeyance of Shi'i legitimist claims is illustrated in the episode of the Shi'i Buwayhid amirs' (932-1055) conquest of Baghdad. They took over governmental powers, but did not attempt to install a legitimist Shi'i leadership, nor were they pressed to do so by their favoured Shi'i ulama. Instead they maintained the puppet Abbasid Caliph. The history of 'orthodox' Shi'ism thus far does not lend support to the view that Shi'ism is inherently revolutionary and a constant challenge to the legitimacy of the government. As we shall see, the subsequent history of Iranian Shi'ism under the Safavids did not alter the general picture. But under the Qajars, Iranian Shi'ism assumed a distinctive oppositional stance, and this is one of the main supports for the thesis that Shi'ism is inherently revolutionary. We shall turn to a consideration of Shi'ism under the Qajar presently, but before doing this, let us look at other strands of Shi'ism which do not conform to this picture.

The discussion above related to 'orthodox' or Twelver Shi'ism. However, at various points in Islamic history there were uprisings against the state in the name of one or other Alid 'pretender'. The strand of Shi'ism most given to rebellion in the Islamic Middle Ages was Isma'ilism in its various forms (split from 'mainstream' Shi'ism over the succession to Ja'far; the 'mainstream' followed his son, Musa, while the dissidents declared his son Isma'il the rightful successor). To mention the most prominent examples of Isma'ili movements: the Qarmatians (ninth to eleventh centuries) who rose against the Abbasid caliphate and established a Shi'i community, praised by its supporters as a communistic egalitarian state, and reviled by its opponents as a corrupt tyranny; the Fatimids (909-1171) who established a rival caliphate centred in Egypt which rivalled and threatened the Abbasids and their Seljukid masters; and the order of the Assassins, in Iran and in Syria (thirteenth century), whose members engaged extensively in the activity which gave their name to political killing. We should first note that at their inception, all these movements (and many others besides) were centred around a charismatic leader with a claim to Alid descent, or to be acting as an agent for such a descendant. We should follow Khomeini in making a clear distinction between the charismatic/sacred attributes of descent on the one hand and the claim to the function of government by a just *faqih*. The claims for leadership and for the Imamate by the 'pretenders' in question did not rest upon knowledge gained by study and training, but upon the attributes of holy descent (which naturally includes knowledge as an inherent endowment). The second point that we should note is that the doctrines and philosophies of these movements remain separate from the mainstream of Shi'i or Sunni theology and eventually disappear, perhaps leaving traces in the popular religiosity. Either the movement in question inaugurated a separate sectarian community as in the case of the Qarmatians, in which case their doctrines were strictly segregated and anathematised by the 'mainstream' ulama, and eventually disappeared with the final demise of the community. Or, as in the case of the Fatimids, the ascent to the caliphate created a new mainstream which gradually compromised with and approximated to orthodoxy. When the original leader or his immediate successor established a dynasty, like the Fatimids, they were concerned to establish their power on a secure institutional basis. The heterodox enthusiasms which had brought them to rule then became an embarrassment, and the rulers turned to more orthodox sources of doctrine and law. Here again, the heterodox doctrines of rebellion are diluted and routinised.

As we shall see, the Safavid ascent to power (in 1500) was at the head of a heterodox Sufi-Shi'i movement of this type, the 'extreme' elements being subsequently suppressed and Twelver Shi'ism established as the state religion.

Heterodox and messianic movements have continued to appear in Iran right up to the mid-nineteenth century and to exert various degrees of influence on some of the ulama and sectors of the populace, the last significant movement being Babism (mid-nineteenth century). A discussion of these movements is out of place in this context. What has to be noted here is their separateness from and opposition to mainstream orthodoxy.

If the argument for the revolutionary nature of Shi'ism should claim as supporters these examples of heterodox and rebellious Shi'ism, then it cannot go on to consider Khomeinism as part of this tradition (and in fairness no one to my knowledge has put forward this view). Khomeini remained very much within the mainstream of Shi'i thought, which considered 'extreme' (*ghuluww*) Shi'ism as heretical. His innovations are firmly within this mainstream.

The Safavid Dynasty (1500-1722) which instituted Shi'ism in Iran was brought to power by militant tribesmen inspired by heterodox enthusiasms mixing popular Sufism with elements of Alid veneration. Shah Isma'il, the first Safavid king, was the descendant of a holy (Sufi) dynasty with temporal ambitions. They adopted Shi'ism, some say, to differentiate themselves and their claims for spiritual and temporal power from the Ottoman state and to appeal to the generally heterodox sentiments of the populace, especially the tribesmen.

The success of the Safavids and the institution of their state led to the problems of routinisation and of control of their militant followers. The Shi'ism of the populace was heterodox. As against that, the early Safavids imported (literally) orthodox Twelver Shi'ism in the form of ulama from the traditional Shi'i stronghold of Jabal 'Amil, in what is now the Lebanon. Throughout the reign of the Safavids, the ulama had high posts in the state administration and generous endowments of land, both directly as personal endowments and indirectly in the form of *Waqf* (religious endowment for mosques, schools and charities). In general, the elite of the ulama enjoyed power and wealth and high status and were closely involved in state institutions.

The example of the Safavids fits in very well with the pattern of relations between religion and government in dynastic Islamic states. Its charisma is one of descent which is the basis for its claim to leadership. Once the power of the lineage is established, its religious affiliations move towards orthodoxy and the establishment of specialist religious institutions; these in effect, separating off religion from other state functions. The ulama, established and honoured, are nevertheless subordinated to temporal power. They are entirely involved in sustaining and furthering the legitimacy of Safavid rule. They constructed a Sharifian lineage (that is, descent from the House of the Prophet) for the Safavid family, sometimes with connotations of the Shi'i Imamate. The Safavids' claim to be 'God's shadow on earth' (an ancient, pre-Islamic, notion of Persian kingdom) is not questioned by the ulama elite. There were no doubt always dissenting voices among the ulama who questioned the claims and conduct of kings and their courts. But this questioning was not to deny the validity and the legitimacy of kingship or of government as such, but only that of unjust, repressive or ungodly kings. Short of the messianic reappearances of *Imam-ul-Zaman,* there was no other way to truly righteous government. A just king would take the counsel of the pious man of religion, but there was no question of the just *faqih* taking over from the king.[19]

The Qajar dynasty (1796-1926) fared much worse with the ulama. The context of the ulama's power was the general weakness, decentralisation and corruption of the Qajar state. Tribal leaders, big landowners, military chiefs and religious magnates enjoyed singly or in alliance extensive local and regional power. The ulama elite shared in this fragmented power, enjoying extensive land holding and the revenues from religious taxes as well as the allegiance of local communities. There are instances of prominent *mujtahids* leading private armies recruited from fugitives whom they sheltered, and/or students of the religious schools. They were used to collect taxes and to enforce decisions of religious courts.[20] Twelver Shi'ism was the established religion of Iran under the Qajars and the ulama for the most part enjoyed governmental deference as well as the payment of stipends to those engaged on judicial and ceremonial functions. But the autonomous bases of the ulama enabled them to speak out against the government whenever any measures were introduced which threatened their privileges or influence among their followers.[21] This included opposition to any form of secularisation and modernisation, such as the establishment of secular schools and education. It also included opposition to all foreign intrusion or influence, and in this respect their position coincided with that of the national movements. In many instances, the granting of economic privileges and monopolies to foreign companies and individuals directly threatened the interests of merchants closely allied with the ulama. The latter would then lead agitation, demonstration and boycotts. The most notable case was that of the tobacco concession granted by Nasir Ud-Din Shah to the Imperial Tobacco Company in 1891. There were a series of agitations led by the ulama, culminating in a total boycott of tobacco products following a ruling by Mirza Hasan Shirazi, the then *Marja'i Taqlid* (highest source of religious judgement) of Samarra, one of the Shi'i holy shrines in Ottoman Iraq, and therefore outside the reach of Iranian authorities. The campaign was very effective, ending with the cancellation of the concession (with appropriate compensation to the Company).[22] In retrospect, this episode appears as a preliminary to the political campaign in which the ulama also played a prominent part.

Does the Ulama's oppositional stance under the Qajars constitute a precedent or a lead up to the doctrine of *Wilayat Al-Faqih?* Perhaps this question is best answered in the words of Hamid Algar (in the conclusion to his authoritative study of religion under the Qajars):

> intervention in political affairs to gain permanent control thereof never appears to have been even a distant aim of the Ulama. The continued occultation of the Imam meant, inescapably, the absence of all legitimising authority from worldly affairs, so that the political attitudes of the Ulama could, in the final analysis, be only a question of opposition. Any wish to reshape definitively the norms of political life in the laws of the state was foreign to the Ulama in Qajar Iran. Thus it was that the forces of renewal passed them by, (Algar, 1980, p. 260).

The clear implication is that the Ulama's political involvement was basically oppositional rather than revolutionary or innovative. Certainly the replacement of the Qajar kingdom by an Islamic government controlled by the clergy was not 'even a distant aim of the Ulama'.

Conclusion

To return to the question of 'fundamentalism' raised at the beginning.

'Fundamentalist' seems to be applied to those doctrines and movements which oppose secular governments in Muslim countries by insisting on the necessary unity of religion, state and society in Islam. We have shown in the foregoing discussion that this political stance does not entail an ideological homogeneity.

The exponents of these doctrines are 'fundamentalist' in the sense of their emphasis on deriving their political and social ideas from the fundamental or original sources of Islam, the Quran and the Sunna — this, as we have seen, to the effective exclusion of the Islamic political or juridical precepts which developed over the many centuries of Islamic empires. But these factors do not distinguish the so-called fundamentalists from many of the Islamic reformers, like Abdu and some of his disciples, who also believed in the renewal of religion and society from the original sources, and in the unity of religion, society and the state in Islam, and yet came to very different conclusions, far more accommodating to 'modern' (that is European inspired) institutions and practices which they believed to be compatible with those original principles. This shows clearly the problems of thinking of Islam (or any other religion) as an essential unity and totality whose 'fundamentals' are clear and discernible. Every return to the 'sources' constitutes a construction of these sources in line with the desired conclusions.

Another aspect of many of those who fall within the general classification of fundamentalism is the innovatory nature of their pronouncements within the Islamic tradition. Ideologically they are operating within Western-inspired political paradigms of the nation state and 'the people'. Many of the movements in question, like the Muslim Brothers and the Islamic components of the Iranian revolution, were looking to the common people for support against Western-orientated dominant social groups, institutions and parties: theirs is a populist nationalism with 'Islam' as the identifying emblem of the common people against the 'alien' social spheres in their own country which had excluded and subordinated them.

One thing Al-Banna, Shari'ati and, in places, Khomeini, are agreed upon is that the achievement of an 'organic' Islamic society and state in which the people and the leadership are of one mind and purpose must start with the reform of the hearts and minds of the people in an Islamic world; this will form the basis of the good society and state:

> Our duty as Muslim Brothers is to work for the reform of selves [*nufus*], of hearts and souls by joining them to God the all-high; then to organise our society to be fit for the virtuous community which commands the good and forbids evil-doing, then from the community will arise the good state.
> (Hassan al-Banna, pp. 62–3)

The traditional Islamic political ideal of the good prince who rules justly among the people and enforces Islamic observances here gives place to a leadership which reforms hearts and minds, which then becomes in turn the basis for a just Islamic state; an organicism which starts from below, from the roots, and the roots are the people. Of course Islamic men of religion in past centuries sought to reform and enlighten. What is new in this case is the specific and explicit link between this reformation and the good Islamic state. The just ruler and the pious soul were both long-standing ideals in Islam (as in most other religions and doctrines), the innovation is to make personal piety and the good community the conditions of a just state.

We have seen that Ali Shari'ati made this linkage both at the moral level (enlightenment of hearts to recognise and follow the Imam) and at the 'sociological level', that is in terms of systematic social processes which link 'people', 'society' and 'state' (after having conceptually made these distinctions). This 'sociological' level is a distinctively 'modern' element not clearly present in the thought of Hassan al-Banna (although present in Islamic thought since the late nineteenth century).[23] But even in Al-Banna's thought a linkage is made at the moral level which is not common in traditional Islamic thought. The nature of the state in the historical empires would not suggest such a people/society/state linkage. For the most part, the state appeared as an external addition to society, albeit one which is necessary to institute order and security and to provide the conditions for Islamic observances. The succession of princes and dynasties must have seemed quite arbitrary and certainly not due to some systematic 'social' condition. Even in the ideal text-book Islamic state in Ibn Taymiyya's *Al-Siyasa al-Shar'iyya* the rights and duties of the ruler and his subjects appear in the form of complementary rights and duties; the one to rule justly and competently in accordance with the Quaran and the *shari'a*, the other to obey and follow. The unity of piety and justice was an ideal realised only in the Medina community of Muhammad and his immediate successors. But that ideal is contained in a community in which 'state' and 'society' are not differentiated and in which 'government' is synonymous with 'leadership'. When the state acquired institutional and military forms distinct from the community, then the 'ideal' relationship shifted to one of complementarity of rights and duties. The piety and solidarity of the ruled community did not feature as a *systematic* condition of the power of the state. The justice or corruption of the ruler could prove a good or bad example for his subjects, but was not considered a condition for their piety or virtue. What was at issue was the moral quality and answerability to God of rulers and ruled, separately as persons or communities, rather than a systematic linkage between them.

Notes

1 Abdu advocated a unified Islamic state/society; but one in which the law was sufficiently flexible to accommodate the institutions of the modern state and economy without compromising what he considered to be the basic tenets of Islam. He had a great admiration for the achievements of contemporary European nations and was strongly influenced by contemporary currents of European thought, notably Auguste Comte and Herbert Spencer (see Hourani, 1962, pp. 130-60).

2 The word 'imam' has a multiplicity of senses which makes it confusing for the reader not familiar with Islamic usage. Most generally, 'Imam' means leader of a community: in this sense all Islamic princes, including all the caliphs, can be called 'Imams'. 'Imamate' refers to the position and function of leadership. The prayer leader in any congregation is also called Imam, and the term may also be used as a title for specially prestigious Ulama. In addition to these usages, the Shi'a have a special notion of the Imamate. They believe that the leadership (Imamate) of the Islamic community should be assumed by designated descendants from the House of the Prophet through his daughter Fatima and her husband (the Prophet's cousin) Ali. Nevertheless, the Shi'a followed a succession of twelve designated Imams (each designating his successor) in the line of Ali. The third Imam Hussain, son of Ali, led a rebellion against the Umayyad caliphate which was defeated, culminating in his martyrdom. The succeeding Imams lived for the most part pacifically under the Abbasid caliphate, assuming the role of supreme religious leader of the Shi'i community. The Shi'a believe their Imams to be infallible by virtue of having special super-human powers of knowledge and enlightenment with which to guide the community. The twelfth Imam, Al-Mahdi, 'disappeared' in Samarra', near Baghdad, in 873. After a short period of communicating with the community through appointed deputies, the communication ceased altogether and then ensued the period of the 'Great Occultation' which has lasted to the present day. The 'absent' Imam is still the reigning Imam ul Zaman (the Imam of all time), but his guidance is withheld from the community until such time as he returns. The expectation of his reappearance has assumed the dimensions of a Messianic hope. As we shall see, Khomeini's doctrine of government and the controversies surrounding it revolve around the question of leadership and government of the community during the period of the Occultation. These are the beliefs of the 'mainstream' Shi'a, known as Twelvers or Imami. But historically, and to the present day, there have been many schisms around the question of succession to the Imamate which have resulted in a number of sects, notably the Isma'ilis, the Druze and the Alawis.

3 A prominent example is that of Ali Abdulraziq who argued in 1925 that the caliphate is not a necessary part of the Islamic religion, and that for most of its historical existence it was a secular institution operating by the rule of force and not contributing significantly to Islamic observance or spirituality. Interestingly, he also derived his argument from the 'fundamentals' of Islam. See Hourani, 1962, pp. 183-92.

4 Each Sunni community subscribes to one of four schools or doctrines

(Madhahib) of law, all considered equally 'orthodox' and mutually acceptable to one another.

5 'It has been suggested that it may have been regarded as good form by Muslim rulers to allow vigorous and penetrating sermons to be addressed to them on specific occasions', Watt, 1973, p. 80.

6 *'Ijtihad'* means independent exertion in the use of reason to arrive at judgments relating to religious law. It is widely accepted (though by no means unanimously) that the Sunni schools of law had closed the 'gate of *Ijtihad'* at an early stage in the ninth century, thus making it incumbent upon legal scholars to follow authority and precedent. In Shi'ism *ijtihad* is a complex issue, and opinions on its legitimacy have varied. The dominant current view favours *ijtihad* by designated senior clergy with a high level of learning with the title of *mujtahid*.

7 'Sunna' means 'path' or 'norm' and refers to the traditions, conduct and example of the Prophet. Orthodox Muslims are designated 'Sunna', that is followers of the 'path'. In fact, the Shi'a accept the authority of the Sunna equally, although they may differ in the versions of the traditions they accept and in their interpretation.

8 For a detailed account, see W.M. Patton, 1897.

9 For a history of the house of Sa'ud and its relation to Wahhabism, see H. St John Philby, 1968.

10 For a history of the Ikhwan movement, see J. Habib, 1978.

11 I am indebted to Parvin Javadi-Motlagh and to Abbas Vali for acquainting me with the contents of this essay, for which I could not find an Arabic or English translation.

12 See Hourani, 1962, pp. 222-44.

13 Joseph Eliash (1979) in an article on 'Misconception regarding the juridical status of the Iranian ulama' considers the claim of some Shi'i ulama, echoed by some Western scholars, that in the period of absence of the Imam, the ulama act as his general agents, and while not fully participating in his charisma, nevertheless have equal claims to the following and obedience of believers. Eliash shows that this claim cannot be supported by reference to the traditions (Hadith) of the Imams and cites one Hadith of Imam Ja'far (the supposed protagonist of the disputed view), which clearly

> does not delegate to the judges the exclusive and infallible authority of the Imam to interpret the law and commands them to adhere strictly to the Koran and to the traditions and the rulings of the Imams when pronouncing their own judgement....Moreover the Hadith confers on the community the right to dispose of the judge if it finds out that he has based his judgement on an exceptional (shadhdh) tradition rather than on a well-known (mashur) tradition. [p. 15]

This would clearly subvert the claim for nearly absolute authority made by Khomeini for the *faqih*.

Maghniyya (1979) (a Lebanese Shi'i*'alim*) in a generally respectful and sympathetic critique of Khomeini, makes similar points. Maghniyya also argues (pp. 99-103) that the religiously specified taxes from Muslims (*Khums* and *zakat*) are not intended for state expenditure, but as alms to be distributed to poor Muslims.

14 For an elaboration on this point, see Zubaida, 1969.

15 This section refers to the essays collected under *On the Sociology of Islam*, 1979.

16 All Quranic quotes are from Arberry, 1964.

17 *Sha'b* is here used in the sense of 'race' or 'stock', much like the older usage of 'nation' in English.

18 For a statement of this view, see Bernard Lewis, 1985. Arjomand (1979), Eliash (1979) and Floor (1980) have effectively questioned this view with arguments relating to the history of Iranian Shi'ism (Arjomand), its doctrinal bases (Eliash) and the political alignments of the ulama in recent Iranian history (Floor).

19 For a discussion of the doctrinal and political positions of the ulama under the Safavids, see Arjomand, (1979).

20 See Algar, 1980, p. 19.

21 See Floor, 1980.

22 See Keddie, 1966.

23 For an account of the influence of nineteenth-century Western social thought including Comte and Spencer on Abdu and other contemporary thinkers, see Hourani, 1962, pp. 135-40.

2

The quest for the Islamic state: Islamic Fundamentalism in Egypt and Iran

'Islamic Fundamentalism' is a term which has been created in current discourses on the Middle East and elsewhere which has an identifiable but not strictly limited range of reference. It refers to modern political movements and ideas, mostly oppositional, which seek to establish, in one sense or another, an Islamic state. The model for an Islamic state is sought by these movements in a 'sacred history' of the original political community of the faithful established by the Prophet Muhammad in Medina in the seventh century and maintained under his four successors, the *Rashidun* (rightly guided) caliphs (in Shi'i Islam, it is only the rule of one of them, Ali). Identifying the essential elements of this model, and the way in which they can be constructed into a contemporary state and society, varies widely according to different political and ideological positions. I would argue that all 'fundamentalism' is modern in that it attempts to reconstruct the fundamentals of an ideational system in modern society, in accordance with political and ideological positions taken in relation to current issues and discourses. Identification of the fundamentals and their combinations are effected in relation to these current political processes. In what follows I shall examine the development of themes and issues in Islamic political discourse and activity in two Middle East countries in which these developments have been prominent and influential, and which provide strikingly contrasting examples. I shall concentrate primarily on Egypt, concluding with a general sketch of religion and politics in Iran to draw out the main contrasts. I shall discuss these developments in the context of their relation to the ideas and realities of the modern nation state, at first in anticipation of this political form and by reference to European examples, and later in the project to Islamise the nation state, or to

38

deny it in favour of a universal conception of faith. In Egypt modern political Islam started in the second half of the nineteenth century in anticipation of a modern state on the European model which it mostly welcomed, but constructed in terms of 'original' Islam, as against the degenerate religion of the dynastic polity it opposed. Subsequent movements in Egypt assumed the model of a modern nation state and sought ways, intellectually and politically, to Islamise this model. Unlike Egypt, religious developments in Iran remained largely within the religious establishment, which feared and resisted the modern state (itself a very different pattern from the Egyptian), then acquiesced in its inevitability while retaining an important base of autonomy in relation to that state. This was to be a crucial factor in the leading role it came to play in recent political events.

The terms 'modern state' and 'nation state' do not refer to an unvarying common form, but more to combinations of elements and characteristics constituting perhaps an 'ideal type'. To use Max Weber's [1] characterisation, the modern state is 'legal-rational', in that government rests on codified law which regulates hierarchies of office with specified powers, obligations and limits, thus constituting a specific type of bureaucracy. The form of society which typically corresponds to this state and provides the conditions for it is one in which extensive social division of labour has led to individualisation of economic and political subjects from communal and collectivist organisation of tribe, village, kinship or other corporate forms. The constituents of the state are then individual citizens with legal personalities and specified rights and obligations. Whether such a state has a democratic representational form or not, its political processes and struggles involve the organisation and mobilisation of citizens in constituencies of support based on common interests or ideological commitments. A certain degree of general literacy is essential for the communications which form an important part of this form of politics. Literacy in a common language is also an important constituent of the ideological conceptions of common national belonging, what Benedict Anderson (1983) has called 'imagined communities'. In reality, as we all know, primordial loyalties of ethnicity, religion, regional origins and so forth play a very important part in the politics of modern states, but these loyalties are cast in the political idiom and mode of political parties employing methods of organisation and communication characteristic of this model of the modern state. [2] I shall have occasion in what follows to elaborate on these different political modalities.

The currents of Islamic fundamentalism I shall discuss here have developed discourses and practices which refer, explicitly or implicitly, to the modern state. The creation or the transformation of the modern state along the lines of the 'sacred history' of Islam is a recurrent theme. There are fundamentalist currents which do not fit into this mould, most notably the Wahhabi movement which culminated in the formation of modern Saudi Arabia (see Chapter 1, pp. 10–13). I would argue (see Zubaida, 1986) that this is an example of a historical genre of tribal movements which start with religious zeal and culminate in routinised dynastic states, which is precisely what happened in Saudi Arabia. It is quite distinct from Islamic politics in the context of the modern state (although it did have important intellectual effects in that context).

The event which above all others has focused world attention on 'fundamentalism' was the Iranian revolution of 1979. For the European and American media and their audiences it was an object of fascination and fear: a demonstration to many that the deep-rooted bases of 'traditional belief' cannot be overridden with 'modernisation' which is only a superficial veneer. To 'Third World' nationalists and some 'Third Worldists', it represented not merely an anti-imperialist revolution, but one with the special distinction of cultural authenticity, challenging the most insidious dimension of imperialism, the cultural. In other Islamic countries, especially in the Arab world, the impact was tremendous. Naturally enough, those already inclined to Islamic affiliations drew great inspiration and strength from the demonstration effect of the revolution; suddenly their ideas were firmly on the world stage and within the realms of political possibility. What is even more important, however, was the impact on other oppositional political groups and individuals, including those on the left, who have traditionally opposed Islamic currents, usually ranged to the far right of the political spectrum. Here was an Islamic revolution which was populist and anti-imperialist, which had sported some of the vocabularies and slogans of the left. For some it seemed that, unlike the 'imported' ideologies of Marxism or nationalism, Islam in its political and 'progressive' form is more accessible to the people, springing as it does from their historical cultural roots. Political Islam acquired many recruits, a political respectability and viability, it became firmly established in the political mainstream. This was to the embarrassment and discomfort of political regimes which had adopted or encouraged Islam as a means of discipline and control (Saudi Arabia), or as a counter against the left (Sadat in Egypt).

The Iranian revolution underlined the salience of political Islam in current Middle East and world politics. But it is clearly neither the starting point of political Islam, which has a long history in the modern world, nor the political or sociological prototype of Islamic political movements elsewhere. It is important to emphasise this point, because it is often assumed, both by the Islamic propagandists themselves and by some Western commentators, that there is some unity underlying the Islamic phenomenon, provided by the receptivity of Middle Eastern peoples to religious appeals, which they understand and accept more readily than they would 'imported' politics and ideology. The argument I shall present here is that the significance and outcome of Islamic politics can only be determined in the contexts of particular institutions and struggles, which in the case of Egypt are vastly different. This difference, I shall show, cannot be explained in terms of the contrast between Sunni and Shi'i Islam. Let us turn to a consideration of these contexts and conjunctures.

The historical background

While the concern of this paper is primarily with the modern world, a brief glance at the historical background is nevertheless essential. The very use of the term 'political Islam' may be at issue: what other form of Islam is there? Islam has been political since its inception, it may be argued, a unity of state and the community of the faithful. That is at least the theory of Islamic jurisprudence, but the practice for most of the centuries of Islamic history is quite different, a fact also recognised in theology and jurisprudence. Islamic empires, at least since the time of the Umayyads, have maintained a *de facto* distinction between the state and society, and religion entered both but in different ways, and except for brief periods, was neither dominant over nor coincident with either state or society. The state consisted of the ruling dynasty with their retainers, functionaries and soldiery. The early Islamic armies which conquered the vast territories which later constituted the Islamic empires consisted of Arab tribesmen. As such the Caliph could be seen as the chief of the community, the state as the political form of the community, and the soldiers as the faithful in arms. This state of affairs was not to survive dynastic rule, under which the Arab armies were disbanded and replaced by professional soldiers, mostly Turkish. This state, now structurally and socially separate from its subjects, remained theoretically the Islamic state. Its head still bore the title of Caliph (successor and deputy to the Prophet), who encouraged and facilitated Islamic worship, punished heresy and generally upheld the symbols and rituals of Islam. In the constitution of the state Islam was confined to particular institutions, almost exclusively the legal institutions. The law, however, was in practice only partially based on religious sources, and it only applied to limited spheres of mostly private and civil statuses and transactions. The ruler and his servants were bound by the law only in theory and in the most general ethical terms. Models and procedures of government were drawn from pre-Islamic imperial traditions of Persia and Byzantium. The primary source of legislation was by decree of the ruler, although this in theory should not contradict the principles of *shari'a* (Islamic law). Some taxes are specified in *shari'a*, but most of the forms of taxation were in addition to those stipulated; some rulers even taxed the sale of alcoholic drinks, thus legaly admitting what in religious terms is prohibited. In the sphere of the state, therefore, religion occupied a distinct but limited and subordinate position. Middle Eastern polities were in practice as Islamic as their European counterparts were Christian.

In the context of society, the first point to note is the diversity of religious manifestations. The most important divide is that between the city and the non-urban sphere of nomads and tribesmen of desert and mountain (in Middle Eastern geo-history, these are the two main spheres, the rural being an appendage of one or the other, see Zubaida, 1986). the nomadic was considered by the orthodox (often quite rightly) to be the sphere of heterodoxy and the refuge of heresy outside the reach of political and religious authority. Scriptural orthodoxy claimed pride of place in the city: it was the official state religion, and one of the main connecting links between state and civil society. The religious institutions of the state were manned by personnel drawn from the strata of urban notables, the same strata which included merchants and landowners. These were also the leaders of urban society and the intermediaries between the state and the other urban strata. Orthodoxy existed side by side with Sufism, and since about the eleventh century, in harmony with it. In terms of belief and ritual, Sufism is a mystical, spiritual and gnostic stream within Islam, but beyond this general characterisation exhibits, in turn, considerable diversity. To sum up, religion took diverse and overlapping forms, many of which bore only a tenuous relation to orthodox, scriptural Islam.

Modern Islamic political thought has to be seen in the context of a conjuncture between this historical background and the European impact. The reformist intellectuals of the Ottoman Empire and of Iran, concerned at the weakness and backwardness of their countries in the face of European might, believed that the superiority of the European powers (mainly Britain and France) did not depend solely on economic and military power, but that behind these factors lay a socio-political system which produces awareness and commitment among the people and an effective organisation of state and society. Ottoman, including Egyptian Islamic intellectuals argued that the perceived inferiority of their countries was not attributable to Islam as such, as Europeans may think, but to the degeneration and corruption of Islam. Islam was seen to have anticipated the European systems. This line of thought was shared by two major figures in the late nineteenth century, often cited as the founders of the reformist movement in Egypt, Jamal Eddin al-Afghani and Muhammad Abdu.

Political Islam in Egypt

Egypt was the Middle Eastern country which experienced the earliest direct European conquest and thereafter its continued presence and influence. It started with the Napoleonic invasion, soon followed by the modernising rule of Muhammad Ali, who attempted, with some success, economic and administrative reforms. These included institutions of modern education and scholarships for promising students to France. French and other European literature and social thought were eagerly taken up by a wide circle of intellectuals, including, significantly, some with religious education and training. Muhammad Ali's successors (dynastic descendants) took Egypt into ever-closer involvement with and dependence upon Britain and France, culminating in debt crises and more direct economic, military and political controls by these powers throughout the nineteenth century and for the first half of the twentieth. These developments included profound social and cultural effects: considerable measures of industrialisation and urbanisation, capitalist penetration of important sectors of agriculture, with consequent break-up or loosening of old communal bonds. Together with the limited development of education and literacy, these developments created more or less politicised publics, especially in the major cities, who were increasingly aware of the inequities of foreign domination, and of the gap between the promise of European ideas of liberty and the realities of continued restrictions under dynastic rule. Islamic political thought has to be considered in this context.

The picture of religion in relation to society and the state given in the foregoing historical sketch still applied to nineteenth-century Egypt. Muhammad Abdu's reforms were aimed first at religious ideas and institutions, and then at the wider society.[3] Religious institutions, including the great university of al-Azhar in Cairo, were still partaking in the wisdom of the Middle Ages, and teaching medieval geography, mathematics and science as well as the religious studies of theology and jurisprudence. This archaic scholasticism existed side by side with popular religiosity imbued with magic and saint worship. Abdu, himself a prominent *'alim* (a learned man of religion) succeeded in enlisting the support of the authorities in reforming and modernising these institutions. But the task which he and his mentor Afghani had set themselves was much wider: it was to liberate Islamic countries from their weakness and backwardness, and their subjugation to the European imperial powers. They attributed this weakness to ignorance, corruption and fragmentation characteristic of Islamic polities and societies including the religious institutions. But these failings, they argued, were certainly not intrinsic to Islam, quite the contrary; witness the glories of the Islamic past, both in knowledge and in might. In particular, the socio-political system which contributed so much to the might and civilisation of the West was anticipated by Islam many centuries previously. The Islamic community founded by Muhammad in Medina in the seventh century exemplified all the principles of citizenship and democracy in a purer and clearer form. For while in Christianity religion is separated from the state, in Islam the state is one with the *umma*, the community of believers; religion, state and people form one body. In the Medinan community the state was but the plurality of its citizens unified by faith and obedience to the commands of God. No man could rule over another because rule belonged to God alone. The army was but the citizenry in arms. Institutions like *shura*, the imperative that the ruler consult his followers in all important matters, and *bay'a*, the collective oath of allegiance to a new leader before he could assume the *Khilafa* (caliphate) – the succession to Muhammed as commander of the faithful – ensured representativeness and responsibility of rule in a form more original and direct than the equivalent institution in modern Europe. What Muslims needed now was not so much to follow Europe, but to revive their original heritage, which had been subverted by the dynastic empires, and forgotten in the degeneration and corruption of religion in the later centuries.

It may be instructive to draw a parallel between Islamic thinkers seeking reform in the revival of original elements of their history with their European (especially German) equivalents in the eighteenth and nineteenth centuries. For Goethe, Schiller, Holderlin and Hegel,[4] the ancient Athenian republic fulfilled a similar function as the Medinan community for our Islamic thinkers — a model of the unity of the state and civil society, and the identity of private individual and citizen, in contrast to the social, political and psychological fragmentation which they perceived in their contemporary world. Some, like the young Hegel, saw in the French Revolution the possibilities of a regeneration at a higher level of the Athenian model. But it is the significance they attached to religion which is of particular interest here. They contrasted the subjective and individualistic elements of Christianity to the civic and folk religions of Greece and Rome, and attributed the fragmentation of life in contemporary society at least in part to the prevailing religious spirit. We do not know whether Abdu or any of his followers knew about this discussion, though we do know that Abdu was familiar with contemporary European thought, and was specially impressed with Auguste Comte and Herbert Spencer.[5] What is interesting, however is that he presented similar arguments when contrasting Christianity with Islam: Christianity separated religiosity from politics and public life, whereas Islam, as we have seen, he considered to be an eminently political and civic religion. But unlike the German thinkers who could not argue for a revival of ancient Greek religion, Abdu's Athenian republic was Islamic Medina; all he was doing was advocating a revival of true and original Islam.

Abdu is not normally identified as a fundamentalist but rather as a liberal reformer with a nineteenth-century faith in progress through enlightenment. The major contrast between Abdu and, say, the Muslim Brotherhood (see below) is his liberalism with regard to the application of Islamic law, particularly elements of the penal code and the restrictions on women. At the present time the insistence on these elements of *shari'a* is the hallmark of fundamentalism,[6] and by these criteria Abdu is not a fundamentalist. It may be argued that this insistence on the letter of the Quran is a defining characteristic of fundamentalism. But any call for the application of the *shari'a* must implicitly accept many interpretations and elaborations beyond the letter of the holy sources. Abdu was doing no more than the Islamic jurists have done throughout the ages in using very wide and vague principles of legal methodology of deduction and analogy in arriving at judgments. A fundamentalist position calling for the application of the *shari'a* must accept that any version will already contain many constructions which have a very tenuous connection to the holy sources. What underlies the contrast between Abdu and later fundamentalists are their different attitudes to European ideas and models: whereas for Abdu Europe, the oppressor, was at the same time the model for progress and strength, for the later fundamentalists the West was both oppressive and culturally threatening. The insistence on the Quranic penal code and on the restrictions on women are emotionally and symbolically potent proclamations of cultural identity and antagonism to the Westernised sectors of society who have betrayed this heritage. While Abdu is clearly not a fundamentalist in the current sense, his construction of the 'sacred history' as a model for the modern state was a very important episode in the quest for this Islamic state.

An event which symbolised the institution of the modern state in the former Ottoman lands was Ataturk's abolition of the caliphate in 1924. The modern state which Abdu sought had arrived, but with hardly any Islamic trappings in its organisation or ideology. Ataturk's republic was explicitly anti-religious. Iraq, Palestine and Syria were under European mandates, and Egypt, while nominally independent was in reality a European colony. Islamic presence within the state, in so far as it existed at all, was confined to the law of personal status. The loss of the caliphate stimulated diverse reactions throughout the Islamic world, from the caliphate movement in India, to the various schemes advanced by would-be candidates for the vacant position among Arab rulers and dignitaries, including the Egyptian monarch.[7] At the level of politico-religious ideas, the most prominent response was that of Rashid Rida (d.1935),[8] a religious intellectual and disciple of Abdu. He sought a formula for re-establishing the caliphate under modern conditions of separate nation states (see Chapter 1, pp. 15-16). His solution was a caliph who would enjoy spiritual authority in all the Islamic lands by virtue of his learning and religious stature, and possibly of his descent from one of the respected Arab dynasties who claim the ancestry of the Prophet. This authority would be superimposed on independent sovereign governments, much like the papacy in the Catholic world. Politically Rida's advocacy came to nothing. Like Abdu, Rida exerted considerable intellectual influence, which had practical consequence in the religious and educational spheres. But neither of them succeeded in transferring his ideas into the field of political struggle or of incorporating them into the modern state. It was the Muslim Brotherhood which took the quest for the Islamic state into the political field of popular agitation and organisation.

The Muslim Brotherhood

This is the movement which, in one form or another, has been the most prominent fundamentalist current in Sunni Islam since its inception in Egypt in 1928.[9] While clearly influenced by the ideas of Abdu and Rida, it eschewed the European influences of Abdu's reformism and the intellectualism of Rida, aiming for a popular and populist appeal, with considerable success. The Brotherhood was founded by Hassan al-Banna, a school teacher in Isma'iliya in the Canal Zone. By all accounts al-Banna was a person endowed with great charisma and a prophetic zeal. He was struck by the corruption and degradation of Muslims, especially the young, of his time, and their subordination politically, economically and culturally to the dominant foreigners. He launched the Brotherhood as a movement for education and reform of hearts and minds. He taught the children in the daytime and their parents at night. The movement soon grew and spread to many parts of the country, acquired premises and funds. It very soon acquired a political dimension, calling for the Islamic reform of society and government. It became bitterly opposed to the secular, liberal-constitutional parties, especially the Wafd (the main democratic party in Egypt before the Free Officers' revolution in 1952), and in the process was firmly identified with the right. At times the Brotherhood flirted with the Royal Palace and participated in its intrigues against the elected Wafd government. Its members participated in the nationalist agitations against the British in the Canal Zone and then as volunteers in the Palestine conflict. It clearly had a potent influence in the lower ranks of the armed forces. Eventually (early 1940s) it developed its own armed 'secret apparatus' and engaged in political assassinations, the most prominent victim being the prime minister of Egypt, al-Nuqrashi, killed in 1949. Al-Banna himself was soon to fall in what was evidently a reprisal killing by the secret police. The Brotherhood, it would seem, had close connections with the Free Officers movement which staged the coup d'etat in 1952, and enjoyed official favour in the early days of the new regime. But they were soon to fall out with Nasser after he took over in 1954, and he was to become the target for an assassination attempt, after which the Brotherhood was fiercely suppressed. In spite of the flourishes of Islamic rhetoric, Nasser's regime was essentially secular, and the dominant official ideas were those of nationalism and socialism. The bitter enmity between Nasser and the Brotherhood persisted and flared in another episode in 1965 when the police claimed to have discovered an armed plot against the government, arrested many of the cadres of the Brotherhood and executed some of the leaders, including Sayyid Qutb, theoretician of more recent trends to be discussed in a following section.

The original aim of the Brotherhood was the reform of hearts and minds, to guide Muslims back to the true religion, and away from the corrupt aspirations and conduct created by European dominance. The early politicisation of the movement placed this objective in the context of a virtuous community and an Islamic political order. Hassan al-Banna, in an essay entitled 'The Reform of Self and Society', wrote:

> Our duty as Muslim Brothers is to work for the reform of selves [*nufus*], of hearts and souls by joining them to God the all-high; then to organise our society to be fit for the virtuous community which commands the good and forbids evil-doing, then from the community will arise the good state. (Hassan al-Banna, n.d., pp.62–3)

The main plank of their (rudimentary) political thought is a construction of the 'sacred history' similar to what we have already outlined, the recreation of the early Medinan community of the Prophet; their most persistent slogan is 'the Quran is our constitution'. But their model of the 'sacred history' is quite different from the liberal-constitutional image which emerges from Abdu's construction. In their version piety, order and authority play a central role. They advocate a presidential system with an elected *shura* (consultative) council, also part of the 'sacred history' model, postulated as an equivalent to a parliament. However, al-Banna strongly objected to political parties, arguing that they represent sectional and egoistic interests which divide and corrupt the body politic of the *umma*. This element in their thought reinforced their identification, by their opponents, with fascist organic-statist ideologies. The social and economic programme for such a regime is even more rudimentary and vague than the political thought. First is the axiomatic duty to facilitate and enforce the conditions and means for Islamic piety and ritual observance. This includes facilities for women, including working women, to maintain appropriate standards of dress and of insulation from contact with men. After that it is the maintenance of social justice as specified in the Quran. This of course gives wide scope for interpretation. Some thinkers from the ranks of the Muslim Brothers advocated Islamic socialism (see for instance Mohammad al-Ghazzali 1951). These treaties always start with a denunciation of Marxism and materialism, then elaborate on the inequities of capitalism seen as a system of *riba*, usury, which is forbidden in Islamic law. Al-Ghazzali interprets the sacred sources as supporting a distrust of private property, all goods belonging to God and disposable by those who rule justly in His name, the Caliph or his equivalent in an Islamic order. Private property is only justified if it fulfils a social function. The programme of an Islamic government must, therefore, include nationalisation and land reform. Some commentators have remarked on the similarity of this picture to the Nasser regime's 'Arab socialism' which was to follow. But as we have seen the Brothers were to denounce that regime as ungodly tyranny, and one that neglected all the tenets of Islam. These ideas of Islamic socialism have persisted in one form or another among progressive intellectuals with an Islamic orientation, but not so much among the Muslim Brothers as such. They have maintained vague notions of social justice, but have not used the vocabulary of socialism, or shown any hostility to private property. An obvious interpretation of this reticence regarding socialism is the maintenance of a clear ideological boundary against the rhetoric of the Nasser regime, and its apparent friendliness in foreign affairs to the socialist block. This hostility to socialism and to socialists has crystallised even more clearly in the ideas of the new Muslim Brotherhood which emerged into semi-legal public operation under Sadat in the 1970s and continues to the present day. Many of the leading personalities of the Brotherhood found refuge from Nasserite repression in Saudi Arabia, and the Saudi connection has been maintained as an important source of moral and financial support to the present time. This connection will no doubt have had significant political influence. More recently, persons and organisations associated with the Brotherhood have been very active in business and finance, especially with the rise of the Islamic banks and investment companies.

In every respect the Muslim Brotherhood, from its inception, has operated as a political party, now legal, now clandestine. It is the first organised Islamic popular movement in a modern urban setting. Its organisation and ideology assume potential constituencies composed of individualised political subjects, a high proportion of whom are literate and approachable through the printed word. Its activities and strategies assume the space of a centralised modern state, and are directed at its institutions and powers. Part of their strategy is the infiltration of military and police establishments. The primary objective of the establishment of an Islamic state is construed within the context of a modern nation state. In fact of all the political parties operating in recent Egyptian history the Muslim Brotherhood is one of the most modern in its assumptions and operations. Alongside the various small parties of the left, it relied primarily on organisation and mobilisation of support on ideological-political appeal and on an individual basis, as against the predominant politics of notables and of patronage networks characteristic of the general political scene, including many aspects of the organisation of support for the leading Wafd party. Nasserism in its heyday enjoyed widespread popular support and enthusiasm, but much of that was spontaneous and unorganised. And where it was organised, it was based on a government party closely interlinked with authority. Finally, in terms of the territorial scope of its operation, the Brotherhood shared the dilemma of Arab political ideologies in the oscillation between a particular national perspective (Egyptian) and a pan-Arab or, sometimes, pan-Islamic one. Its political organisation and activity was primarily in Egypt, but Brotherhood organisations were founded in other Arab countries, notably in Syria and Jordan, and more recently in the Gulf and in Tunisia. But while there is considerable contact and sometimes co-operation between these different national organisations, each in effect constitutes a unit in the national politics of its location. [10] The political space of its operation is in effect the multitude of Arab political entities, each organised as a separate nation state, but with a formal commitment to 'unity' theoretically shared by all, but in practice a dead letter.

The most notable extra-Egyptian activity in the Brotherhood's history is its participation in the Palestinian conflict, in itself part of Egyptian national politics.

In case the foregoing passages create the impression that the Brotherhood was a continuously coherent party, I should add a note about its fissiparous tendencies, particularly under conditions of stress. After the death of Banna, and then under Nasserite repression, conflicting factions were formed which engaged in various struggles. Often, there was no strong central control or discipline over the activities of members and factions, some of whom pursued their own projects, without reference to others. Many members and followers were dissatisfied with the weak leadership which prevailed in the organisation after Banna. The development of dissident groups and currents, to which we shall now turn, was, in part, a reflection of this situation.

Recent fundamentalist currents

While the Muslim Brotherhood has maintained its position as a leading actor on the political stage in recent years, it was the other more militant Islamic groups, like the so-called *Takfir wal Hijra*, and *Jihad* who assumed the most spectacular roles, especially with the assassination of President Sadat in 1981. To understand properly the ideology and organisation of these groups and their difference from the Brotherhood, we have first to consider the ideological strand which inspired them in the first place, the ideas of Sayyid Qutb.

Sayyid Qutb (1906-65) was one of the main intellectual figures in the Muslim Brotherhood. A school teacher who was also a known and respected man of letters, he spent two years in the United States (1949-51) on a training programme, and was familiar with the major strands in modern Western thought. He joined the Brotherhood in 1951 and was put in charge of *da'wa* ('missionary') activity. Under the Nasser repression he spent 1954-64 in prison, released in 1964 only to be rearrested a few months later, implicated in an arms plot, condemned to death and executed in 1965. He wrote many books on Islamic religion and its modern social and political implications, including a highly original commentary on the Quran (see Carré, 1984). *Ma'alim fil Tariq*, 'landmarks along the path' (Qutb, 1980), was one of his last books. It contains the ideational basis for much subsequent radical thinking. Let us consider the main ideas of this work.

The project of re-enacting the episodes of the 'sacred history' features prominently in Qutb's thought, only the episodes follow early Islamic history more precisely. The 'first Islamic generation' of Muhammad and his followers constituted themselves as a nucleus of believers separate from the *jahili* (ignorant, barbaric) society around them. As such they strengthened themselves in faith and numbers in spite of the waves of persecution they suffered. When they were sufficiently strong and confident in their faith, they broke away from *jahili* society in a *hijra* (flight, migration) from Mecca to Medina, where support was already assured. From there they waged an armed assault, a *jihad* (holy war) against the unbelievers, and with the help of the Almighty, triumphed and prevailed. They instituted the rule (sovereignty) of God (*hakimiyyet allah*) as against the heretofore prevalent rule of man. But this holy realm only lasted for a brief period, to be subverted after the death of the Prophet and his close companions into a dynastic corrupt rule of man by man. *Jahiliyya* was restored, and it prevails to the present day. The task of the believer now is to follow in the footsteps of this first Islamic generation. A vanguard of believers must be formed which would insulate itself from *jahili* society. Given that the believers will have to live within *jahili* society (as Muhammad and his early followers had to live within Meccan society), the insulation will have to be a psychic or emotional insulation (*in'izal shu'uri*). This vanguard, again following the example of the sacred history, would then strengthen itself in faith and numbers, and then launch a *jihad* against *jahili* society, which will only end when the rule of God prevails throughout the world (and Qutb made it clear that he meant the whole world, and not just the Islamic world). This would not entail any coercion in converting people to the true faith, but only the removal of the coercion of the rule of man; only then will individuals be able freely to choose their faith. Qutb contended that Western civilisation, while successful in providing material wealth (which merited his approval, because Islam is not an ascetic religion, but enjoins the production and enjoyment of wealth), has reached a point of crisis because of spiritual bankruptcy. Communism is no solution, as it has proved itself to be a guise for tyranny and corruption. Only Islam can maintain the material achievements of the West, but in the good society, under the rule of God.

Qutb, however, was quite insistent that economic and social considerations were only secondary; Islam is not a social doctrine, its concern is not social justice or freedom or any other ideological ideal, it is nothing but a faith. The sole object of the Islamic vanguard is to implant this faith in the hearts and minds of the believers. Part of this faith is to bring about sovereignty of God, so it has a necessary political project: to overthrow the rule of man and end the state of *jahiliyya*. *Jihad* is, therefore, an integral part of the faith. The effect of this element of Qutb's thought is to rule out as irrelevant the comparisons of Islam to democracy, to socialism or any other -ism. Islam is nothing but itself, a faith and a doctrine.

The political implications of Qutbic thought are quite startling. It departs radically from the central concerns of mainstream Islamic politics as represented in the different strand of the Muslim Brotherhood, or in reformist Islamic thinking. It implies that purportedly Islamic countries, like Egypt, are not really Islamic but part of the realm of *jahiliyya*. In terms of conventional religion it is a serious infraction to declare a Muslim (i.e. one who professes Islam) to be an infidel (*takfir al-muslim*). Politically it requires an abandonment of the populist stance of the Brotherhood in favour of vanguardist secret politics of cells (the Brotherhood reserved this kind of politics for its 'secret apparatus', the armed conspiratorial branch). In our terms, it means an explicit rejection of the political idiom of the modern nation state and of modern political ideologies in favour of a universalist project based on faith. These implications were realised to various degrees by the radical groups of the 1970s and 80s.

Modern radical groups

In the 1970s two main groups emerged on the political scene in Egypt; the 'Military Academy' (*al-faniyya al-askariyya*) group, deriving this name from the attack on the military academy in 1974 (as a prelude to a failed coup d'etat), and the so-called *takfir wal hijra* (inadequately translated as 'repentance and holy flight'), but which referred to itself as *Jama'at al-Muslimin* (the Society of Muslims).[11] This group came into prominence with the kidnap and then assassination of the Minister of Religious Foundations in 1977. The so-called *al-Jihad* (holy war) group, some of whose members were responsible for the assassination of President Sadat in 1981, is reckoned to be a continuation of the 'military academy' group. The founders and core members of these groups were among those incarcerated and tortured in Nasser's prisons. It is related that their jailers often ridiculed their convictions and taunted them that the Almighty was indifferent to their sufferings. These attitudes led many of the younger internees to the conviction that their jailers and the state which employed them could not be Muslims even when they professed Islam, they were *kuffar* (infidels). Sayyid Qutb's view of contemporary society as a *jahiliyya* from which the true believers must separate themselves until sufficiently strong to conquer it for Islam gave a coherent theoretical expression to these sentiments. These ideas are at the basis of the doctrines of the modern radical groups.

Jama'at al-Muslimin, was the group that took these ideas to their logical extreme. Under the leadership of Shukri Mustafa, they considered themselves to constitute the only true Muslims; anyone called to join but refusing is an infidel. The life and property of all infidels are licit to the believers. Their separation from *jahili* society was accomplished within urban spaces by housing their members in 'furnished apartments', a term which has specific significance in current Egyptian vocabulary. In modern Cairo, property values and rents are so high that to rent a house or a flat which is subject to rent control requires considerable capital outlay in 'key money'. The poorer entrants into the housing market, as well as various marginals like prostitutes and petty criminals, are pushed into 'furnished apartments' (which do not in practice have much furniture), mostly located in the outer suburbs. It was in this space of marginality and transience that the true believers found their separation from *jahili* society. In common with the other radical groups they indicated their separation by refusing to recognise the religious and social institutions of *jahili* society. For instance, they refused to pray in the official mosques, and they arranged their own marriages without the customary monetary payments (*mahr*), or the parties and ceremonies. Some of the Society of Muslims went further and effected a total spatial separation, a *hijra* (following the example of the Prophet and the early followers in the sacred history) into the mountains and caves of Upper Egypt, where they engaged in worship and physical training.

What is the political significance of this separation? First we must note an important difference between the two groups. While the Society of Muslims declared all the people outside their group to be infidels, the *jihad* group declared only the rulers to be infidels, while ordinary people were Muslims. Their task, therefore, consisted in attempting to remove these rulers and restore the rule of God (the assassination of Sadat was fully consistent with this view). The view of the Society of Muslims required taking on the whole of society as *jahili* enemies, a much more difficult task. Both groups display characteristics of a messianic view of the world. This is not in the sense of postulating the coming of a messiah, but in aiming to achieve a perfect state of socio-political being without even a remotely realistic account of the current situation nor a strategy for achieving such a state, except perhaps a ritual one. An element of this ritual is their insistence on the imperative of *bay'a*, the duty of every Muslim to swear allegiance to an *amir* and thereafter to obey his commands. In this step the group constitutes itself as a political society in the ritual sense of being subject to the rule of a Muslim prince, who will govern in accordance with God's commands. The question of how this microcosm of the Islamic body politic is to achieve its victory over *jahili* society and its rulers is answered primarily in terms of spectacular gestures.

All the Egyptian Islamic currents under consideration have been located outside the religious institutions and hierarchies, and often in opposition to them. But individual *'alims* or shaykhs (clerics for lack of a better English equivalent) have participated in leadership of movements: Abdu, as we have seen was a shaykh, but one who found the religious establishment archaic, and embarked on a programme of reforms. More recently, some of the most vociferous demands for the application of the *shari'a* in Egypt have come from clerics. But these mavericks do not speak for the religious establishment, which is generally quiescent in relation to the government of the day. In this respect the religious institutions in Egypt still follow the Ottoman pattern of forming part of the state, for the most part supporting its policies, or at least not voicing strong opposition, unless some outrage is being committed against religion. To conclude the discussion I want to identify a number of salient contrasts between the Egyptian context I have outlined and recent Islamic politics in Iran.

Islamic politics in Iran

The difference in religion between Iran and Egypt which immediately comes to mind is that between Shi'ism and Sunnism. There is a view that Shi'i Islam is inherently revolutionary or dissident.[12] The recent revolution in Iran, followed by Shi'i militant activism in various other parts of the world, notably the Lebanon, has lent credence to this view. I have argued elsewhere

(Chapter 1, pp. 26-32) against this view. The gist of the argument is that Shi'ism has not been a uniform phenomenon unified by a historical essence, but that many diverse groups, sects, movements and dynastic states have claimed the designation of Shi'ism, and that these diverse Shi'is have for most of Islamic history been quietist, quiescent or active participants in government. This is not to deny the Shi'i inspiration of many dissident and rebellious movements, they are part of the diversity.

The specific character of modern Iranian Shi'ism is not to be sought in some inherent essence of Shi'ism in general, but in the recent history of Iranian society and state. The key element, I would argue, is the mode of institutionalisation of religion in relation to the state. Whereas in the Ottoman world, including Egypt, religion was firmly attached to the state, in Qajar Iran religion, alongside other major social spheres, was autonomously instituted. The Qajar state (1796-1926) never managed to bring local and regional powers under its full control; it ruled primarily through the manipulation of alliances and loyalties, especially among the tribal factions, among whom the Qajar dynasty became *primus inter pares*. Religious magnates formed part of local power structures involving landlords, tribal chieftains, and sometimes wealthy merchants. These presided over intricate networks of tribal and urban factions, often including groups of armed retainers. *Mujtahids* (clerics of high rank) were often wealthy landlords in their own right, as well as controlling revenues from religious endowments (*waqfs*). [13] Every *mujtahid* had a network of followers who deferred to him in matters of belief and the regulation of daily life, in fact it was (and still remains) the duty of every believer to enter into a relationship of this kind (*taqlid*, imitation) to a *mujtahid*. This relationship entailed the payment of a religious tax, like the tithe in Europe, to the *mujtahid*, who would in turn dispense this revenue as he saw fit for charitable and religious purposes. Religious schools and their students were maintained partly from this source. In effect, through the control and dispensation of the various revenues, the *mujtahids* presided over considerable networks of patronage and following, including in some cases private armies composed of students and other dependents, who were sometimes employed in the collection of religious revenues from recalcitrant followers. It should be noted, however, that these *mujtahids* did not constitute a centralised church with overall control of religious matters; they were related to one another by informal bonds of kinship and marriage, mutual recognition of rank, and acceptance of each other's certification of students.

The notable aspect of Islamic politics in Iran is that, until the 1960s and 70s, it was largely confined to the sphere of the clergy and the religious institutions. This is carried over to the Islamic revolution of 1979, which was led by a prominent cleric and later dominated by the clergy. Until Khomeini first came to prominence in the early 1960s, the character of Islamic politics was largely reactive, that is the clergy reacting against social and political developments which limited their powers and privileges. Whatever reformist religious and political thought there may have been among the clergy remained subordinate and obscure; Iranian religion did not produce anyone remotely like Muhammad Abdu. Modernist intellectuals found no common grounds or sources of inspiration in religion, which they associated with reactive and reactionary clergy. The political alliance between liberal-nationalist intellectuals and sectors of the clergy in the Constitutional Revolution of 1906 was not based on ideological affinity, but on common objectives against the absolutism of the Qajar monarchy and the increasing dominance of its European backers.

The course and the pace of development of the modern state in Iran[14] is quite distinct from the Egyptian example. European domination in nineteenth-century Iran was indirect, and while having important consequences for some sectors of trade and craft, did not extend far enough to create any major social dislocations or upheavals. The Qajar state remained rudimentary and decentralised with little in the way of a state bureaucracy or standing army. The Constitutional Revolution of 1906 and the struggles which followed it represent, perhaps, the preliminary steps in the formation of a modern state, but the establishment of centralised state powers and institutions only really took off after Reza Khan's (later Shah) takeover of government in 1924. He then proceeded to consolidate his power by eliminating one by one the alternative sources of power nourished under the Qajar state, starting with the tribes and the landed aristocracy. The religious sphere, too, lost many of its privileges and prerogatives, especially in the fields of law and education as well as sectors of religious endowments. For the most part, the clergy acquiesced to the new *status quo*, and many of them lent voice and influence to positions of social and political conservatism which favoured the government. However, the bases for their institutional autonomy were not entirely eliminated: they still had the mosques, the religious schools, the religious charities, and the sources of revenue from the contributions of the pious. All these maintained bases for autonomy, organisation and networks of patronage and influence. These were to be crucial factors in facilitating their leading role in the revolution.

The rule of the two Shahs of the Pahlavi dynasty maintained successfully repressive regimes which, for most of their rule, made organised political opposition difficult if not impossible. The exception was the period of the Second World War, when the British and the Russians deposed Reza Shah for fear of his sympathy for the Axis powers, and installed his young son on the throne in a regime more or less under their control. This was the period during which political organisation and activity flourished. The parties which came to prominence were the Tudeh (communist) party, and various nationalist and constitutionalist parties, allied after the war in the coalition called the National Front. It was the electoral success of this coalition which brought Dr Mossadeq to power as the prime minister who nationalised Iranian oil in the early 1950s and provoked the CIA-inspired coup d'etat which restored the full powers of the Shah. After that, political repression proceeded apace, and during the 1960s and 70s any oppositional political organisation was ruthlessly crushed, and even clandestine, underground organisation was successfully undermined.

Khomeini and his immediate followers among the clergy seem, in retrospect, to have effected a break with the defensive then acquiescent stance of their predecessors. They first came to public attention in 1963, in episodes of religious opposition to a number of proposed government acts: land reform, opposed by some on the grounds of incompatibility with Islamic protection of private property; extension of voting rights for women; and certain legal privileges and exemptions for US personnel in Iran. Khomeini's pronouncements were most emphatic and clear on the last issue; his attitude to the first two is not so clear, though the balance of opinion seems to be that he was opposed to all the measures. At that point religious opposition seemed to run along the traditional pattern of reactive resistance. But Khomeini showed none of the reserve of his predecessors in his vocabulary of denunciation of authority, including the person of the Shah. This earned him imprisonment and then exile, ultimately to the Shi'i holy city of Najaf in Iraq, to a niche in the celebrated seminary there, a traditional refuge for Iranian clerics. It was at the Najaf seminary that he delivered the lectures on Islamic government which were to constitute his doctrine of *velayat-e-faqih* (the guardianship of the jurist), which represented such a radical departure in religious political thought in Iran, in that it preached an alternative form of government based on Islamic law as promulgated and interpreted by a just and competent *faqih* (see Chapter 1, pp. 16-20), no longer merely a defence of the religious sphere but a proposal for an alternative government within it. This doctrine was to be written into the Iranian revolutionary constitution for an Islamic *republic*: the Iranian clergy (or a section thereof) have finally entered the field in the ideological contest for the modern state. And their stance in this enterprise was 'fundamentalist', in that it evoked the supposedly original tenets and conditions of the Islam of the Prophet and of the Shi'i Imams.

I have argued (in Chapter 1) that Khomeini's doctrine of government, although constructed in the vocabulary of Shi'i discourses and authorities, and avoiding any reference to Western ideas or ideologies (except to denounce them in general), is nevertheless based on the assumptions of the modern state and nation, and in particular on the idea of modern forms of popular political action and mobilisation. His basic doctrine of *velayat-e-faqih*, assigning the duty of government of Muslims to the just *faqih* (jurist), represents a radical departure from the mainstream of Islamic political ideas, Sunni or Shi'i, which had generally recognised and accepted the assumption of rule by princes who possess adequate power to maintain order and unity in the Islamic community, providing they are Muslims and enforce and facilitate Islamic worship. For the prince to be a *faqih* was never a required qualification. In this regard it is significant that Khomeini incorporated one European concept into his political vocabulary at the time of revolutionary agitation, that of the 'republic'. Perhaps Khomeini's modernist innovation, otherwise implicit, is manifested in the term 'Islamic Republic', a form of government never before conceived of in an Islamic history dominated by dynasties whose rule was for the most part accepted by Sunni and Shi'i jurists. Relying as he may have done on modern ideological assumptions, Khomeini never had the chance before the revolution of participating in modern forms of political organisation. The political organisation on which he relied during his exile and in the conduct of the revolution was that of the traditional networks already mentioned. During Khomeini's exile, a group of senior clerics associated with him maintained the networks of support and patronage, and collected the religious dues on his behalf (see Bakhash, 1985). Some were detected by the security services and suffered spells of persecution and imprisonment, but their organisation could not be eliminated, located as it was in the complex of mosques, bazaars and religious schools, which were never fully under the control of the regime. When the chance of open political action presented itself, the Islamic clergy was the only group that enjoyed organisation and resources which could be mobilised and directed in a concerted fashion. They also had leadership with great force and talent in the form of Khomeini. Alone of all the possible leaders he demanded the abdication of the Shah and the end of the monarchy in favour of an Islamic Republic, while all the secular leaders were making feeble demands for concessions on civil rights. He never hesitated or showed any inclination to compromise or prevaricate in spite of all the pressures. At the same time he gave vague indications of commitment to democracy and social justice, primarily through the radical vocabulary he adopted. His entourage in exile included many prominent Western-educated intellectuals like Bani Sadr and Yazdi, which strengthened the impression of a progressive openness to modern political objectives. These factors led many democratic and left forces to acquiesce in Khomeini's overall leadership with more or less enthusiasm. Thus a fundamentalist revolution was achieved with the full support of secular democratic forces who were later to become its victims.

The foregoing discussion raises the question of the extent to which Islamic revolution in Iran was based on popular support arising specifically from religious commitment. This is a very difficult issue to determine with any measure of confidence. The great majority of Iranians are Shi'i Muslims. Part of the legend and ritual of Shi'i involves celebrations of the martyrdom of the Imam Hussein and his family and followers in the battle of Kerbala in the seventh century. Some writers[15] have attributed great significance to this motif as symbolising the struggle of righteousness against oppression and tyranny, a view shared with the modern radical Shi'is. The fact of the matter is that Shi'is throughout the world have been celebrating these rituals of mourning over the centuries without realising any necessary political implications, except on the occasions on which political interpretations are explicitly constructed in relation to contemporary struggles. This is precisely what happened in the agitations leading up to the revolution. At another level, many conservative religious figures, in and outside clerical circles, have maintained a distance from the revolution, and some have spoken up against Khomeini's political interpretations of Shi'ism. Radical Shi'i thought outside the clergy, such as that of the influential Ali Shari'ati (see Chapter 1 pp. 20-6), does not share Khomeini's specification of Islamic government. As for the common people, the rural masses are not known for their orthodox piety or particular attachment to the clergy (often associated with landlords and authority). The old urban strata of merchants, craftsmen and the networks in which they are involved have had long-standing association with the clergy, related by kinship and business connections. These groups were clearly and significantly involved in the revolution, but not necessarily through religious commitment. It is difficult to ascertain the political commitments or religious faith of the recently urbanised inhabitants of the shanty towns around Teheran and the other major cities. We may guess that they were volatile and changeable, and certainly susceptible to agitation by any oppositional political group which could reach them, and the Islamic networks may have been the only avenue through which they could have been reached against the vigilance of SAVAK (acronym for the Shah's all-powerful secret police). In any case, the degree of participation of these groups in revolutionary agitation is uncertain. The groups whose action was particularly important for the success of the revolution were the oil workers, the bank employees and the government workers, whose combined strike crippled the Shah's regime. These groups are not particularly known for their religious commitment. Many of the bureaucratic workers are modern-educated, and though some may be personally religious, they would normally hold secular political objectives. Historically, the oil workers are known for their leftist inclinations, and constituted one of the most fruitful bases for communist organisation when it was possible. It would seem, therefore, that the significance of religious commitment for revolutionary support was a variable factor. It is certainly not a given disposition of a religious population to follow Islamic leaders and slogans. The leading role of religious ideas and personnel was politically and ideologically constructed in relation to a situation in which clerical forces were uniquely in possession of organisation and resources, while all other opposition groups were weak, unorganised and unprepared. [16]

The revolution in Iran was made possible by the convergence of many economic and political contradictions (see Chapter 3, pp. 64-7). Like other revolutions it was not inevitable, but was produced by a favourable conjuncture of factors, one of the most important being Khomeini's powerful and uncompromising leadership supported by networks of organisations revolving around religious institutions and personnel. It was this conjuncture which made the revolution, and made it an Islamic revolution. I have tried to show that the importance of religion in the modern history of Iran was due to the fact that it remained the only major sphere not completely incorporated and controlled by the state, and as such retained the possibility of autonomous action and organisation. This is quite different from the popular explanation of the Islamic revolution in terms of the effect of some religious essence inherent in Iranian culture and most readily appealing to the hearts and minds of Iranians.

Conclusion

I have surveyed the currents of Islamic fundamentalism in Egypt and, to provide a contrast, in Iran in the contexts of their ideological and political relations to the modern state. I have argued that the differences between the movements and ideologies in the two countries are not reducible to the differences between Sunni and Shi'i Islam, although some aspects of this difference are significant, such as the Shi'i doctrine of the imamate, and the Shi'i cult of martyrs. But these distinctions cannot explain the varying characters of Islamic movements in the two countries and the political significance of these movements. I have tried to explain them in terms of the different histories of the different modes of institutionalisation of religion in relation to the state in the two countries. I have also argued that these Islamic discourses and politics are modern in so far as they involve the construction of the sacred history of Islam in forms which relate to models of the modern state. These themes and arguments will be pursued in relation to different contexts and situations in the chapters to follow.

Notes

1 For a discussion of Max Weber's characterisation of the modern state see Beetham, 1985.

2 For a wider discussion of the question of the modern state, see Chapter 6 below.

3 For an account of Abdu's thought see Hourani, 1962, pp. 130-60.

4 See Plant, 1983, pp. 16-40.

5 Hourani, 1962, pp. 135-40.

6 While committed to the ultimate implementation of the Quranic penal code, some Muslim Brothers (see al-Ghazzali, 1948) have held that these prescriptions would only be just under conditions of general social justice in a truly Islamic society.

7 See G. Baer, 1983, pp. 44-5.

8 See Enayat, 1982, pp. 69-83.

9 For a history of the Muslim Brotherhood see Mitchell, 1969.

10 The politics of the Syrian Muslim Brotherhood, for instance, is significantly influenced by the sectarian (Alawite) composition of the ruling Ba'ath faction in a predominantly Sunni country.

11 More detailed accounts of these groups and their activities can be found in Ibrahim (1980), al-Ansari (1984) and Kepel (1985).

12 A recent statement of this view is contained in Lewis, 1985.

13 For an account of the relation of the ulama to the Qajar state see Algar, 1980.

14 For an analytical history of modern Iran see Abrahamian, 1982.

15 For a discussion of the political significance of mourning rituals see Fischer, 1980, pp. 12-27, 170-80 and 213-16.

16 For a wider discussion of the question of the participation in the revolution of different social groups, see Chapter 3.

3

Classes as political actors in the Iranian revolution

The constitution of classes as political actors is a common feature of the sociological approach to politics. Perhaps Marxism can claim the most elaborate theorisation in this area, but the vocabularies of class and politics are by no means confined to Marxism. There is a general logic underlying all these forms of explanation, which is that a social class, by virtue of a particular position in society, acquires particular interests, has a peculiar form of social experience, and on the bases of these factors develops a common consciousness, world view or ideology, which in turn forms the basis of a political orientation and particular dispositions to political action or inaction. That is to say, classes as political subjects are formed at the level of socio-economic experience, and as such presented as ready-made political actors to the political process. Political processes and institutions are, thus, passive recipients of political actors formed by socio-economic forces. In the discussion which follows I shall examine critically class characterisation of political actors in the Iranian revolution, both Marxist and non-Marxist. I should note that these vocabularies of class are by no means confined to Iran, but have a much more general usage.

Class explanations are foregrounded in the literature, explicitly or implicitly by a 'structural context', what I shall call the 'crisis scenario'. Let us first sketch out this scenario.

The crisis scenario

There seems to be a widespread agreement in the literature that there were accumulating structural strains in Iranian economy and

64

society in the years leading up to the revolution. There may be some disagreement about the precise nature of these strains or their causes; Abrahamian[1] identifies two contrasting explanations of the causes of revolution: one that the Shah modernised too fast for his backward, traditional subjects, and the other that he did not modernise fast enough for the contemporary Iranian situation. Abrahamian argues that each interpretation contains half the truth. His explanation is in terms of uneven development, fast socio-economic development and political underdevelopment. This theme, perhaps not as explicitly and cogently argued as in Abrahamian's text, recurs in the recent literature on the revolution. The so-called 'white revolution' starting with the land reforms of 1963 initiated a period of rapid economic development and modernisation which was accelerated at a considerable rate with the dramatic escalation of oil revenues in 1973. Economic growth in turn brought about far-reaching social changes. Both economic and social developments were uneven and contradictory. Land reform ultimately favoured the richer peasants, agribusiness and the landlords in the more capitalist sectors, to the impoverishment of the poorer, landless peasant sectors. Policy with respect to agriculture in fact led to relative falls in output and necessitated the import of foodstuffs at a vast scale. High-tech agriculture in one area coexisted with the lack of the most basic facilities such as electricity supply in the majority of villages. The rate of rural–urban migration accelerated. Education, health and other welfare provisions expanded at an impressive rate on paper, but levels of illiteracy, infant mortality and provision of medical services remained unfavourable even by Third World standards. The benefits of economic growth were in general very unevenly distributed by class and region in a predictable direction: more benefits to the rich and the better paid sector of the workforce, much greater benefits to Tehran and the central Persian-speaking areas, and much less to provinces such as Azerbaijan, least of all to the ethnic fringes like Kurdistan.

The push factors of land reform and rural unemployment and the pull factors of expanding urban economies, especially in the construction and services sectors, led to an acceleration in the rate of rural–urban migration, extending the ranks of the urban poor in the slums and squatter settlements of South Tehran and other large cities. These groups may have benefited marginally from the oil boom, but for the most part remained in poor and insecure housing, lacking basic facilities and services and restricted to casual and uncertain employment.

The expanding state sector became the major employer of labour (estimate of one in two of the Tehran labour force). This was related to the extension of education and higher education. At the lower levels there was a marked increase in literacy rates in the twenty years preceding the revolution, but literacy rates remained low by Third World and regional standards. Literacy was an important qualification for more secure employment in government or industry. At the higher levels, graduates from Iranian and foreign universities were absorbed into the echelons of government bureaucracy.

Certain social groups and strata derived considerable material benefits from this situation. Business interests were among the foremost beneficiaries but with distinct differentiations in distribution of benefits: bankers, industrialists and merchants who formed part of the clique surrounding the Shah and the Royal Family, and those who constituted the patronage networks deriving from this clique, benefited disproportionately. High government and army functionaries shared in these benefits through partnerships or 'commissions' (including the lucrative percentages on military purchases). Business strata outside these circles and networks, especially bazaar merchants, did enjoy considerable benefits, but were excluded from the favours enjoyed by the former group, such as cheap credit and easier access to licenses and foreign contracts. Bazaar merchants were also subject to pressures and harassments by state agencies, such as being blamed and punished for the high levels of price inflation.

Of the Western-educated groups, high-level state employees and professionals were well favoured in terms of pay, conditions and style of life. Salaried white-collar groups also benefited, but to a lesser extent. Sectors of the working class, such as the oil workers at the height of the boom, received reasonable pay and enjoyed relative security of employment This did not apply to all industrial workers, many of whom suffered low pay, poor conditions and insecurity. Generally, material benefits of the salariat and the wage earners were regularly eroded by the high levels of inflation.

The 'crisis' was engendered by two processes, one economic and one political. Economically, deflation and monetary controls followed the 'heating up' of the economy, high levels of inflation and high levels of state expenditure. Decline in the construction industry marked the slowdown that hit the casual labourers of the urban poor hardest. Remedies for inflation included a half-hearted price freeze, which was enforced most severely in the bazaar, blaming inflation on profiteering merchants. More generally, expectations of growth and rise in the standards of living among the more privileged waged and salaried sectors were disappointed. A classic situation of 'relative deprivation' was engendered.

Politically, the discontent related to the exclusion from the political process of groups and strata whose education and experience had led them to expect and demand participation. The expansion of education and of higher education, and the recruitment of increasing numbers of the educated into government service enhanced expectations of political participation, as did the integration into the national political arena of increasing sectors of the urban and urbanised population through the breakdown of particularistic barriers of village and community. But the Shah's strategy continued to maintain a highly autocratic style of government, confining political power to a small clique in the court and the armed forces, and even then manoeuvring these cliques against one another so that they could never pursue policies and activities independently from him personally. High ranking administrators, planners and experts were regularly bypassed or ignored by the Shah and his clique, sometimes treated like office boys. In effect the Shah's policies created groups and strata who were educated and articulate, many employed in formally important decision-making positions, who were materially favoured but politically excluded. The bitterness and discontent of these groups were demonstrated in the strikes of government and bank employees which constituted such an important step in the revolution.

As already indicated, some version of this 'crisis' is commonly accepted in the literature, some idea of economic and political contradictions besetting the Shah's regime and constituting the basic grounds for the revolution. Perhaps we should note in passing that some other Middle East and Third World countries, especially those dependent on oil revenues, can be characterised in similar terms. It goes without saying that in themselves these contradictions do not constitute *necessary* causes of revolution.

Class analysis

In the structural picture sketched above, can the political forces and actors be identified in terms of 'class' defined in the Marxist sense of relations to the means of production? The first thing to note is that there have been very few actual analyses in these terms, and that these have come mostly not from academic sources but from the political left, both in Iran and abroad. There is no shortage of academic writers on Iran with Marxist commitments, but to my knowledge they have confined themselves for the most part to programmatic statements about the desirability of class analysis, and then proceeded with accounts and analyses which use 'class' in a descriptive sense rather than as a rigorous Marxist concept. Abrahamian's book, already cited, is a case in point. His project is to write a political sociology of twentieth-century Iran, in terms of the interaction between political organisation and social forces. In the 'Introduction' to the book he postulates two categories of social forces, ethnic groups and social classes. But the author is clearly uneasy about the classical Marxist definition of class in terms of relations to the means of production, which he qualifies in the following terms:

> It [the book] will apply the term 'social class' to the broad horizontal layers composed of individuals with common relationships to the means of production, common interaction with the means of administration, and, in a developing environment, common attitudes towards economic, social and political modernisation. (Abrahamian, 1982, p. 5)

Further on he tells us that his conception of class is 'neo-Marxist', following E. P. Thompson,

> that the phenomenon of class should be understood not simply in terms of its relation to the mode of production... but, on the contrary, in the context of historical time and of social friction with other contemporary classes. (Ibid., p. 6)

There seems to be a deliberate vagueness about these form-ulations, borne of a recognition that strict Marxist concepts of 'class analysis' are too limiting for social and historical analysis. He brings in 'common interactions with the means of administration', and 'common attitudes' alongside mode of production. In the Marxist, and other sociological schemes, 'attitudes' are dependent variables, to be explained in terms of class, not defining criteria of class. The effects of these qualifications is that any group can be referred to as a class. The term loses any conceptual sharpness and

68

becomes a descriptive and shifting category, which is how it is commonly (and outside Marxism, legitimately) used in any case. In this respect Abrahamian makes a gesture towards Marxism, but one whose theoretical effects are indeterminate, at the most a general orientation towards the analysis of political phenomena in terms of social and economic relations. The result is very good analytical social history, but hardly class analysis in the Marxist sense. It will be seen from the arguments presented here that this is not meant as a criticism.

To examine the logic and the viability of Marxist class analysis in relation to the Iranian revolution we need a coherent example of such an analysis. I have not been able to find one such analysis in the academic literature, although, as we have seen, there are many commitments to it. In effect, 'class analysis' becomes for many people on the left the absent prince, whose reappearance in the fullness of time will reveal all. It is important, therefore, to see what class analysis would look like, and the analytical and political problems it would raise. Rather than construct a hypothetical class analysis of my own to illustrate these points, I shall address the only coherent class analysis I could find, that emanating from the Tudeh (communist) party of Iran after the revolution. [2] The precise terms of this analysis are clearly influenced by current political considerations, and as such may be considered a less legitimate example than one emanating from an academic source. It nevertheless illustrates very well the theoretical logic and conceptual problems of such an analysis, which is the main object of this exposition. The basis of this theoretical position is the supposition that political actors are formed at the level of economic-class relations, and as such given to the political field which is a passive recipient of such actors. The logic of this position is qualified, but not systematically altered by the more liberal or 'sophisticated' Marxist positions which assert the 'relative autonomy' of the political.

The Tudeh party analysis follows the Marxist scheme in which classes are defined in terms of their relations within the mode of production. In its application to Third World countries this is frequently complicated by the international context of hypothesised dependency of economic and social formations on a world market dominated by advanced capitalism. In the case of Iran, feudal institutions and classes are no longer relevant factors (especially after the land reforms of the early 1960s). Following these considerations, the Tudeh party analysis identifies the following classes and fractions, which are here listed with some comments and qualifications.

The bourgeoisie, in turn divided into: 1 The comprador or 'dependent' bourgeoisie, variously defined, but always with emphasis on its dependence on foreign capital for its operation and reproduction. Strictly speaking this would include practically *all* of capital and capitalists under the Shah, and the Tudeh party analysis follows this logic. Not only are business cliques surrounding the court included in this category (some Marxists restricted the comprador designation to this group), but also leading bazaar merchants involved in foreign trade. Practically all major industrialists, whatever their social location, would also fall in this category, given that most industries operated under license from or in partnership with foreign capital.

2 This leaves very little room for the national bourgeoisie, those operating in relation to production cycles totally inside Iran. If there were any such, then they would consist of owners of small scale factories and workshops, petty traders and moneylenders (even then, many of the capital goods used in production or trade would be imported). In the political vocabularies of the left, this category is easily associated with the petite bourgeoisie. In the analyses of the Tudeh party, the national bourgeoisie is distinguished from the sectors of the petite bourgeoisie engaged in production, such as artisans and craftsmen, by the criterion of participation in the labour process; that is, the national bourgeoisie employs labour, while those sectors of the petite bourgeoisie engaged in production work directly in their enterprises.

3 The petite bourgeoisie: the widest and most diffuse category in the various vocabularies of the left, and one overburdened with political roles. Not only does it include the 'classic' petit bourgeois categories of small businesses and workshops, but in the Tudeh analysis it embraces the whole of the service sector, which in turn includes government bureaucrats, professionals, and most sectors of the clergy. The whole intelligentsia thus becomes, by definition, petit bourgeois.

Even more surprising, the Tudeh analysis includes many categories of peasants and rural artisans in the category of 'traditional petite bourgeoisie', albeit in the process of dissolution by capital.

The peasantry (including the rural poor), by the time of the revolution, divided into a kulak class of capitalist farmers, petit bourgeois/petty commodity producers, as already mentioned, and landless labourers, many of them in the process of migration.

The working class: regularly employed wage workers in industry and the services. In Iran this constituted a small but expanding and politically significant group. One of the most important industries, especially in the boom years of the mid-1970s, was construction. Many of the workers in this sphere were casual, and may have suffered from the deflationary decline of construction after 1975. Were they 'working-class', or did they shade off into the next category?

Lumpenproletariat, or the 'marginal' urban poor. Mostly recent rural migrants in squatter settlements and slum housing on the edges of Tehran and the other major cities. Casual labour, services like portering, and street pedlars. High level of unemployment and under-employment.

One of the problems which a rigorous class analysis would have to face is how to locate within this classification two broad categories of actors who were obviously central to the revolution: the intelligentsia and the clergy. Either they have to be allocated to one of the class categories, or they have to be shown to *represent* particular class interests. We have seen that in the Tudeh party analysis they are both for the most part (arbitrarily) allocated to the petite bourgeoisie. On the other hand, some writers have remarked (quite correctly) that the clergy are strongly differentiated in terms of property and income ranging from substantial land-owners to low-paid preachers. The Shah's reform of religious institutions such as *waqfs* (religious endowments) and the increasing separation of functions such as education and law from those institutions, had also resulted in the impoverishment and insecurity of growing sectors of the clergy, as it was being proletarianised. The Shah also attempted (with some success) to incorporate as many members of the clergy as possible into state institutions, including the official Rastakhiz party and even the notorious SAVAK (security apparatus). In broad outline these statements are correct. But do these economic differences correspond to political affiliations? Some writers have suggested that they do: J.-P. Digard (1982, p. 87), for instance, at the end of an article on Shi'ism and the state in Iran, states that the Iranian clergy do not constitute a single class, but that following the Marxist scheme of classes, they should be differentiated according to the different economic and social positions and relations in which they are involved. He does not elaborate, but presumably such an analysis would have as its object the relationships between class and religio-political positions of the different sectors of the clergy. Do we conclude, for instance, that the poorer clergy would adopt more radical or revolutionary postures? This is not supported by evidence. We do know, for instance, that the poorest clergy, the village *akhunds*, tended to identify with the landlords and with authority as against the poor peasants. It is more likely that the political behaviour of the clergy relates more to the institutional networks of which they form a part, than to their class position. For example, the dispossession of the religious institutions of their privileges and statuses by the Pahlavi state constituted a much more important factor in the divisions and political allegiances of the clergy than particular class positions. This, of course, includes economic factors, such as the obstacles to career opportunities and to social mobility of ambitious young clerics, which could be resolved, for some, by co-operation with state agencies and institutions, but which for others led to heightened discontent and militancy. These considerations include economic factors, but not in terms of class relations.

With regard to representation, some writers have related particular clergy leaders and factions to classes. The most persistent association is of the clergy to the petite bourgeoisie and the national bourgeoisie. Some writers have argued particular affiliations between personalities and class groupings: James D. Cockroft (1980), writing soon after the revolution, stated that Khomeini represented the petite bourgeoisie, while Shari'at-Madari related more to the national bourgeoisie. The plausibility of these statements (never argued in any detail) seems to rest on the perceived affinity between policy positions and attributed class interests.

Class analysis would then have to put the classes in motion in relation to the revolution. All the classes listed with the exception of the comprador bourgeoisie had grievances against the Shah's regime (although most of them also benefited from it at some stage). The agitation against the regime (however it may have started and under whatever leadership) set in motion in 1977 found a ready response among those classes who participated in various ways. But for a Marxist class analysis, the working class must receive particular attention. There is wide agreement, however, among Marxist writers, both political and theoretical, that the Iranian working class was too small and not sufficiently organised or experienced to lead the revolution. However, one section of the working class, which may be seen as a vanguard, did play a crucial role; those were the oil workers whose strike was such an important step in the revolution. In the early days of the revolution, some observers on the left saw this event as an indication of the future action and organisation of the workers who must enter into the struggle to determine the direction of the revolution. The bourgeois stage of the revolution must give way to a proletarian conclusion. If the Tudeh party believed this version it did not act accordingly. Its actions indicated a policy of accommodating itself to the role of subordinate (but hopefully influential) ally of the regime. It identified the regime as progressive in that it favoured the poor and the oppressed (*al-mustazefin*), and in that it had radical economic policies of nationalisation and land reform as part of its programme. Above all it was anti-imperialist. The class nature of the regime was not highlighted, except in that it embraced 'national' and progressive classes.

In class terms, the real heroes of the revolution would appear to be the petite bourgeoisie, a petite bourgeoisie so broadly defined as to include the politically most active groups: the intelligentsia and most of the clergy. The fact of the matter is that the various sections of the intelligentsia are *the* political classes in most Third World societies. To preserve a semblance of class analysis, these groups have to be given a class designation. *Petite bourgeoisie* in Marxist lore (starting with Marx's *Eighteenth Brumaire*) is an ambivalent category: it is 'progressive', but within limits, and when these are reached it can become reactionary. Without rigorous specifications of the limits, a commentator can choose when to assign the respective labels. 'Petite bourgeoisie' becomes a category which is socially elastic and politically malleable, which explains the ubiquity of its reference in Third World contexts. In fact this category in its catch-all application has little, if any, analytic value. Descriptively it would be clearer and more accurate to speak of the 'intelligentsia'. We should hasten to state the obvious and say that groups so designated are not politically homogeneous, for the simple reason that political activists throughout the ideological spectrum are recruited from these groups. And the determinants of their ideological commitments may include 'economic position' (which is not necessarily to say 'class position'), but more often cultural or institutional affiliations, and most importantly, their place in the political process itself. To illustrate these arguments, let us examine in some detail the significance of the 'bazaar' as a political category.

Example: the bazaar in politics

The 'bazaar' in the major Iranian cities is first identifiable as a spatial location for particular commercial and craft activities. Socially it comprises a number of different types of agents. At the apex are the wholesale merchants involved in domestic as well as international trade. Social and commercial networks connect these merchants within the bazaar and outside it into other cities and into the rural areas where agricultural and craft products are bought and sold. Other agents include retailers, pedlars, craftsmen, porters and food vendors. These agents are identified with the social and cultural entity of the bazaar in the form of networks of patronage and reciprocity as well as formal institutions and organisations of guilds, religious brotherhoods, mutual aid associations and charities.

As already noted, the social networks extend outside the bazaar, and one connection which has been emphasised in the recent literature is that to the clergy. Some of the bazaar merchants have social and kinship networks which overlap with those of some of the higher clergy; some of the clergy are involved in bazaar activities as merchants, investors or land-owners selling produce. Some bazaar networks overlap with religious fraternities which may be involved in mobilising funds and support for particular high-ranking clerics and their sponsored charities. The emphasis in these statements should be on the 'some', and it would be a mistake to identify the clergy and the bazaaris too closely, as we shall see.

In terms of class, the bazaar clearly contains a whole spectrum of classes, including all the categories of bourgeoisie listed above, and is recognised as such by authors who consider it in any detail. What part does this play in the political affiliation and activity of its members? If the top bazaar merchants are part of the comprador or dependent bourgeoisie, then they clearly do not share political positions with other sectors of that class. Many of them were prominent in the organisation and finance of the revolutionary struggle (not always out of religious loyalty, as we shall see, but many through National Front affiliations). In economic terms, they only differed from the court-based cliques in matters of institutional and social locations of capital, credit and investment, not in scale, structure or foreign dependence. These differences were generated and maintained by political influence and favour, including extensive corruption, for the court-associated capitalists. They enjoyed cheap credit, government grants, easier access to import

74

licenses, and did not suffer the harassment meted out to bazaar merchants over prices. The bazaar merchants responded by instituting their own bank and credit facilities, thus accentuating the distinction. So, it would seem that however the bazaar merchants are classified economically, their systematic political and economic differences from other prominent sectors of the bourgeoisie are generated at the political level. It can also be said that the bazaar represents a distinct political space (which is not to say that it is politically homogeneous) organised by the social networks and cultural identities, and that its politics and economics are best understood in terms of these socio-cultural factors. This was clearly manifested in the role the bazaar played in the revolution. Its institutions and networks organised funds and communications and mobilised people for demonstrations and strikes. Its cultural and institutional links with the clergy and religious institutions were crucial in the co-ordination of these activities. But it must be emphasised again that the bazaar is not politically homogeneous, and that its apparent homogeneity with respect to the revolution only reflects the fact that the revolution represented a coalition of forces. Let us examine this question in a historical context.

It is commonly stated that a tripartite opposition front has characterised Iranian political upheavals since the closing decades of the nineteenth century, consisting of clergy, bazaar and liberal nationalists. It is generally thought that the first two were 'organically' linked by traditional culture and outlook and economic and kinship connections and that the third (liberal nationalists) were uneasy partners whose alliance was a tactical one against a common enemy. This picture is inaccurate in many respects and certainly in relation to the recent revolution. It may have been true of the Constitutional Revolution. In the other great upheaval of this century, the Mossadeq episode of the early 1950's, the religious forces (and especially the clergy) were only marginally involved, and for the most part in opposition to the National Front. The main contending forces there were entirely 'secular', the royalist supporters against the liberal nationalists, with the left (Tudeh party) playing a significant if ambiguous role. On that occasion a number of bazaar merchants could be counted among the forces of the National Front, and without clergy connections. On the other hand, in the disturbances of 1963 in which religious, clergy forces were prominent, the bazaaris were not directly or prominently involved (except, that is, in the shrine city of Qom, the centre of the disturbances). In the recent revolution, the bazaars were not homogeneous in their political allegiance; there are indications that many of the merchants continued to support the National Front,[3] whereas others had closer connections with the clergy, and no doubt many others had no definite political allegiance but joined in the action against the Shah's regime.

The conclusion that we may draw from the foregoing is that the bazaars constituted more or less definite economic, social and cultural entities, but differentiated entities. Politically they were not homogeneous, but on balance at the particular conjuncture of the recent revolution, oppositional. As a locus of opposition the bazaar was very important in that it contained social networks and stocks of money which were outside the control of the state and its agencies and which could be mobilised in opposition to the state. In the process of revolution, this proved to be of decisive significance.

On the basis of the foregoing analysis, we may conclude that social and economic divisions in Iran do not correspond easily to the abstract scheme of classes which are conventionally associated with Marxist analysis, in particular various classifications of the bourgeoisie. Political forces do not correspond to economic divisions. Groups which can be distinguished as political actors are formed on the basis of cultural and institutional characteristics. Above all it is important to realise that political conjunctures of institutions and struggles themselves play a crucial role in the differentiation and consolidation of political forces. That is, political forces are not just constituted at the economic and social levels and then enter the political arena ready-made. For instance, the factionalisation of the clergy and their followers in the Islamic Republican Party in the years following the revolution cannot adequately be explained, if at all, in terms of the social or economic differentiation of the clergy, but has to be seen in terms of political interests and strategies formed in relation to the party, the state and the religious institutions.[4]

Trends in Marxist thought in Western Europe in recent years have attempted more subtle political analyses in terms of class and class fractions, ostensibly derived from the work of Antonio Gramsci and elaborated by Nicos Poulantzas among others. From this point of view it may be objected that the foregoing analysis relates to a 'crude' Marxist analysis, and that it is possible to relate institutions and cultural attributes to capital and class in a more 'complex' fashion. Critics of this approach[5] have argued (effectively) that it ultimately rests on the same reductionist logic of 'representation' of economically determined class forces at the political level as the supposedly 'crude' variants. Gramsci's political writings have emphasised the extra-economic considerations of the class struggle: a class aspiring to a dominant or 'hegemonic' role must broaden its conception of its interests to include strategies for moral and national leadership. Interactions between classes would then reflect these considerations. However, for Gramsci, political actors are still class actors, class being defined in the classic Marxist terms outlined above. Classes are formed outside the political process and given to it, at which point they interact in ways which modify the suppositions of 'crude' Marxism. Poulantzas's theoretical formulations attempt to delimit a space of 'relative autonomy' for the political, and a role in the determination of classes. But the economic remains determinant 'in the last instance'. Hindess (1980) has shown how this attempt does not succeed in escaping the determinist logic of Marxist class analysis, but in fact reproduces that logic in more elaborate theoretical terms. It is important to emphasise that these are not individual failures of Gramsci or Poulantzas, but systematic products of Marxist theory, which, if it did not impose definite constraints and limits would not be much of a theory. The only way to escape these constraints is to use class vocabulary in a loose, descriptive manner, the path taken by Abrahamian as described above.

Classes and 'elective affinity'

The term 'elective affinity' was used by Max Weber to designate the relation between a class or status group and a particular world view which can be understood in terms of the peculiar interests and experiences of that group. In his sociology of religion, Weber (1965, pp. 80-94) attributed particular forms of religiosity to social groups variously designated: peasants have an affinity to 'natural' and magical religiosity, warrior castes incline to belief in fate and destiny, and urban artisans and merchants are attracted to ethical religion stressing reciprocity and personal responsibility. The Protestant Ethic thesis follows this logic in stressing the elective affinity between entrepreneurs and artisans and puritan protestantism. Another concept with similar theoretical effects is that of *weltanschauung* or world view, advanced by Karl

Mannheim, and in varying forms by Marxist writers such as Georg Lukács and Lucien Goldmann. They attribute particular world views to classes or other groups, to be understood as expressions of the particular social-historical experience of that group. This type of connection is implicit in many of the accounts of forms of religiosity. In relation to Middle Eastern Islam, Ernest Gellner[6] has elaborated this type of account in the contrast he draws between urban and rural–tribal forms of religiosity: scriptural–puritanical vs. charismatic–magical–devotional. Following strands of this type phenomenological reasoning from Gellner, Bourdieu and others, Michael M. Fischer (1982) attempts to characterise the prevalence of political fundamentalist Islam as 'the revolt of the petit bourgeoisie'. Both the urban petit bourgeoisie and the urban (sub-) proletariat contain a high proportion of recent rural migrants. For the proletariat, the search for security and meaning in a de-centred world is bewildering, but has no determinate consequences in terms of politics or religion. Fischer argues that the petit bourgeoisie display a more definite direction. In their search for distinctive status, they attempt to differentiate themselves from their rural origins and from the Europeanised elite (presumably a style not readily available to them in any case?). They aspire to the traditional urban styles, which in religious terms is puritanical and fundamentalist (a disputable attribution). It is the second, educated generation of this petit bourgeoisie, argues Fischer, which constitutes the cadres of revolution whether leftist or religious:

> If the traditional petit bourgeois class is a reservoir for conservative puritanical status concerns, their children often constitute, in modernizing states with, expanding educational facilities, a pool of educated discontents, unable to find suitable employment. Many of these 'intellectuals' turn to political solutions: their education gives them both a somewhat broader vision of the operation of the socio-economic system and the political means that might be used to change it. It is an important fact that in many countries intellectuals tend to be, in more or less equal numbers, either religious fundamentalists or Marxist revolutionaries. (Fischer, 1982, pp. 112-13)

Fischer then points out that the leaders of the Mujahidin in Iran both claim the support of the petit bourgeoisie for their cause, and denounce Khomeini as a petit bourgeois reactionary. This distinction, he argues, is one 'between fathers (conservative shopkeepers) and sons (revolutionary high-school and college graduates)'. The idea of the generational dialectic (in the cultural-historical if not the strictly genealogical sense) is an interesting one, and indeed there is a great deal which is of interest and value in Fischer's article, but in the process of making these connections he managed to identify intellectuals as children of the petit bourgeoisie. Even a catch-all category of the petit bourgeoisie (shopkeepers, clerks, teachers and craftsmen) cannot quite cope with this burden. The Mujahidin, for instance, recruited children of merchants, professionals and clergymen among others. The statement in the above quote which can be endorsed with some certainty is that intellectuals provide recruits for both the left and the religious groups, and one may add to many other 'isms' of ideological politics. The identification of intellectuals with the petit bourgeoisie both by Marxists, as we have seen, and by other sociologists, facilitates the attribution of various kinds of world views and political affiliations to this diffuse category. I have tried to show that there is little justification for this attribution.

Weber's attribution of types of religiosity to social types may have some kind of surface plausibility. But these are ideal types, plausible at the level of 'understanding', but cannot stand by themselves without supporting argument or evidence. Weber intended them as provisional categories to organise research, not as substitutes for it. At the level of understanding many other speculations are equally possible and plausible; for instance, why should hard-headed merchants, accustomed to calculation and the demands for guarantees and collaterals, accept the unsecured promise of salvation by faith as against the guaranteed absolution of sins offered by the Catholic Church acting as agents for the Almighty? All plausible links between social groups or classes and particular ideological tendencies can be challenged on the bases of alternative speculations and contrary historical examples. Marxists, in the European context, have also drawn essential links between classes and political ideologies, such as that between the petit bourgeoisie and fascism. And yet in other contexts, as we have seen, the petit bourgeoisie appear as revolutionary, or at least 'progressive' forces. The material and ideal interests of social groups are clearly important determinants of their political affiliations and actions. But these interests are, in turn, shaped and defined in many respects by political conjunctures and processes, rather than being intrinsically given in their socio-economic positions as such.

The Islamic character of the Iranian revolution did not arise from the religious world views of particular social classes, but from the peculiar historical position of the religious institutions in Iran. Many forms and patterns of religiosity and of irreligion coexisted in Iran before the revolution, including different forms of political Islam. Leftist, populist and modernist Islam as preached by Shari'ati and followed by the Mujahidin was perhaps the most prominent form of political Islam, popular among students and other young intellectuals. Khomeini's form of political Islam, perhaps best summed up in the doctrine of *velayat-e-faqih* (see Chapter 1), was for the most part confined to conspiratorial networks of clergy, their students and immediate followers. Shari'ati's Islam may be said to have articulated the aspirations and frustrations of young radicals attracted to Western philosophies of liberation, but antagonistic to the cultural imperialism of the West and more willing to find these philosophies in indigenous sources. It could hardly be said to express the world view born out of the existential experience of the Iranian petit bourgeoisie as a class. Even less could Khomeini's then obscure doctrine be attributed to the world view of any class. It was developed within a particular circle of clergy and their students, in relation to political ideas and aspirations. Religious Iranians were not for the most part political as Muslims, but some were politicised by agitation and organisation emanating from that circle, as well as the more eclectic ideas and sermons of Ali Shari'ati and related 'liberationist' Islamic ideas. Political Islam was constructed as a revolutionary ideology in a particular political conjuncture and can only be understood in terms of that conjuncture.

The Pahlavi dynasty, from the early decades of this century, has attempted with considerable success to eliminate any possible social or institutional base of autonomous political action or organisation. After the Mossadeq episode in the early 1950's, all political parties, trade unions and oppositional ideas and publications were systematically and ruthlessly suppressed. After the oil revenues explosion of 1973, even more efficient repression was supplemented by incorporation into the state of potentially troublesome elements, notably many sectors of the intelligentsia. The only two social spheres which retained a tenous and increasingly threatened degree of social and organisational autonomy were the religious institutions and the bazaars. So, when the Shah in 1977 responded to a combination of internal problems and international pressures by introducing a small and grudging measure of political liberalisation, the secular intellectuals, lacking political organisation or experience, responded with meetings and petitions for civil rights which lacked clear political objectives. The only political force which was well organised, provided with funds, possessed of a strong leadership and having a clear strategy was the network of clergy and their students and supporters which consisted of Khomeini's associates and disciples. Aided by a populist and radical rhetoric, it was able to hegemonise the multitude of forces which were eager for revolutionary transformation, but lacked the organisation and resources to act autonomously. It was that political conjuncture which raised Khomeinist Islam to the leading position in the revolution, providing common symbols and slogans for diverse forces. There was no intrinsic or organic link which tied that type of ideology to particular social classes.

I have discussed two forms of argumentation which constitute classes as political subjects in the Iranian revolution. Theoretically and politically the Marxist approach is very different to that pursued by Fischer among others which attributes a special affinity of certain classes to particular ideologies and political positions. But the two do have an important element in common: they both suppose that social classes are pre-formed as political subjects by economic and social processes and as such act in the political arena. That is, the political process is given no distinct, or at best, a subordinate effectivity in the formation of political subjects and actors, it is a passive receiver of actors constituted elsewhere. It is this common element which has been challenged in this chapter, which has argued in favour of an analysis of the constitution of social forces in relation to political conjunctures.

Notes

1 Ervand Abrahamian, *Iran Between Two Revolutions* (Princeton, 1982). The discussion of the background to the recent revolution is in Part III, pp. 419-530.

2 The account of Tudeh party analysis is drawn from various party publications, in particular *Dunya* no. 3, 1980, and no. 2, 1981, and *Mardum*, no. 342, August 1980. The research into these publications was part of work carried out jointly with Abbas Vali on a research project 'Religion and the Intelligentsia in the 1979 Iranian Revolution ', 1981-4, funded by ESRC.

3 Interviews with bazaari informants conducted in the course of the

research project cited above.

4 For a detailed discussion of this subject, see Abbas Vali and Sami Zubaida, 1985.

5 See, for instance, Barry Hindess, 1980.

6 Ernest Gellner, 1983. This is a theme running through most of the essays in the book.

4

Class and community in urban politics

'Vertical' and 'horizontal' solidarities

A regular theme in the social science literature is the distinction between class and community as alternative bases of social solidarity. This distinction has its origin in an evolutionary assumption, part of the classic evolutionary dichotomies, such as 'status' to 'contract', 'mechanical' to 'organic' solidarities, *Gemeinschaft* to *Gesellschaft*. The first term of each couple refers to a state of society based on primary solidarities of kinship, tribe, patronage and other forms of traditional obligations and bonds, the second to some version of modern society with an elaborate social division of labour, secondary and often impersonal forms of association and solidarity. Communal solidarities are typical in the first form while solidarities based on positions in the division of labour (including class) are typical of the second. These are schematic, 'ideal typical' characterisations; when it comes to the study of concrete, historical societies, these different types coexist in more or less complex patterns.

Some of these ideas and typologies are implicit or explicit in more recent writing on Third World countries. They are also involved in the political and ideological alignments in and with regard to these countries. Strictly evolutionary logic, whether Marxist or modernisation theory, would conclude that with capitalism or modernisation the second form of the couple must emerge, and with it secondary bases of association and solidarity, including classes, political parties and trade unions; for modernisation theory this would constitute elements of nation-building. The persistence of some of the old bases of primary solidarity or their transformation in modern forms, such as political parties, would be seen as transitional forms, survivals, failure of the full evolutionary process because of traditional sentiments or uneven development or reactive and distorted forms of capitalist development resulting from dependency, all depending on the theoretical position. Against these lines of thought are cultural essentialists or conservatives who have rejected the evolutionary schemes in favour of cultural continuities. Their line of argument contends that Western forms of political thought and organisation are culturally specific, and as such alien to African and Asian cultures. The imposition of Western political constitutions in these countries simply results in some form of continuity of the traditional solidarities. Nation states, parliaments, political parties, trade unions are really superficial forms acting as guises for the real solidarities of tribe, ethnicity or patronage. 'Politics' in the sense of ideologically based solidarities and commitments, whether or not based on class or other secondary social associations, is a Western phenomenon, it is contended (see Chapter 6). A version of the cultural essentialism argument has special appeal for some Third World cultural nationalists: the idea of a cultural heritage which does not admit class divisions and factional ideologies, but insists on the unity and solidarity of the community-cum-nation. Cultural nationalists from 'negritude' theorists to Muslim Brothers have advanced some version of this ideology. But, naturally, contrary to their Western counterparts, Third World essentialists reject the idea of tribal ethnic divisions.

The contemporary student of the Middle East is faced with several theoretical dilemmas. One of them is the question of the suitability of concepts and theories of class for the analysis of contemporary societies in the Middle East and the explanation of political forces, configurations and events in these terms. Versions of cultural essentialism which deny or subordinate general political sociology will be considered in Chapter 6, including the problems of explaining the socio-economic and political transformations of recent times in their terms. The study of these transformations within a general political sociology, however, would still have to face the fact that solidarities and political alignments and forces cannot be explained simply or primarily in terms of class and related concepts (perhaps no more than they can in Western societies!). It is not so much the *persistence* of old forms of primary solidarities as their political and ideological reconstruction in relation to the new situations. I should like to consider as examples two recent important and influential studies of Middle East countries, each one beginning with a consideration of this very problem of the social bases of political forces and configurations: Hanna Batatu, *The Old Social Classes and the Revolutionary Movements of Iraq* (1978), and Ervand Abrahamian, *Iran Between Two Revolutions* (1982).

Batatu defines class in terms of property and hierarchy: '"class" is, in essence, an economically based formation, though it ultimately refers to the social position of the constituent individuals or families in its varied aspects' (Batutu, 1978, p. 6). That is to say (if we unravel the ambiguous formulation) 'class' refers to social position which is economically determined. 'To be more explicit, I find it difficult not to agree with James Madison, Karl Marx, and Max Weber that "property" and "lack of property" form the fundamental elements of the class...situation, and that this antithesis contains the seeds of an antagonistic relationship' (Batatu, 1978, p. 7). But following classic sociological and Marxist formulations, Batatu contends that solidarities on the bases of these relations and 'consciousness' of this antagonism are not always realised or explicit, but can be a passive sentiment. Class as a basis for stratification and solidarity only became important in Iraq after the incorporation of the country into the world market associated with the coming of the British imperial system in the nineteenth century. Prior to that private property was a shaky asset, subject to interference and confiscation by the politico-military rulers. The salient bases of stratification and solidarity were 'status', determined by military and political power (pashas, shaykhs, aghas, etc.), religious rank (sadah/ashraf, and Sufi shaykhs) and lineage (tribal, religious and merchant aristocracies), the last two being interlinked. Status stratification also marked the hierarchical ranking of religious and ethnic communities. Property and wealth, primarily in the form of revenues from land, taxation and tribute, was derived from power and status, rather than determining it. It is not clear whether for Batatu class relations and sentiments were non-existent under these conditions, or that they were there (by definition?) but dormant.

Batatu goes on to argue that Ottoman centralisation and legal reforms in the middle decades of the nineteenth century, as well as the increasing intrusion of the capitalist world market into Ottoman territory, brought about changes which facilitated the creation and acquisition of private property in land. Some of the old powerful status groups consolidated their positions on the bases of private property, such as tribal chiefs who acquired personal title to tribal lands, or the *sadah* who converted their *waqfs* and other sources of revenue into private holdings. These various, and previously separate, status groups converged in the twentieth century, under the modern Iraqi state, into land-owning classes, politically united on the basis of common class positions, and divided sometimes by the scale of their holdings, for instance into small and large land-holders. These economic developments also lead to the formation of new classes on the bases of property and lack of it, and act as a stimulus for class sentiments in the old poor classes such as the peasants. But the old principles of stratification in terms of status are by no means eliminated; some of them, such as religious status and communal attachments, coexist with class, but are presumably transformed under the new conditions. Observed political configurations can be explained, therefore, in terms of complex interactions between class and status factors.

Ervand Abrahamian's formulations are even closer to the ideal typical model of alternative horizontal and vertical bases of stratification. His project is to write a political sociology of Iran as against previous forms of writing which may be characterised as broad historical surveys, studies of particular aspects or parts of the politics and small community studies:

> The present work intends to examine the politics of modern Iran by analyzing the interaction between political organization and social forces. These forces can be categorized generally as ethnic groups and social classes. The book will use the phrase 'ethnic group' to describe the vertical groupings of individuals with common ties of language, tribal lineage, religion, or regional affiliation. It will apply the term 'social class' to the broad horizontal layers composed of individuals with common relationships to the means of production, common interactions with the mode of administration, and, in a developing environment, common attitudes towards economic, social, and political modernization. (Abrahamian, 1982, p. 5)

Abrahamian concludes his Introduction by pointing out that his conception of class is 'neo-Marxist', following E.P. Thompson, 'that the phenomenon of class should be understood not simply in terms of its relation to the mode of production...but, on the contrary, in the context of historical time and of social friction with other contemporary classes' (p. 6).

Both authors, in their different formulations, are keen to establish a sociological framework for the analysis of politics. In highlighting the concept of 'class' and associated themes, they are trying to establish the suitability of these general concepts for the analyses of Middle Eastern societies, implicitly against the particularistic approaches which would emphasise historical and cultural specifities and the categorical distinction between 'Islamic' and European societies. At the same time they are clearly uneasy about too precise and strict concepts of class, such as the classical Marxist conception. Batatu appeals to James Madison and Max Weber as well as Marx, and his formulations contain almost deliberate vagueness: 'in essence an economically based formation'; 'to do with property'. Abrahamian's formulation brings in 'common interactions with the mode of administration', and common attitudes (surely to be explained by class, rather than constituting part of its definition?), alongside 'means of production'. The effects of these qualifications is that any group can be referred to as a class. The concept loses any conceptual sharpness and becomes a descriptive and shifting category, which is how it is commonly used in any case.

Vague as these formulations may be, they assume a particular logic of explanation. Political forces are constituted from social solidarities, whether of community or of class. These solidarities are social processes presented as givens to the political sphere. Political institutions and processes themselves play little part in the constitution of political forces. These are constituted as social solidarities developed on the basis of common interests or of traditional loyalties and bonds or a mixture of the two. My object here is to extend to other cases and examples the argument advanced in the previous chapter against these assumptions. I argue that the constitution of political forces relates to various and shifting bases of social solidarities, but, crucially, these varieties and shifts often result from changes in political and economic conjuncture, including state structures and policies: the profound consequences for social and economic organisation and solidarity attributed to the Ottoman *tanzimat* is a case in point. A related point which I should emphasise is that communities and classes are not in themselves political forces. Under particular conditions political forces may be *constituted* on the bases of class or community, and this constitution is in itself a political process. Witness the constitution of the Shi'i community in Lebanon as a political force in the last ten years, but not in its previous long history; or the constitution of sectors of the Iraqi working class as a political force through the political activity of the Iraqi Communist Party. These social entities are not given to politics having been formed by social processes elsewhere; as political forces and concepts they are formed through the political process itself.

Both Batatu and Abrahamian are aware of these problems in their introductory formulations: Abrahamian's 'common interactions with the mode of administration', and Batatu's statement that prior to Ottoman reforms class factors were insignificant because of the insecurity of property, and therefore relations to the means of politico-military power were paramount. I should like here to highlight and crystallise these aspects, not just before the Ottoman reforms, but for more recent history. In doing so I shall draw upon analyses given by Batatu and Abrahamian (and others) in the body of their substantive studies, for these studies provide ample illustrations for my argument, notwithstanding their introductory discussions of concepts.

Example: early nationalist politics in Damascus

The first example I should like to consider is drawn from Philip S. Khoury's *Urban Notables and Arab Nationalism: The Politics of Damascus 1860-1920*(1983). Khoury starts with an endorsement of Batatu's formulations regarding 'class'. Classes are not always class-conscious, and their members may act according to individual or factional interests. This is especially the case under conditions which prevailed until the middle of the nineteenth century, when property is dependent on political manipulations, and members of the same class (merchants, or tax-farmers) are rivals for official favours:

> Indeed, for class members to feel obliged to close their ranks and clarify their common interests as a class on 'crucial' political issues, there must be a need. Otherwise, intra-class (or even ethnic) conflict, expressed in terms of vertically structured factionalism, rather than conflict between classes, is likely to be the active force behind the emergence of particular social and political movements. (Khoury, 1983, p. 4)

In Khoury's account, it is only after the Ottoman Land Code of

1858 favouring private property in land, and the effect of the upheavals of 1860 which shook the local power structure and brought the notables under much firmer central control, that we witness the formation of a class of landowner-bureaucrats. This was constituted by a convergence of previously distinct status groups of leading ulama, *aghawat* (garrison or tribal chiefs) and merchant-moneylenders. The point of convergence is land-ownership reinforced by the assumption of office in the now centralised Ottoman bureaucracy. These factors constituted a class which, while not strictly speaking a 'ruling class' (the rulers still being the Ottomans), was the most powerful native class, acting as an intermediary between the Ottomans and Syrian society.

This account would appear to fit in with the ideal-typical model of change from community-patronage based solidarities to those based on class, a change brought about by the incorporation of the Ottoman Empire into the Western capitalist world market system. But the accounts and analyses in Khoury's text show nothing of the sort. The previously disparate elites do converge into a more homogeneous ruling group, with more direct links to and dependence upon Istanbul. But this convergence does not appear (from Khoury's account) to have generated any more solidarity. The great families are rivals for office, for connections, influence and favours with the Ottoman state. They each have their network of patronage through which they attempt to control and mobilise various sectors and quarters of the urban population (although many of the elite families had moved out of the quarters over which they presided as patrons and protectors and into common elite quarters). Even under the common threat of Turkification and exclusion from office of Arab elites under the Young Turks, the Damascene notables show little solidarity and break ranks in pursuit of individual advantage. In the last decades of the Empire, the division of the Syrian elite into Ottomanists and Arabists, and the roots of Arab nationalism among the latter, again do not seem to have been predicated upon class divisions. The split often occurred within the same family. The factors which appear to have been most important in determining the allegiance of each member were relations to the Ottoman government, and whether the person in question enjoyed office and rank or was excluded. Without entering the argument on whether they constituted a class in any strict sense, we can say that they did not exhibit the solidarity of class. The factors that divided them and determined their political affiliations appear to have been differential access to political influence, prospects of office and the economic advantages attendant upon these factors. The conventional Marxist and other sociological characterisations of class are in terms of economic factors determining social solidarities and political allegiances. In this instance it would seem that economic advantage was determined by political power and influence, a process which generated rivalry rather than solidarity. It may be the case that if the social order at the source of political power and economic advantage was under threat from popular forces, the elite would close ranks. But the question did not arise in this form. The conclusion I wish to draw from this example is that here the political process, forces, actions and solidarities were determined neither by class nor by community, but by the political institutions and processes themselves in interaction with various social groupings.

Do these conclusions, however, only apply to nineteenth-century examples? Have the socio-economic transformations of later times altered the bases of social solidarities and political actions along the lines indicated by the ideal–typical model outlined above? Certainly, Middle Eastern societies have been transformed many times over since the Ottoman Empire, and among the changes have been the formation of institutions and solidarities apparently or really based on class affiliations, including political parties and trade union movements of considerable force in some countries. Any account of contemporary politics would have to give these phenomena their due weight. Equally, in many instances, communal, ethnic and religious solidarities and forms of patronage have been constructed and reconstructed in many forms and continue to play important roles in politics. But, I should like to argue, these forms of solidarity are just as inadequate, in themselves, as accounts of political affiliations, institutions and processes as they were in relation to the nineteenth century. Political processes and conjunctures play crucial roles in the constitution of economic difference, social solidarity and political forces. Let us consider two examples drawn from recent history.

Example: the politics of the Sunni-Shi'i split in Iraq

One of the frequently cited examples of the importance of communalism in modern Middle East politics is that of the

Sunni-Shi'i split in Iraq. The Sunni supremacy of Ottoman times is maintained into the politics of independent Iraq, with the Royal Family and the great majority of the political and military elite being Sunni. This supremacy is maintained after the displacement of the monarchy (except perhaps for the years of Qasim's rule, 1958-63). The Ba'th ruling circles are drawn predominantly from the Sunni cities and regions of north-west Iraq. The majority of Shi'is (who constitute the numerical majority of the Iraqi Arab population) are peasants inhabiting the south of Iraq. Three groups constitute the Shi'i elite: the ulama of the holy cities, the merchants in Baghdad and the southern cities (and Shi'is have predominated in commerce, especially after the exodus of the Jews in the early 1950s) and shaykhs-landlords of the southern tribes (that is, until the land reforms of the Qasim period, after which the situation becomes complicated and ambiguous). The conventional picture of communalist politics is that the Shi'is, because politically disenfranchised, are oppositional. While Sunnis have identified with Arab nationalism (the other Arab states being predominantly Sunni), those Shi'is who have followed modern political ideologies have tended towards left-wing identifications, notably the Communist Party. The regions, cities and quarters where the party had its strongest support were those with predominantly Shi'i populations, while the northern and western Sunni regions and cities, and the Sunni quarters of Baghdad, were associated with nationalist politics.

No one can deny the importance of the Sunni-Shi'i distinction in modern Iraqi politics, one which is highlighted after the Iranian revolution and the war which followed. But against conventional ideas of communal solidarities in politics, the diversity of political significances must be emphasised. In line with my general argument, I must also show that political differentiation within the Shi'i community is as much the product of political institutions and processes as it is of class and economic factors. Under the monarchy, southern Shi'i shaykh-landlords were a prominent part of the political establishment. They were first brought into political prominence during the British occupation and mandate as loyal clients who would act as a counter to any ambitions to real independence by the Hashemite rulers (also British clients, but ones who were not always reliable because they might pursue independent policies for political or ideological ends). Exploitative 'feudal' landlords associated with authority and imperialism, they were prime targets for denunciation by the modern 'progressive' intelligentsia, nationalist and leftist, amongst whom Shi'i intellectuals were strongly represented. The attitudes of ulama and merchants to the landlords were mixed and shifting, depending on political conjunctures and alliances. The ulama, in any case did not constitute a unitary political group, but different members and factions had associates and patrons in different political corners, ranging from communist sympathisers to those on the payroll of Western embassies.

One aspect, already mentioned, deserves particular attention: that of differential nationalist-communist affiliations by community. The Arab Sunnis of Iraq, the argument runs, are a minority, whose traditionally dominant position is threatened by the entry into national politics of Shi'is and Kurds. The appeal of Arab nationalism is that it relates the Sunnis to an Arab world in which Sunnis are the predominant majority. The Shi'is, underprivileged and excluded from government and authority, tend towards radical solutions, which do not include Arab nationalism, as this would only subordinate them further to a Sunni world. This is not a complete picture. We have already noted the diversity of Shi'i politics. In relation to Arab nationalism, it is probably true that traditional and conservative nationalist parties, like the Istiqlal Party (active in the 1940s and 1950s) were predominantly Sunni. But the subsequent radical nationalisms of Nasserism and Ba'thism did attract many Shi'is. The leadership of the Ba'th party in the 1950s included some Shi'is (the dominant Sunni Takriti leadership was to emerge later after a number of internal shuffles and purges, see Farouk-Sluglett and Sluglett, 1985). Equally, at various points in its history, the Communist Party included many Sunni Arabs in its leadership. It is true, however, that in the public mind, communism in Iraq has been associated with Shi'is (and Kurds). Batatu (1978, pp. 649-50;699-705) acknowledges this association, but puts it in proportion, by showing that numerically the representation of Shi'is in the Communist party was no more, perhaps a little less, than their representation in the population at large. The community disproportionately represented in the party in the 1950s and 1960s were the Kurds. The Arab Sunnis, initially (1930s and 1940s) dominant in the leadership of the party, had by the later 1940s and 1950s fallen in numbers in the membership and the leadership. However, quite apart from numerical representation discussed by Batatu, the association of communism with Shi'is in the Arab regions of Iraq, is crucially based on the prominence of the communist presence, in organisation and activity, in the Shi'i cities of southern Iraq, including the shrine city of Najaf, and the Shi'i quarters of Baghdad, notably the shrine suburb of Kadhemeyya. Clearly, the great majority of the inhabitants of these Shi'i areas were not communists, and not particularly sympathetic to communism. But equally, one may assume, there could not have been strong enough hostility to communists to eject them from these areas. It is a scrupulously observed rule of the Iraqi Communist Party to avoid any controversy regarding religion, and certainly never to criticise or denounce religious beliefs and institutions. Many of the communist activists were presumably sons, brothers, friends and associates of local families. At the same time these cities and quarters, being Shi'i, have a long history of clandestine organisation, and of distrust of governments. In addition, the Shi'i shrine cities, in common with other old cities and quarters, have forms of urban organisation and architecture of narrow streets and alleyways, of hidden courtyards, and in the case of Najaf, reputedly, a network of underground passages, all providing a suitable environment for clandestine organisation (which also explains the present government's anxiety to demolish these old quarters to make room for avenues and squares). In the massacre of communists signalled by the Ba'thist coup d'etat of 1963 the Shi'i quarters of Baghdad, especially Kadhemiyya, were prime targets. Batatu (1978, pp. 983-5) points out that on that occasion all the districts of Baghdad which offered resistance to the coup were without exception Shi'i. However, he warns against drawing easy conclusions regarding the communalist nature of communist affiliation. Many of the Sunni communists, for instance, took refuge in the Shi'i areas in which they could count on protection. In any case, most of the Shi'i areas were also the poorest in Baghdad. Although Batatu warns against easy class explanations, he nevertheless emphasises the importance of class sentiments in this instance. So it would appear that the two possible explanations are 'community' and 'class', neither of which is by itself fully adequate. We are back in the conceptual world of the alternative ideal types we started with.

Class factors in the sense of economic underprivilege or oppression clearly have considerable weight in the explanation of political affiliations and action. However, it must be emphasised that class belonging in itself does not explain political solidarities. It is the activity of the Communist Party in agitation, recruitment, trade union organisation and general propaganda which must be given the credit for politicising sectors of the working class and the poor in the major cities. In any case, as most people would recognise, the class element is only part of the story; is the other part 'community'? If it is then it is community in a special sense, certainly not in the sense of communal solidarities passing on to political solidarities. We have seen that politically Iraqi Shiʻis are very diverse, ranging from 'feudalist' landlords with reactionary and imperialist affiliations, to merchants, ulama, peasants and modern intelligentsia with a wide variety of shifting political sentiments and affiliations. As for most groups, however designated, the majority are likely to be non-political or 'apathetic'. The remarkable fact about Iraqi Shiʻa, however, is the extent to which they have been prominent in politics, not any particular characteristic affiliation, but general participation. Rather than saying that they have a propensity to communism, it would be more accurate to say that they have a propensity to politics. As we have seen, Shiʻis were also represented in the Baʻth party. The Iranian revolution and its aftermath have politicised the Iraqi Shiʻis further and in different directions than previously, more distinctively religious. What we have here is not so much definite political affiliation based on community, but rather a distinctive *political culture*. This political culture of distinction from orthodoxy and ruling authority and sometimes of opposition and resistance, of secrecy and dissimulation, and of doctrinal disputations, had a definite location in cities and urban quarters to which it gave its stamp. It would be interesting to direct study and analysis in these terms, but prior to such analysis we can only speculate on the significance of the historical articulation of Shiʻi cities, regions and institutions, first to the Ottoman Empire, then to the Iraqi state, in the constitution of this political culture. I should make it clear that I am not postulating this political culture as in itself a political force, but that it may become an important ingredient in the constitution of political forces at particular historical conjunctures.

Urban political organisation

The ideal type picture of social development sketched in the opening passages entails a typical course of urban political development. Communal solidarities are spatially located in well defined quarters with strong boundaries. Intensification of the social division of labour, population increase, class differentiation and conflict, the creation of centralised nation states and the consequent shift in the bases of social solidarities lead to the decline of traditional urban quarters and the dispersion of their populations along class and status lines. The modern city is spatially stratified in terms of class, status and differential access to services and amenities.

The picture of the historical Middle Eastern city which emerges in the literature fits in with the ideal type characterisation of the initial stage. Cities are divided into quarters on the bases of religion, ethnicity and craft; the quarters are units of social solidarity and dependence, with their own organisation and leadership, often bounded by walls with a gate which is locked at night or in situations of threat. The government did not always successfully ensure the security of the subjects, often indeed quite the contrary, as soldiers, functionaries and tax collectors were often the source of the threat. The class heterogeneity of each quarter played an important part in the security function: the wealthy, the notables and the religious dignitaries of each quarter acted as patrons and intermediaries with authority for their weaker and poorer fellow residents. By the same token these notables could mobilise the members of their quarters when demonstrations of political support were required. How did this picture alter with modern developments? Did it move along the course indicated by the ideal type model?

Philip S. Khoury's (1984) study of Damascus urban politics during the French mandate provides an interesting illustration. Under Ottoman rule Damascus fitted in with the classic picture of quarter-based urban organisation and solidarities. The socio-economic and political changes of the nineteenth century had altered the bases of political power and of political formations at the top, and part of that change was the greater dependence of the elite on connections to Istanbul and on holding office, and a proportionately lesser dependence on previous power bases in the quarters. Some residential class differentiation did take place with the movement of some elite families from the quarters of their support and into more class-homogeneous wealthy neighbourhoods, but residential movement did not necessarily disrupt the ties of patronage in the quarters of origin. These changes do not appear to have significantly altered the structure and organisation of the quarters, which retained their significance as the main units of urban social organisation and of political mobilisation of the popular classes. In this latter respect they played an important part in the events leading up to the Arab nationalist agitation and support for Faysal in the last days of the Ottoman Empire and the allied occupation. This mobilisation continued in resistance and opposition to the French Mandate. However, the 1920's witnessed significant changes, partly brought about by the high volume of rural migration into the city, and partly with the continuing advance of the processes of economic, cultural and consequently residential differentiation. The influx of migrants altered the density and organisation of the quarters and attenuated the ties of patronage. The new opportunities for gain and the new bases of political influence offered under the new regime drew more of the elite families away from their connections in the old quarters. But others, notably the families which assumed the leading roles in the nationalist struggles against the French, retained important bases in the quarters, which formed a crucial foundation for their political influence, and reservoirs for popular demonstrations and agitations, that is to say, the old quarters, in spite of the changes continued as the locus of popular politics in the nationalist agitations of the 1930s. But this type of politics is indirect; the population of the quarters do not join the nationalist parties as such, they participate in politics under the leadership of their patrons and respond to their commands, and would readily shift their political allegiances in accordance with that of their patrons. The patrons maintain their influences by rendering services to their clients, either directly or through intermediaries.

This example highlights a familiar feature of political organisation and mobilisation in many Middle East (and other) countries: modern ideological politics and political parties mobilising support on the basis of 'traditional' networks of patronage and primary solidarities. This form of politics proceeds alongside and in interaction with the politics of the intelligentsia and sometimes of the working classes and trade unions, based more on ideological solidarities. 'Traditional' is put in inverted commas to indicate the superficiality of the designations. Clearly, the old quarters and the socio-economic bases for their existence are transformed. The conduct of politics in accordance with patronage networks does not indicate continuity or survival. Patronage politics occurs in a great variety of situations and conditions, including aspects of political party organisation in the United States today. In itself it does not indicate a homogeneity in all the situations in which it occurs. The old solidarities were based on common residence, mutual security and self-defence, local administration of the quarter, and local economic interests and relations, if not always of production and commerce, then of provision and of taxation. Patronage relations were enmeshed in these networks and functions. But already in Khoury's Damascus of the 1920s the patrons were moving out of the quarters, and those who still maintained contacts often did so through intermediaries. This impersonality and instrumentality of patronage relations becomes increasingly prominent in later periods, and patrons and clients need not have any traditional connections of community or quarter.

Some urban quarters, however, acquired renewed political significance under modern conditions, sometimes based on elements of their historical functions of security and protection. This is well illustrated in the example of Shi'i cities and urban quarters in Iraq which we have already considered. A quarter like Kadhemiyya in Baghdad may have lost all the old forms of local administration, and the rigid physical and social boundaries which enveloped it, but elements of its Shi'i cultural identity, attitudes to ruling authority, and perhaps of its architecture and spatial organisation, make it a hospitable environment for clandestine dissident politics. As such the quarter is protective and supportive of the politics of some of its members (communism) which may not be generally shared, but which fit in with its general ethos. It can also become a refuge for fellow dissidents from the outside, as we have seen. As a sphere of dissident politics outside the direct control of the state, especially a repressive totalitarian state, it becomes a target for persecution and repression. The bazaars of the major Iranian cities (which we considered in Chapter 3), though different from urban quarters in that they are not confined to a location as such, nevertheless show similar features. They also represented spheres of activity, potentially political, which are autonomous from state control. Both in Iran under the Pahlavis and in Iraq under the Ba'thists, the governments have attempted to eliminate all potential spheres of social and political action not under their control. To that end the late Shah took concerted steps against the bazaars (and the religious sphere), aimed at incorporating them and destroying any elements of autonomy. These attempts included urban planning measures which sought ultimately to demolish the bazaar areas in favour of wide avenues and supermarkets. Similarly in Iraq, urban planning has created spacious squares around the shrines of Najaf on the site of the old quarters and markets. Similar measures are planned in other Iraqi cities, especially in Kurdistan. The politics of urban locations and cultural identities may well continue in some countries until and in so far as these repressive measures of urban planning are successful.

5

Components of popular culture in the Middle East

The 'Middle East' is a geocentric European term. Against this vague geographical designation we may be inclined to point out the great diversity of societies, languages and cultures, or to counterpose a less ethnocentric (though no less problematic) designation such as 'the Mediterranean' which includes Europe and non-Europe. Yet, at the level of culture and social organisation, a number of common elements and themes may be distinguished, some specific to the Arab world (or at least its Eastern wing), but many common also to Iran and Turkey. In this respect, the Middle East may be seen to constitute a civilisational area, formed historically out of common subjugation to the great empires of Persia, Byzantium and the Muslim Caliphates, out of the waves of Islamisation (though I shall argue that the common cultural elements are not specifically Islamic), and out of the intermingling of peoples and cultures brought about by these processes. This entity is differentiated, but the lines of differentiation are often those of desert, mountain, coastal plain and city, which cut across the linguistic and 'national' differences.

The cultural uniformities take the form of variations on common themes. Perhaps the most accessible is that of culinary culture: kebabs, stuffed vegetables, mutton stews with vegetables, sweet pastries with ground nuts. Another is that of popular religion and magic; witness the striking universality of beliefs and rituals concerning the 'evil eye' (some transcending the Middle East to Southern and Eastern Europe), or the common themes and characters of mythology, such as those concerning al-Khidr or Alexander, some of which will be explored below.[1]

I should perhaps emphasise that I do not wish to argue for some historically constituted cultural essence. Historically, there are many transformations and upheavals which must have included cultural elements, and ancient cultural elements are transformed in modern contexts, as we shall see. These changes may have differential effects on different countries or regions, but over time they seem to percolate into most areas, not necessarily in similar forms. To pursue the culinary example, we may point to the general and almost uniform effects of the introduction of the tomato to the region, and its eventual adoption into all aspects of the cuisine, such that it is difficult now to imagine what Middle Eastern food was like before the ubiquitous tomato.

The most easily comprehensible similarities are at the level of literate, intellectual culture. Philosophy, theology, mysticism, poetry and music, constituted for the most part common universes of discourse in which the educated elites of the various parts of the region participated. This does not imply consensus, for there were great and running conflicts in the intellectual and political history of the region. But these were fought on common discursive grounds, with themes and issues comprehensible to all the parties. The common elements at this level are more understandable because there are clearly identifiable traditions, channels and institutions of learning, law and religion. In this respect the institutions of religion and learning were not dissimilar to those in Europe.

At the popular level, the uniformities in elements and themes of culture are seemingly paradoxical. The conventional picture of social organisation and solidarities under the dynastic empires which emerges from some of the historical accounts is one of fragmentation into a number of distinct communities, often with specific territories in tribal land, village or urban quarter.[2] Urban society (from which we draw our main examples) appears from these accounts to conform to the model of the 'plural society' developed in relation to more recent colonial multi-ethnic situations,[3] communities which are socially, culturally and spatially distinct, based on religion, ethnicity, tribal or regional origin, often internally self-governing. These co-exist with one another and participate in a common economy, sometimes with particular communities having specialist functions. They are under the rule of a common authority to whom they all pay taxes, but with differential privileges depending on religious status; orthodox Muslims (whatever the official orthodoxy happens to be) being regarded, at least formally, as part of the community of the state. The so-called *millet* system of the Ottoman Empire is a formalisation of this situation. But the elements of the 'plural society' are supposed to keep separate cultural identities, with their own languages, religions and customs. My contention here is that if Middle Eastern societies conformed to this picture, then the common cultural themes which I shall try to illustrate are all the more remarkable. This degree of communality of culture would suggest a society with a much greater density of interaction, a social division of labour and associated social relations cutting across communal boundaries. The model of the isolated communities could only have been true of particular periods of social and economic decline and political instability. In periods of prosperity and stability, such as the heyday of the Abbasid dynasty, or the golden age of Arab Spain, or favourable interludes under Mamluke rule in Egypt, there are many indications of the intensity and variety of social and economic interaction across communal boundaries.[4]

Two long-term processes are central to the cultural history of the region: Islamisation and Arabisation. After the initial Islamic conquests, Islamisation proceeded apace, and a substantial proportion of the population of the region, probably a majority, were Islamised in the first century of Islam. In its first two centuries, Islam also attracted Turkish tribes and dynasties which subsequently carried its banners even further afield. In this process the Islamic religion was adopted and adapted in a wide range of social and cultural settings. The resulting forms of Islam varied accordingly, ranging from institutionalised orthodox, literate/scriptural forms to syncretistic beliefs and practices at the popular level. Considerable sectors of Middle Eastern populations were not, however, Islamised, but retained their faiths as Christians, Jews and Zoroastrians, as well as other minor religions. In many respects Judaism, Christianity and Islam share a common historico-cultural universe, which remained an important element in their coexistence as well as their conflicts.

Arabisation is the more remarkable of the two processes. True it is the language of Islam and of the original conquerors. But so often in world history the conquerors maintain an aristocratic court language separate from those of the conquered. It is clearly not simply a function of Islamisation: Iran was thoroughly Islamised but not Arabised, while Egypt retained a large Christian population which was eventually Arabised. Nor did Arabic supplant fragmented unwritten 'tribal' languages, the languages it replaced were Aramaic, Greek and Persian. The Arabisation of the state (but with important Persian and Turkish elements) is not enough to account for the generality of the process; state language does not have to be that of the ruled. The large scale of settlement of Arabian tribesmen in the conquered territories would not explain the phenomenon; linguistic diversity in close spatial proximity is not uncommon. Only an extensive social division of labour which cuts across communal and tribal boundaries, and brings people from different social and cultural locations into close interaction can lead to this homogenisation of language. Arabisation is yet another indication that the conventional picture of the communally fragmented society was not always true of the region.

One implication of the foregoing argument is that Islamisation (and even less Arabisation) were not simply the impositions of an Arab-Muslim ruling class. The indications are that this ruling class, discernible in the early decades of Islam, especially under the Umayyad Caliphate, were, if anything, anxious to maintain their distinction from the subject peoples. But Islamic civilisation was shaped more definitely during the Abbasid period, in the second century of Islam. This was a much more cosmopolitan period, in which the cultural as well as the ruling elites, included many people of Persian origins, and incorporated dominant features of Hellenic and Persian provenance. The language of this cosmopolitan civilisation, however, was Arabic. This context of Arabisation would indicate that the process was not the result of 'impositions', but rather the product of wide-ranging mixing and interaction of peoples and communities, participating in an economically and culturally complex, and relatively open society.[5]

Language is the most important element of cultural uniformities, but it is not the only one. Language, of course, facilitates other common elements. Indeed the Arab world does contain more uniformities within itself as against Turkey and Iran. But it should be emphasised that linguistic and cultural boundaries are fluid. Southern Iraq, for instance, combines its Arab make-up with extensive Persian linguistic and cultural elements, probably through Shi'i affinities. North-Western Iraq, along with Greater Syria, though Arabic-speaking, share many Turkish cultural and linguistic elements. The Arab linguistic and cultural effects in Iran and Turkey are well known, as are the Persian influence in Turkish culture. Moreover, within the Arab world there are many linguistic minorities: Kurds, Turkomans, Armenians and Persians. In so far as they are urbanised they partake in many of the cultural uniformities in question.

In what follows I shall illustrate the discussion with examples.

Some of these are drawn from written sources and records. Others are based on personal knowledge, confirmed by informants, of different parts of the Middle East, but particularly Iraq. It may be argued that, as illustrative examples, these are as valid as ethnographic records.

Religion and popular culture

The distinction of popular religion from orthodox, scriptural and juridical religion is well established and documented. There are many popular religious manifestations, however, which have orthodox underpinning and support. Such are, for instance, the celebrations of the Prophet's birthday, or for the Shi'a the mourning ceremonies for Hussain. Equally, Sufi organisations and practices have, at least since the eleventh century, been accepted by orthodoxy, and become a regular part of specifically Muslim life (but, of course with recurrent schisms ánd conflicts). But apart from these specifically Islamic manifestations of popular religiosity, and other specifically Christian or Jewish examples, there is a whole range of common features which transcend communal confessional boundaries. It should also be pointed out that the *jinn*, the mythical underworld agents of much popular religiosity, across the confessional boundaries, are well established in the Quran. In this respect the contrast of popular religiosity to orthodoxy is sometimes exaggerated.

One of these common features is the veneration of saints. The tombs of prophets, prominent Sufis and mystics or minor local mystagogues constitute holy shrines with some persons or establishments maintaining them and administering pilgrimages and other services. One of the services they perform is intercession for the supplicant, to facilitate a blessing or ward off an evil. Particular shrines become known for particular types of services, such as facilitating conception for a hitherto barren woman, or curing particular illnesses. Living mystagogues and magicians can also become renowned in a particular area for certain cures, potions or blessings against a range of evils, often to do with the evil eye.

These religio-magical practices have a predominantly *instrumental* orientation. By 'instrumental' I mean the use of these practices as means to attain desired ends or to ward off evils, following, of course, a belief in their efficacy. In Max Weber's classifications of religious orientations, 'instrumental' would be (analytically) contrasted to 'ethical'. In what follows, I also contrast it to 'solidaristic' orientations, in which religion becomes a communal 'marker', rallying believers to communal action in defence of the community and the faith, or for their honour and glory. It is this instrumental orientation and the sets of beliefs which specify the employment and efficacy of religio-magical practices, which appear to be shared across confessional boundaries. A Muslim shrine renowned for its efficacy for certain problems will be frequented by Jews or Christians. The shrine of Shaykh Abdel-Qadir al-Gailani in Baghdad, for instance, was the site of certain rituals for women seeking conception, and as such attracted Jewish women alongside Muslims. But, of course, they had to go there under the cover of an *abaya* (black cloak) as worn by all women in public. The claimed shrines of Biblical prophets in Iraq, such as Ezekiel and Jonas, are sometimes shared, sometimes possessed exclusively, sometimes disputed, between Jews and Muslims, their holiness and intercession sought by both. Living mystagogues can become renowned for the efficacy of their blessings, medicine or magic, and regardless of their confessional identity will be sought after by clients of all faiths. Examples of this communality of practices and their personnel can also be found in Egypt between Muslims and Copts, and in Morocco between Muslims and Jews. At this level of instrumentality the religious boundaries of community become fluid.

These shared instrumental orientations and practices can also be identified at the level of 'do-it-yourself' magic and ritual. The common recurrence of recipes to deal with the evil eye as far apart as Iraq and Morocco is astonishing. The molten lead oracle is one such: a pellet of lead is melted over a fire, then poured into a vessel containing cold water. The shape in which it sets is then 'read' to trace the source of the evil eye and then to destroy it by piercing any protrusion which resembles an eye with a pin. Examples can be multiplied, some perhaps more specific to particular communities or particular regions, but almost always with parallels and overlaps.

Another element of popular religion which is widely shared is religious mythology. Al-Khidr is a recurrent figure in Islamic religion and mythology. The location of this figure in scriptures and traditions is vague: associations with *surat al-kahf* in the Quran, Syriac myths of Alexander, Messianic scenarios, but nothing definite.[6] In popular religion, he is a figure of mercy and rescue, interceding for people in danger and saving them from what appears to be certain death. In Messianic scenarios he accompanies the Messiah and guides him: the Sudanese Mahdi saw al-Khidr alongside the Prophet Muhammad in the dream or apparition which first authorised his mission. In Jewish tradition and popular religion an equivalent figure is Elijah or Eliahu or Elias. Messianic myths have *nabi Eliahu* accompanying the Messiah in his coming.

The figure of 'Khidhr-Elias' is interesting in this respect. He (or they, as we shall see), features in Iraqi and Turkish popular mythologies. It is probable that he also features in the mythologies of other parts of the region, but I cannot say. He shares the intercessionary functions and the benign protectiveness of al-Khidhr and of Eliahu, and would appear to be a composite figure. A (minor) spring festival is celebrated both in Iraq and in Turkey in honour of this figure, but the rituals are quite different in the two countries. Turkish informants specify two brothers, Khidhr and Elias, and the festival marks their annual meeting. In Iraq, this figure is sometimes symbolised by sprigs of myrtle, which in Iraqi Arabic is called *al-Yas*, and this plant is used in various ritual functions. One of these is the Jewish circumcision ceremony, as recounted in the following passage:

> On the evening preceding the eighth day the Chair of Elijah the Prophet is removed from its place in the synagogue and brought to the house of childbirth. Here a Pentateuch is placed on it and covered with rich brocade, and decorated with flowers and with twigs of fresh myrtle and rue....The Baghdadians give a popular explanation for the use of myrtle on this occasion by identifying the name of the Prophet Khidr Elyas, and the Arabic name of the myrtle, el-yas. However ingenious this etymology is, we know that the use of myrtle in burial, wedding, and birth ceremonies goes back to Talmudic times and serves the purpose of protecting from demoniac powers. (Sassoon, 1949, p. 183)

The author, David Solomon Sassoon, a wealthy and philanthropic Jew of Iraqi origin writing in England (work completed in 1932), may not have been aware of the existence or the significance of al-Khidhr in the general Arab-Islamic context, and preferred to explain the custom in terms of ancient Jewish history. The significance of the Chair of Eliahu, and his symbolisation in the myrtle, is indeed to ward off evil spirits and the evil eye, and moreover to protect the small child in a situation of physical danger. This is fully in keeping with the functions generally attributed to al-Khidhr.

In the religious mythology of Egypt and Greater Syria, the Christian equivalent to al-Khidhr is Saint George. The ancient myth of the dragon of the Nile to whom a yearly human sacrifice had to be made so that he would not hold up the water features a saintly slayer of the beast: for the Muslims al-Khidhr, for the Copts Saint George.

It may be argued that these common elements of popular religion and mythology are attributable to the common historical universe of the three religions which we have already noted, and/or to the common cultural history of the region, including pre-Islamic Mesopotamian and Persian religious and magical beliefs and practices. This is plausible, but common ancient origins are never sufficient, in themselves, to account for current practices. It is highly likely that these cultural elements have shared in the upheavals and transformations which have characterised the history of the ancient world. As regards the 'official' religions, it should be noted that most of the popular beliefs and practices are on the margin, or even totally outside these religions, perhaps utilising scriptures and traditions, and holy figures and stories from these, but used for their own constructions which are often heretical from the point of view of orthodoxy. In this respect popular culture is a *bricoleur*[7], cobbling together elements of mythology from a variety of sources for particular purposes in hand.

Instrumentality and solidarity

These elements of communality of popular culture contrast sharply with the image of Middle Eastern urban society noted above: communities based on religion, ethnicity or tribal origin, maintaining strong social and territorial boundaries. This contrast is comprehensible if we consider the social significance of religion in two perspectives, instrumentality and solidarity. In the context of instrumentality, religion represents a set of resources for the fulfilment of particular objectives to do with health, wealth and happiness. This is where popular culture appears as a *bricoleur*, constructing remedies from various elements to suit the task in hand. This is where confessional boundaries are at their most fluid, and where elements from the various religions and from general folk magic are used interchangeably. In Mauss's theory of magic,[8] this is the terrain on which the sacred/communal is usurped for individual ends.

Religion in another perspective is the sphere of social solidarities based on common belonging, with specific institutions and rituals of worship which identifies the believers and separates them from the practitioners of other faiths. The overall unity of the Islamic community, the *umma*, is theoretical, but particular communal solidarities are based, at least in part on sectional identities of faith. Being Sunni, Shi'i, Christian or Jewish is always a highly relevant ethnic marker in addition to being Kurdish or Armenian or from tribe x or y. In situations of communal competition or conflict, individuals respond according to communal solidarity, in which the religious component is essential.

I should emphasise again that these definite communal identities did not always stop social and economic intercourse across their boundaries. In periods of security and prosperity, intensified economic activities and contacts spilled over into social intercourse and cultural interchange. The Ottoman state drew heavily on the skills and presumed loyalties of *dhimmi* subjects – of, at various times, Greeks, Armenians and Jews, who assumed various official positions and functions.[9] This may have alienated them from many sectors of the populace, but will have created social bonds with other sectors. But social relations were necessarily limited by the hierarchy of ritual status, which subordinated the *dhimmis* however wealthy or learned they may be. Social intercourse certainly stopped at intermarriage. As for times of crisis, war, economic hardship, then the communal boundaries were firmly drawn, and each community retreated to the security of its quarter, from which inter-communal strife would occasionally erupt. In a long-term historical perspective, we may postulate cycles alternating between phases of political stability coupled to heightened economic activity, and crises, strifes and contraction of economic functions. The former would be associated with relaxation of communal boundaries and growing social intercourse and cultural interchange, the latter with hardening of communal lines, social insulation and defensiveness. The common components of popular culture may be accounted for in terms of the historical recurrence of the stability-prosperity phase of the cycle.

The two perspectives of instrumentality and solidarity, however, do not exhaust the range of significance of religion in popular culture. There is one very important, but perhaps illusive aspect, which we may call the cognitive or conceptual, cognitive frames of reference consisting of cosmologies, concepts and symbols which form the building blocks of popular knowledge and belief, its 'common sense' and rituals of everyday life. The communality of popular mythology and ritual across confessional boundaries would suggest that elements of this cognitive framework are also shared, at least in particular countries and regions. There is, for instance, the communality of folk knowledge and lore on agricultural matters in Egypt between Muslims and Copts. Even Iranian Jews, who, it would seem, were severely restricted and isolated for most of the Safavid and Qajar periods, produced literary texts, in Persian, using the heroic form of Persian epics, but on Biblical themes.[10]

The wedding ceremonies – an illustration

This section is devoted to a discussion of elements of marriage customs and wedding ceremonies with the object of illustrating two aspects of popular culture: first, communality and persistence of some of its elements, at least in the Arab world, and the limits of religious, and therefore community-specific, inputs; and second, the transformations of these elements under modern social and spatial conditions, while retaining the forms and the terminologies. This will lead to a discussion of the impact of modernity on popular culture.

On reading Edward Lane's account[11] of the marriage customs and wedding ceremonies in nineteenth-century Egypt, I was struck by the many elements of similarity to those of more recent times, familiar through personal knowledge and literary accounts and references, later confirmed by informants from different parts of the region. First, I quote extracts from this account:

[Having first agreed the amount of the dowry (*mahr*), the parties proceed to the ceremony of the contract, *ketb el-ketab* (the writing of the writ).] On the day appointed for this ceremony, the bridegroom, again accompanied by two or three of his friends, goes to the house of the bride, usually about noon, taking with him that portion of the dowry which he has promised to pay on this occasion. He and his companions are received by the bride's wekeel; and two or more friends of the latter are usually present. It is necessary that there be two witnesses (and those must be Muslims) to the marriage-contract, unless in a situation where witnesses cannot be procured. All persons present recite the Fat'hah, and the bridegroom then pays the money. After this the marriage-contract is performed. It is very simple. The bridegroom and the bride's wekeel sit upon the ground, face to face, with one knee upon the ground, and grasp each other's right hand, raising the thumbs and pressing them against each other. A fikee is generally employed to instruct them what they are to say. Having placed a handkerchief over their joined hands, he usually prefaces the words of the contract with a 'khutbeh', consisting of a few words of exhortation and prayer, with quotations from the Kur-an and Traditions on the excellency and advantages of marriage. [...] Before the persons assembled on this occasion disperse, they settle when the 'leylet ed-dukhleh' is to be: this is the night when the bride is brought to the house of the bridegroom, and the latter, for the first time, visits her.

In general, the bridegroom waits for his bride about eight or ten days after the conclusion of the contract. Meanwhile he sends to her, two or three or more times, some fruit, sweetmeats, etc., and perhaps makes her a present of a shawl or some other article of value. The bride's family are at the same time occupied in preparing for her a stock of household furniture (as deewans, matting, carpets, bedding, kitchen utensils, etc.) and dress. The portion of the dowry which has been paid by the bridegroom, and generally a much larger sum (the additional money, which is often more than the dowry itself, being supplied by the bride's family), is expended in purchasing the articles of furniture, dress, and ornaments for the bride. These articles, which are called 'gahaz', are the property of the bride; and if she be divorced, she takes them away with her. She cannot, therefore, with truth be said to be *purchased*. [...]

[Then comes the arrangements for *leylet ed-dukhleh* (the night of the entrance).] Let us say, for instance, that the bride is to be conducted to him on the eve of Friday. During two or three or more preceding nights, the street or quarter in which the bridegroom lives is illuminated with chandeliers and lanterns, or with lanterns and small lamps, some suspended from cords drawn across from the bridegroom's and several other houses on each side to the houses opposite; and several small silk flags, each of two colours, generally red and green, are attached to these or other cords. An entertainment is also given on each of these nights, particularly on the *last* night before that on which the wedding is concluded, at the bridegroom's house. On these occasions, it is customary for the persons invited, and for all intimate friends, to send presents to his house a day or two before the feast which they propose or expect to attend. They generally send sugar, coffee, rice, wax-candles, or a lamb; the former articles are usually placed upon a tray of copper or wood, and covered with a silk or embroidered kerchief. The guests are entertained on these occasions by musicians and male or female singers, by dancing girls, or by the performance of a 'khatmeh' or a 'zikr'. [...]

On the preceding Wednesday (or on the Saturday if the wedding is to conclude on the eve of Monday), at about the hour of noon, or a little later, the bride goes in state to the bath. The procession to the bath is called 'zeffet el-hammam'. It is headed by a party of musicians with a hautboy or two, and drums of different kinds. [...] The procession moves very slowly, and generally pursues a circuitous route, for the sake of greater display. On leaving the house it turns to the right. It is closed by a second party of musicians, similar to the first, or by two or three drummers. [...]

Having returned from the bath to the house of her family, the bride and her companions sup together. If 'A'l'mehs have contributed to the festivity in the bath, they also return with the bride to renew their concert. Their songs are always on the subject of love, and of the joyous event which occasions their presence. After the company have been thus entertained, a large quantity of henna having been prepared, mixed into a paste, the bride takes a lump of it in her hand, and receives contributions (called 'nukoot') from her guests. Each of them sticks a coin (usually of gold) in the henna which she holds upon her hand; and when the lump is closely stuck with these coins, she scrapes it off her hand upon the edge of a basin of water. Having collected in this manner from all her guests, some more henna is applied to her hands and feet, which are then bound with pieces of linen; and in this state they remain until the next morning, when they are found to be sufficiently dyed with its deep orange tint. Her guests make use of the remainder of the dye for their own hands. This night is called 'leylet el-Henna', or 'the night of the Henna'.

It is on this night, and sometimes also during the latter half of the preceding day, that the bridegroom gives his chief entertainment. 'Mohabbazeen' (or low farce-players) often perform on this occasion before the house, or if it be large enough, in the court. The other and more common performances by which the guests are amused have been before mentioned.

On the following day the bride goes in procession to the house of the bridegroom. The procession before described is called 'the zeffeh of the bath', to distinguish it from this, which is the more important, and which is therefore particularly called 'Zeffet el-'Arooseh', or 'the Zeffeh of the Bride'. In some cases, to diminish the expenses of the marriage ceremonies, the bride is conducted privately to the bath, and only honoured with a zeffeh to the bridegroom's house. This procession is exactly similar to the former. The bride and her party, after breakfasting together, generally set out a little after mid-day. They proceed in the same order, and at the same slow pace, as in the zeffeh of the bath; and, if the house of the bridegroom be near, they follow a circuitous route, through several principal streets, for the sake of display. The ceremony usually occupies three or more hours. [...]

The bride and her party having arrived at the bridegroom's house, sit down to a repast. Her friends shortly after take their departure, leaving with her only her mother and sister, or other near female relations, and one or two other women, usually the bellaneh. The ensuing night is called 'Leylet ed-Dukhleh', or 'the Night of the Entrance'.

The bridegroom sits below. Before sunset he goes to the bath, and there changes his clothes; or he merely does the latter at home, and, after having supped with a party of his friends, waits till a little before the 'eshe' (or time of the night-prayer), or until the third or fourth hour of the night, when, according to general custom, he should repair to some celebrated mosque, such as that of the Hasaneyn, and there say his prayers. If young, he is generally honoured with a zeffeh on this occasion. He goes to the mosque preceded by musicians with drums and one or more hautboys, and accompanied by a number of friends, and by several men bearing 'mesh'als'. [...]

Let us first note the sequence and nomenclature of the ceremonies. First, the ceremony of the marriage contract *aqd ennikah*, in which the contract is drawn, *katb el-kitab*, and a *khutbeh* is delivered by the officiating *'fikee'*, i.e. *faqih*. Sometimes this ceremony is called *khutbeh*, and the status of being 'engaged' termed *makhtoub(a)*. This is the preliminary but binding ceremony. The marriage is consummated on the later occasion of *leylet ed-dukhleh*, in Lane's account eight or ten days later, but in more recent times, and for urban middle and upper classes, after a longer period of 'engagement', up to a year. Second, the *zeffehs* (processions). The main occasion is *zeffet el-arooseh*, the one taking the bride to her marital home for *leylet ed-dukhleh*, a subsidiary one is *zeffet el-hammam* (the bath house) culminating in the ceremony of the henna. Other subsidiary processions also called *zeffeh* are *zeffet el-gahaz*, carrying clothes and furniture, and *zeffet el-aris* taking the bridegroom to the mosque and back on the night of the wedding. All these *zeffehs* involve processions taking circuitous routes, moving slowly through the quarters and neighbourhoods of the celebrating households, conducting the celebrations in public with music and various displays, thus marking the status of the celebrants, and marking the event emphatically in public. Third, the henna ceremony, sometimes called *leylet el-henna*, in Lane's account a wholly female affair. Fourth, *leylet ed-dukhleh* (the night of the entrance), and the celebrations preceding and following in the bridegroom's house. Note here that the celebration is not confined to the house but includes the street and sometimes the whole quarter. All these events are marked by the giving and the exchanges of gifts in all directions: groom to bride, between the two households, gifts to servants and subordinates, small gifts of drinks or sweets or coins to the neighbourhood during *zeffehs*, gifts to the couple from friends and neighbours, and so on. Many of these gifts are ceremonially prescribed.

The form, sequence and nomenclature of these ceremonies are broadly shared throughout the Arab world, with some features also in Iran and Turkey. The main variations are those between city, village and tribe. Class differences are also very important, because of the range of expenditure which can be afforded. Many of these elements were also common to indigenous Christians and Jews, but, naturally, with different religious inputs.

Iraqi Jews,[12] for instance, follow a similar sequence of ceremonies. The first ceremony is termed *qaddus*, benediction, during which the marriage contract *ktebbeh* is written, and benedictions over a cup of wine uttered by a *hakham* (rabbi), followed by a party. This is a binding ceremony which can only be revoked by a 'divorce'. The crucial difference of this, and the other ceremonies, from those in Lane's account is that they are not sex-exclusive. The bride is present at the contract ceremony, and so are other women. The couple are then engaged for up to a year or more, after which the wedding ceremonies are celebrated. On the eve of the wedding day is the *leylet el-henna* ceremony, similar in outline to Lane's account. It also follows a festive visit to the bath by the bride with her female kin and friends, but in this case the festivities are not as elaborate as in Lane's account. For Jewish women, the bath is a religiously prescribed ritual bath. The ritual has to be conducted in special approved baths, often attached to synagogues. This means that the bridal bath (at least for orthodox Jews), still takes place in a public bath house, even when people have private baths at home.[13] In recent years, the henna ceremony has become the main wedding party and banquet given by the bride's family. Previously, the ceremony started as a female affair, and was joined by the groom and other men later in the evening. The groom and some of his friends may apply henna to their little fingers.

The main wedding ceremony starts in the synagogue with a religious service, but is then followed by a celebration at the groom's house, usually a smaller and shorter affair than the henna celebrations. That night is known as *leylet ed-dakhla*. For the following seven nights minor celebrations and festivities are conducted in the bridal home. There are ceremonies and rituals surrounding the movement of the bride and groom, sometimes accompanied by music. But these are much more muted affairs than the public *zeffehs* of the Muslims. This may be due to the restrictions on public display by *dhimmis* which operated traditionally, sometimes by law, sometimes custom, and sometimes just plain caution.

Literary references and informants' accounts of different Arab cities and communities would seem to confirm the broad outlines of Lane's account, with local variations in customs and terminologies.[14] I have no information on the generality of these ceremonies and terms among non-Muslim communities in other parts of the Arab world. But the henna ceremony appears to be universal, and is followed in Iran and Turkey.

Note that the religious input into the Muslim ceremonies is confined to blessings and benedictions at various points, and the common recitation of the *Fatiheh*. The *faqih* officiates in the contract ceremony in his capacity as a legal expert and master of ceremonies. The example of the Iraqi Jews shows a similar sequence of ceremonies, but with different and larger religious input, including the celebration of the main ceremony in the synagogue. Another religion-relevant difference is the segregation of the sexes in the Islamic ceremonies (at least traditionally, as in Lane's account), and their mixing among Jews and Christians. The inter-confessional communality of many elements of these ceremonies places them outside any one religious category or origin. Explanation in terms of Arab tribal origins appears equally implausible, because their main locus is urban. In any case, questions of origins are futile. These ceremonies constitute one more example of the common elements of Middle Eastern cultures which are not reducible to religion. These elements, as we have already noted, are not invariants, but subject to the historical transformations of the region. Of these, the recent transformations of 'modernity' are perhaps the most dramatic.

From Lane's account, we may note that the ceremonies are conducted in a context in which the distinction between private and public spaces is fluid or shifting. The *zeffehs* are essentially public displays for whole neighbourhoods or quarters, common spaces to which people do not have to be invited. The main ceremonies in the groom's house preceding and following *leylet ed-dukhleh* are not limited to the house, but take over neighbouring spaces. The lines of exclusion are not those of socio-economic class but of neighbourhood and quarter. Indeed, weddings are the occasions for giving and receiving between constituents of patronage networks which span the different classes of the quarter. The social and spatial transformations of modern cities has altered the nature of these ceremonies, although some of their forms may be maintained.

To rehearse a familiar account of the transformation of Middle Eastern cities as part of the overall processes of transformation of this century. The old quarters were vertical segments of society, with horizontal stratification within (see Chapter 4). Urban growth, and the changing sources of wealth, status and power, the development of new styles of life based on European models, led the rich, the educated and, in general, the diffuse strata called the 'middle classes' to move out of the old quarters and into class-homogeneous residential quarters. The old quarters, where they still survive, have become lower-class areas, often slums, heavily over-populated with waves of rural migrants, and maintaining a mix of residence and small-scale commerce and craft.

There are, no doubt, many wedding ceremonies in some old popular quarters, and in small towns and villages, in Egypt as well as in other Arab countries, which still follow the main outlines of Lane's account. But side by side with these there is a new paradigm of ceremonies associated with the 'modernised' middle and upper classes who inhabit the new class-homogeneous suburbs of the big cities. In the modern ceremonies, the participants are from kinship and friendship networks which are predominantly class-homogeneous, but not necessarily residing in common neighbourhoods. The sequence of ceremonies remains, but the henna ceremony is no longer universal, and where it occurs is not necessarily the wholly female ritual affair, but often becomes another party at the bride's house. Given that these strata do not use public bath houses, there is no *zeffet el-hammam*. *Zeffet el-aroos* remains, but is now a motorcade with blaring klaxons, similar to some European practice. This is the only ceremony which retains a public element, but within the privacy of the private car, and the public impression it makes is for the most part anonymous. The religious element is confined to the contract ceremony. The wedding night is still called by many *leylet ed-dukhla* (or *dakhla*), and is preceded by the main wedding reception/party/banquet depending on wealth and style. The celebration for these groups is always in private spaces, either a private home or a hired hall in a club or hotel. The entertainment is European or cabaret-oriental. For these strata the marriage ceremonies are completely Westernised (but according to their ideas of what is 'Western'), except, that is, for the marriage contract with its minimal religious component. In this respect, the Westernisation of culture is not simply an attitude of mind, but a process which has 'material' underpinning, in economic, social and spatial processes.[15]

The forms and sequences of the ceremonies persist in many old urban quarters. To what extent are they affected by the change in the nature of these quarters, the spectacular growth in population, the inflow of rural migrants and the suburbanisation of some of the original inhabitants, the removal of patronage networks from the spatial locations of the quarters and into more impersonal spaces and relationships? Are the *zeffehs* consequently more anonymous?

Are they motorised to span the much greater spaces which separate residences in the modern city? For instance, in Baghdad up to the 1950s there were *zeffehs* conveyed, with their entertainers and musicians, in slow-moving motor coaches. We should also consider that a high percentage, often a majority, of the popular classes in modern cities no longer inhabit the old quarters, but live in outlying suburbs, sometimes improvised or marginal, sometimes permanent. Do they have the shared public spaces and institutions like mosques and bath houses? Do they have durable social networks of kinship, neighbourhood and patronage on which many of these cultural forms depend? Do they have the social, economic and spatial bases to sustain the old paradigm of wedding ceremonies? Under the conditions of the old quarters, poverty could have been alleviated by local obligations, reciprocity and patronage. Where these are minimal or absent, the constraints of poverty prevail. But of course we cannot assume the curtailment or absence of these networks. New patterns have, no doubt, emerged to suit the conditions. The nature of these patterns is a matter for particular researches.

Attitudes to popular culture

In the example of the wedding ceremonies we saw that contemporary urban conditions have led to the lapse of old cultural forms, at least among the wealthier strata and the intelligentsia. I use 'lapse' rather than 'reject', because explicit attitudes and pronouncements are varied and equivocal. In some cases, of course, it is outright rejection, as a feature of backwardness and superstition, as against progress identified with European models. This latter is what may be called old-fashioned modernism. Current attitudes and pronouncements would usually take account, explicitly or implicitly, of some form of cultural nationalism. This would emphasise the national cultural heritage. But such heritage is not present in everything the 'people' do. Particular readings and definitions of what constitutes national culture must be developed, a project undertaken by intellectuals, politicians and state agencies. These go hand in hand with the transformations of popular culture which are affected by the constraints of the processes of socio-economic and spatial developments, but not necessarily in the same direction. One of the persistent themes in the ideological reconstructions of popular culture is what may be termed 'purification'. Let us consider two forms of this project.

1 National purification

As part of the national heritage, whether Arab, Persian or Turkish, popular culture must be re-written to fit in with the general construction of an essentialised *national* history which establishes the identity of the modern national entity in time. But the history of the region is one of polyglot empires, mixing peoples, cultures, religions and languages. Popular culture reflects this history. The nationalist task is then to purify this culture to conform to the desired image. Foreign elements become superficial accretions, acquired during periods of decline and decadence, even, perhaps, aided by imperialism, which must now be discarded. At a recent symposium on food, an Arab food writer was incensed at the suggestion of extensive Persian influence on Iraqi cooking, and argued passionately for the integrity and originality of the Arab tradition, but was at a loss to explain the Persian and Turkish names of so many of the Iraqi dishes. These attitudes are sometimes enshrined in state policies. Both Iran and Turkey have seen official attempts to purify the respective languages from Arabic elements. State policies to preserve the cultural heritage often lead to the 'folklorisation' of culture, that is the development of selected elements of dress, music and oral literature, to be formalised for staged performances. Only truly national elements are included. An extreme example comes from Iraq, where, reportedly, an official ban was declared (in 1977) on the broadcast of songs containing foreign words. In effect this would apply to practically every classical or old popular song, where Persian and Turkish words and expressions are most common. Clearly this ban was very difficult to operate, and eventually it lapsed.

The economic, social and spatial bases of popular culture are being eroded as part of the general processes of 'modernisation', often as a consequence of state policy. At the same time, state agencies promote a formalised folklore, selected, purified elements abstracted from any lived context and preserved as 'heritage'.

2 Religious purification

A prime object of all religious reform movements in Islam has been the purification of the true religion by casting off heresies, magic, and syncretistic beliefs and practices. Historically, the very fact that attempts at such purification were repeated at various intervals would indicate that these attempts had little success in the long term. Since the nineteenth century, however, religious purification has become part of 'modernising' reform movements, such as that of Muhammad Abdu in Egypt at the end of the nineteenth century, and the Salafiyya movement which followed him in various parts of the Arab world. The prior and more traditional Wahhabism of Arabia proceeded to similar ends regarding popular religion, and in some of its effects and influences it merged with the Salafiyya. In the modern world these reform movements coincided with (and were stimulated by) the overall processes which transformed the region, and which included secularisation of many aspects of society and culture, notably education. Indeed, overtly secular movements, notably Kemalism in Turkey, had many similar aims, objectives and effects to the religious reform movements. Their rejection of popular religion was couched in the language of 'progress' versus 'backwardness', an important part of the campaign for national strength and glory and against foreign domination. The rejection of popular religion became part of the nationalist project, and in this respect merges with national purification of popular culture. A good example is the Istiqlal Party of Morocco, which subscribes to Salafi reforms, and which included in its programme of struggle for independence an opposition to the Sufi orders and rituals which dominate (to the present day) Moroccan religiosity. The attempt after independence to ban or curtail the *mawasim* of saints and other public manifestations of popular religion was short-lived. This is partly due to the deep roots which Sufi orders have in Moroccan society, and partly the result of support from strong political interests, unique features not common to other countries in the region. The more recent radical Islamic movements (at least in Sunni Islam) are no more tolerant of popular religion than their conservative orthodox predecessors, with whom they share an emphasis on scriptural sources and the examples of the Prophet and his companions.

Modern 'fundamentalist' Islamic political movements are usually strongly opposed to secular nationalism. The slogan 'the Muslim's nationality is his faith' is often quoted. Their cultural project involves a rejection of Western ideas and practices in favour of 'original' Islamic percepts. Their construction of 'original' Islam, however, would also exclude most of the beliefs and practices of popular culture, including religio-magical practices, which would be seen as corrupt. In this respect, their cultural project would involve similar, though not identical, effects in terms of 'purification' of popular cultures and life-styles. In a sense, they too are cultural nationalists, their nationality being their faith. Certainly the intellectual and political appeal of modern Islamic ideas and movements, has as an important ingredient cultural purism and the appeal to indigenous sources of ideological inspiration, as against the 'imported' secular ideologies.

I have tried to show in this chapter that popular culture in the Middle East has been polyglot and syncretistic. The religious input in this culture is variable, but seldom orthodox to any religion. What I have called the 'instrumental' orientations of popular religion transcend the boundaries of religious exclusiveness, whether of Islam, Christianity or Judaism, and merge into magic, myth and lore, some of which is drawn from scriptural sources but much of it heretical to all orthodoxies. This would tend to undermine one of the central assumptions of the modern Islamic movements and some of those who observe them in the West, which is that of 'the people' as the bearers and agents of the Islamic heritage. I have suggested that the popular support that these movements may enjoy is more likely to be based on communalist solidarity rather than religious piety or Islamic political consciousness. In so far as it is successful in mobilising popular support, political Islam then becomes a form of populist nationalism, generalising sentiments of communalist solidarity to some notion of the Islamic nation or community. Whether it will also succeed in transforming popular culture and life-styles in its directions (as against those of, say, modern mass culture), is another question.

Notes

1 The question of the diverse origins of Islamic civilisation is widely debated in the orientalist literature. But this debate is primarily concerned with theology, law, philosophy and mysticism, rather than with popular religion and culture. See, for instance, von Grunebaum, 1955 and 1970.

2 See, for instance, Gibb and Bowen, 1950, regarding the Ottoman Empire.

3 For a discussion of the various notions of 'plural society', see Rex, 1973, pp. 243-56.

4 See Goitein, 1967 for a detailed and vivid account of Jewish relations to the wider Arab society, drawn from the *Geniza* documents.

5 See von Grunebaum, 1970 for a discussion of these issues.

6 See the entry under *al-Khadhir* in *The Encyclopaedia of Islam*, New Edition, vol. IV, pp. 902-5.

7 The term *bricoleur* means a do-it-yourself, multi-skill person, but one who follows no systematic knowledge or technique, in contrast to, say, an engineer. Lévi-Strauss, 1966 (pp. 16-17) introduced this term as an analogy to illustrate what he meant by the 'savage mind'.

8 Marcel Mauss, 1972.

9 See Lewis, 1984, chapter 3.

10 Ibid., p. 153.

11 E.W. Lane, 1895, pp. 162-75.

12 This account of the Iraqi Jewish ceremony is based on personal knowledge, supplemented by informants' reports.

13 I am informed that some 'oriental' communities in present-day Israel have elaborate bridal festivities in the ritual baths, and that some baths provide rooms and catering facilities for these festivities.

14 An account of the 'folklore' of marriage in Mosul (al-Daywachi, 1975) reveals similar sequences of ceremonies, but some different terms and expressions.

15 For various discussions on these themes, see the collection of essays in Stauth and Zubaida, 1987 (which included an earlier version of this essay), and in particular the paper by Amr Ibrahim.

6

The nation state in the Middle East

A great deal has been written on the modern state in the Third World and in the Middle East from the standpoint of modernisation theory as well as various neo-Marxist and dependency perspectives. The salience of Islam in Middle Eastern politics in recent years, however, has raised different sorts of questions regarding the compatibility of 'imported' models of the nation state with the histories, cultures and societies in the region. There is no doubt that the ideas of nation, nationality and the nation state spring from particular Western European histories, in particular England and France. But these ideas and practices springing from them have proved highly diffusible to all regions of the world, first to the rest of Europe and the white colonies, then to the rest of the world, colonised or not. In one respect, the nation state has been a 'compulsory' model at independence of former colonies and dependencies, partly for lack of any other respectable models of statehood. That apart, these complex of ideas have proved remarkably popular in the fields of political struggles and contests which have marked the history of the world for the last century. Various brands of nationalism have held sway during and after independence struggles in most Third World countries, and those of the Middle East have been no exception. And yet these ideas and models, and the forms of state which borrowed legitimacy from them, are at issue and on the defensive in the face of the Islamic challenge.

The French revolution 'Jacobin' model of the nation state is perhaps the one which inspired the greatest ideological enthusiasm throughout the world: sovereignty of the people as nation, the state as the sum total of its individual and individualised citizens, the institutions of representation a constitution which enshrines the rights and obligations of citizens and a legal system based upon it before which all are equal. Most Middle Eastern countries acquired constitutions along these lines, then proceeded along lines of politics and administration which departed from these constitutions in theory and in practice, sometimes to the point of complete abrogation. And yet the complex of ideas and ideals associated with this model continued to exercise great influence upon the political actors, ideologies and practices in these societies. The democratic elements of this model may have been played down by various actors ('bourgeois' democracy for Marxists, interests of security and solidarity under threat, and 'people not ready for it yet' for various nationalists), but the idea of the nation and the ideal of popular sovereignty enshrined in some kind of representation, and the institutions of parties, parliaments, etc., all these appear to be durable and repeated features of the political fields which developed in relation to the modern state. And it is these which appear to be the object of the ideological challenge of modern Islamic politics. These failures and challenges have also inspired doubts on the part of academic and other analysts regarding the generalisability of the nation-state model to other historical and cultural contexts.

The object of this chapter is to review arguments regarding the compatibility of the nation-state model and forms of politics with the socio-cultural formations in the modern Middle East. The issues involved include the question of the forms of state organisation and politics, the nature of the political field, the models and assumptions of political organisation and action, and the patterns of differential political participation and mobilisation. The argument will be directed at two types of position. The first is what I identify as cultural and historical 'essentialism', based on the idea that 'Islamic' societies share essential elements which mark their history and determine or limit the possibilities of their social and political developments in the present. This unifying essence is contrasted to another, that of the 'West', whose social and political ideas and models, products of a unique, or rather essential history, are only superficially grafted on to the alien socio-cultural formations of Islam, a graft doomed to failure. This type of argument, in itself quite old and familiar, is now, in the wake of the 'Islamic revival', enjoying a renaissance, among some Western scholars and commentators, as well as among many of the intellectuals and spokesmen of the Islamic movements in the region, with the difference that for the former this historical essence is a dead end or at least a blockage to development, whereas for the latter it is the key to a Utopia. The second is the complex of positions which may be called 'developmentalist', including evolutionism, modernisation theory and dependency theory, all based on the idea that there are systematic processes of historical development in stages which apply to all societies, dependency theory being concerned with the blockage to development by the forces of dependency-underdevelopment resulting from the systematic operations of world capitalism. Within this perspective, every case becomes an exemplification of global processes, the specificity of its politics merged into the great international struggles. It is variants on the 'dependency' position which enjoy widespread currency and it is to these that the critical arguments of this paper will be addressed. It may be objected that the rejection of these systematic positions would result in the reduction of social science discourses to specific narratives regarding people and events, a practice which is familiar in much of the work on the region, whether in the academic literature or in the 'higher journalism', and one which is in any case burdened with implicit general assumptions. The alternative which I propose and demonstrate is quite different: I argue that the specific situations of various Middle Eastern societies and polities can be analysed in terms of general socio-economic processes. They are 'general' in the sense of applying to different societies and cultures, but not in the sense of producing common general patterns of development, as in the case of the various evolutionisms. In this form of analysis, cultural specificity is accommodated, but not cultural essentialism. Culture is a process, part of the historical flux, and cultural patterns are not fixed but reproduced at every generation in relation to different situations and conjunctures. There is no question that Middle Eastern societies are distinct and different in all respects from European societies (and from one another), and that the diffusion of European political models will not produce replicas of European states. The question is what will they produce, and the answer is neither presupposed in some pre-given cultural essence, nor produced simply in terms of global processes.

General socio-economic processes

The context of the rise of the modern state in Europe is constituted by the social and economic developments associated with the rise of capitalism, or, at least, these processes provide the conditions which make possible the basic features of the modern state and associated forms of politics: the separation of peasants from the land, leading to the breakdown of primary communities and solidarities and the individualisation of labour; the accumulation and the concentration of resources, making possible the centralisation of power at the expense of local and regional powers. This is in turn aided by the development of infra-structures of transport and communication, and the development of solidarities based on emerging class and other universalistic interests, marking new forms of political formations and struggles. These features, but on a variable scale of development, have also marked the rise of the modern state in many other parts of the world, usually in relation to Western European economic penetration, political domination and cultural influence. However, this 'dependent development' in itself leaves different traces in the new states and societies, in different patterns partly depending on the scale and type of development in relation to the dominant powers.

The starting point for most Middle Eastern countries is some kind of segmented political organisation consisting of a ruling dynasty whose direct rule does not extend far beyond its capital or seat of power, but which exercises some (variable) authority over its (theoretical) territory by uneasy alliances with local power structures in different parts of the territory, and the manipulation of antagonisms between different magnates, war lords, tribes, and so on. The rulers may develop close ties to the social and economic life of the major cities which are their seats of power, as was clearly the case of Istanbul and some other major Ottoman cities, but not to the bulk of the population in the rural and tribal areas, who remain generally tied to local networks and powers with various relations to the centre. If this is 'Asiatic society' or 'Oriental despotism', then it does not conform to the criterion of centralised power: the ruling dynasty does not usually possess the resources for the range of control which these models specify. It is true that the power of the ruler is not restricted by law or constitution, but it is by the constraints of scarcity and of other powers. The arbitrary and despotic conduct of the rulers can, in fact, only be exercised within the narrow territorial and social ranges of their powers. This form of state does conform to the 'Asiatic' models, however, in that its activities are directed primarily at the related tasks of collecting revenue, and extending, by military might, the territories from which it can collect revenue. The extraction of revenue is, then, the main point of contact between the state and its subjects, but even that contact is relegated to intermediaries like tax-farmers and local magnates. So, with the already noted exception of the major cities, the state remains external to the communities and social structures over which it rules, and in this respect constitutes a major contrast to the modern state.

The ideal type of the modern state in Europe is of one enmeshed in the processes and structures of society. The historical background is that of feudalism, which in many analytical accounts is sharply distinguished from the 'Asiatic' state, as we shall see. Be that as it may, it parallels the situation sketched above in the fragmentation of the polity and its general externality to the society under its control.[1] From this segmented polity, first the absolutist state, then the modern state are seen to develop in close interconnection with the socio-economic processes of developing capitalism. Marx, in a famous passage in *The Eighteenth Brumaire of Louis Napoleon Bonaparte* (1958, pp. 332-3), recounts the growth and elaboration of the French state from the absolutist state (against feudalism), and the acceleration of this process after the glorious revolution. The growth in functions, apparatuses and power of the state follows and parallels the development of bourgeois society and economy, the increasing complexity of the social division of labour, the state powers and organs entering every aspect of this complexity, which provides the dynamic for its growth. This, for Marx, the monster state, acquires its own interests held by its functionaries, which become an imposition and a burden on the society which gave rise to it. For Marx, in that context, the Bonapartist state was the ultimate culmination of this process, in which a government brought in by a military coup d'etat imposes its dictatorial rule over all classes in society, although, ultimately, it maintains and protects the interests of the bourgeoisie, and particularly the bankers.

What emerges from Marx's account, apart from the negative characterisation of the bourgeois state, is the firm anchoring of that state in the processes of the division of labour in bourgeois society. That is, the modern state, although an externalised and coercive imposition upon society, is nevertheless a product of the very processes of development of that society. This conclusion can be put in an entirely different theoretical language, that of Parsonian functionalism, by saying that the differentiation of structures and functions of economy and society create new control functions which are assumed by new organs of state. In these terms, the modern state is an organic outgrowth from the processes of development of society and the economy. Is this, then, the point of contrast between the ideal type of the modern Western state to that of the modern Third World state? It can be argued, as we shall see, that the latter is not an outgrowth of the society as such, but an imposition upon it from outside, by the colonial powers or other international processes and conjunctures. This state is then maintained by its dependence on external forces and resources (metropolitan centres, world market, etc.), in an externalised and oppressive relationship to the social formation. The Western state, however coercive it may become, is enmeshed in relations of reciprocal determination with society and shares in its contradictions and conflicts. It does not constitute a monolithic unity facing society, but a multiplicity of organs and centres, not always in harmony, nor always driving towards common aims and objectives, whereas the Third World ('peripheral') state, because it derives many of its powers and resources from outside its social unit, acts unidirectionally upon that society, attempting to eliminate or displace possible rivals for power within it, disrupting its social units and structures, all in an attempt to make it governable and developed. In this process, and under conditions which inhibit adequate economic development (itself, it is argued, the product of dependence), ruling cliques intensify their oppression and intrusiveness and control to maintain their powers. This would then explain the failure of development of democratic polities or of the 'law state' in most of the Third World. These themes will be elaborated and explored in what follows, particularly in the section on Paul Vieille's characterisation of the 'peripheral state'. It will be argued that, in relation to the Middle East, the processes postulated here have a certain validity, but must be heavily qualified in relation to particular countries, and in the context of many other different developments.

The other explanation of the failure of the modern nation state in the Middle East which will be considered is that in terms of the uniqueness of the modern state to Western history, and the historico-cultural obstacles to its formation in the Islamic world. These views will be critically considered below, but we may agree on one basic point. Nothing in the socio-economic processes considered above entails the concepts or the practices of the nation state; these are the products of particular histories not subsumed under these general processes. However, there are some coincidences between the consequences of these processes and the nation-state model of society: individualised citizens, equal

126

because divested of given statuses deriving from the communal organisations broken down by these processes; centralised state, co-ordinating functions in a given territory; maintenance of order and protection of citizens who are no longer sheltered by their primary associations, in short Weber's 'monopoly of violence'; the state rules according to laws which define functions, obligations and capacities of its functionaries and in relation to the citizens; the diversified and interdependent social formation cannot be left to the arbitrary whims of rulers and functionaries or it would soon collapse, hence the *Rechtsstaat*.

General socio-economic processes in relation to the Middle East

These socio-economic processes of differentiation through intensified social division of labour, the breakdown of old communities based in agricultural production and traditional crafts, the individualisation and migration of labour, all these have taken place in practically all parts of the region, some as early as the beginning of the nineteenth century, but at different rates and in different forms. Egypt, for instance, witnessed wide-ranging social and economic transformations of this nature since the start of the nineteenth century, stimulated by extensive intervention by the European powers, then the formation of a 'modernising' government under Muhammad Ali.[2] It continued to be a principal stage of European and native economic enterprise and development well into the twentieth century, with far-reaching social and political developments. At the other extreme Iraq, a backwater under Ottoman rule, only came on to the modern international scene in relation to British strategic calculations at the turn of the century and into the First World War. The socio-economic transformations in question occurred relatively late, primarily in relation to the later flow of oil revenues. Iran, similarly, first experienced the direct impact of European economic interventions late in the nineteenth century in the form of a parasitic scramble for markets and monopolies, relatively external to Iranian society and economy, tied up with the revenue hunger of a patrimonial segmentary state which persisted into the twentieth century. These different time scales were to have important consequences for the patterns of formation of modern political structures in these countries, compounding the differences in their particular societies and histories, and making any general formulations about 'Islamic' societies rather facile.

The political consequences of these different patterns of development are particularly pertinent in the area of state–society relations. Egypt is again a case in point. The interventionist, 'modernising' state of Muhammad Ali, in pursuing its military and financial objectives, entered into many areas of social and economic activity, effecting transformations which left the imprint of state on society. In addition to regulating and directing agriculture and the creation of an industrial sector, it also introduced military conscription, most unpopular, but bringing young men from different social and geographical spaces together, a preliminary step to some kind of 'national' awareness. Through education and training for government service, it created a class of civil and military functionaries of the middle level, made aware of ideas of national identity by their education, and made more intensely aware of it at personal level by the exclusive monopoly over the higher echelons of service by the Turko-Circassian aristocracy. The economic and military reverses in the fortunes of Muhammad Ali and his dynasty did not significantly reverse these developments. The subsequent reduction of the country into a colonial then semi-colonial dependency, but with a national government struggling now against the British, now against the Palace, contributed towards the formation of a definite national political field. The question of political fields will be raised systematically later. For the moment we can say that levels of political participation varied with events and conjunctures, but as early as 1882, the Urabi movement (see pp.151–2 below) could mobilise wide sectors of the urban population and was certainly not confined to the intelligentsia. It can be argued that this long history of the interaction and interpenetration of state and society in Egypt, added to the particular features of the country, such as relative homogeneity of the population, has produced quite unique state-society relations, which in contrast to some other countries in the region, is not totally marked by the externality of the state and the alienation of society. Even the Nasserite episode would not fit so easily into a category of military dictatorships, or of 'Nasserite' type of state which would include Algeria, Iraq and Syria.

To conclude this section, we may state the obvious in saying that processes of economic development and of social transformations have occurred all over the world in the last two centuries or longer in relation or in response to European capitalist expansion. These processes have taken different forms and consequences under different structural and conjunctural conditions. Common features of these processes have included, in some measure, the breakdown or transformation of primary communities, urbanisation, individualisation of labour, intensification of the social division of labour, the emergence of new forms of government and institutions, widening of education and literacy, technologies and networks of communications and transport, and new ideational formations, often significantly influenced by European ideas, especially in relation to political community and the state. Much of this is 'diffusion' rather than 'evolution'. In making these general statements about 'the rest of the world' outside of Europe, we should not forget that much of European development also occurred in terms of reactions and diffusions of one country in relation to another. The cases of Germany and Italy in relation to England and France are particularly significant, let alone the developments of the smaller countries of Central and Eastern Europe. Each country, although influenced by and reacting to developments in others, developed its own particular political patterns and institutions. This is a point we should keep in mind when considering the contrast of some general notion of the Middle East, the Arab or Islamic world to some equally generalised Europe. Schemes of explanation of the variation in historical patterns of state-society formations in Europe can be extended to serve as explanations outside Europe. In short, very specific and unique histories can be written in terms of general socio-economic processes in relation to particular given configurations and conjunctures. A notable example of a pioneering work which carries out this task comparatively, which includes in its treatment European as well as Asian countries, is that of Barrington Moore (1967) in *The Social Origins of Democracy and Dictatorship*.

Historical specificity or cultural essentialism?

I have argued that specific histories can be written in terms, at least partly, of general socio-economic processes. Some arguments for specificity, however, subordinate or disregard these general processes in favour of basic cultural specificities which direct and limit the possibilities of development. This is implicitly cultural *essentialism*. Analytically, historical specificity is distinct from the cultural essentialism. To argue for historical specificity is to show

how, for any given social formation, a series of historical conjunctures, each with its own patterns of socio-political processes, have led to a distinctive configuration. Cultural specificity is argued in terms of particular inherent and continuously active cultural elements which favour certain socio-political developments and inhibit others. An example of the possible slide from one to the other is Max Weber's construction of the uniqueness of Western history in terms of the cumulation of conjunctures:[3] Roman law, separating person from office, carried over by the Roman church; feudalism featuring multiplicity of powers and jurisdictions, inscribed in law and later incorporated into the centralised state, which becomes a 'law state'; universalising elements of Christianity distinguishing the medieval city from its classical and oriental counterparts; the Protestant Ethic and its consequences; all culminating in the uniqueness of Western capitalism, bureaucracy and rationality. But this historical cumulation can easily slip into the postulation of an 'essence' of the West which unfolds in the historical process, much like the Hegelian Spirit. Although Max Weber would never have argued along these lines, this is, nevertheless, the impression gained from reading his Introduction to *The Protestant Ethic and the Spirit of Capitalism*.

In relation to the Middle East, it is often argued that the Islamic polity is distinguished from its Western counterpart by the fact that, historically, the religious and the political community coincided in the *umma*, unlike the Western separation between church and state. The logic of this statement is that historical origins explain all subsequent historical development, it becomes an essence which underlies and limits all subsequent history. The present as a moment in that history 'contains' all that history in its structure. This would also provide the logic for the related statement that the 'failure' of the nation state in 'Islamic' countries is due to the fact that the notion of a territorial state with individualised citizenship, secular law and principles of sovereignty, is alien to the 'Muslim mind'. It is contrary to the political models of Islamic history: the dynastic, patrimonial state (if it can be called a 'state' at all, that being a Western concept for a different phenomenon), and the all-inclusive Islamic *umma*, which knows no territorial 'national' boundaries, but operates with the concept of *dar-ul-islam* (the house of Islam), which distinguishes the domains of Islam from those of the infidels. These contentions, common to 'Orientalist' thought as well as to the modern Islamist movements, suppose that the 'imported' political models and ideas of the nation state and secular political ideologies are superficial grafts, alien to peoples and governments, and are bound to fail in the hostile environments.

Explanations in terms of cultural specificities, sliding into cultural essentialism, are well illustrated in the work of Bertrand Badie (1986), *Les deux états: pouvoir et société en Occident et en terre d'Islam*, which presents a detailed argument for the historical and ideational distinction and contrast between the 'two states', the Western and the Islamic. We may distinguish two related levels of the contrast drawn between the two states, ideational and institutional.

The ideational level treats the question of legitimacy. In the Christian West there is a multiplicity of philosophical options at this level, and different combinations have characterised the development of political thought and institutions in the different European countries and North America. But all these combinations seem to coincide, for Badie, in the establishment of political spaces distinct from the religious, governed by systematic considerations of legitimacy and legality, and by individualised political actors, all in distinct contrast to Islamic political cultures. Consider, for instance, the concept of 'natural law', proceeding from Thomist-canonist constructions. In this conception, man enjoys a delegation of authority from God, and is able to exercise his God-given reason. He is able to comprehend justice even without knowledge of the Revelations, as the pre-Christian Romans did in their laws. Within this conception, justice is the domain of human reason and endeavour; all rule is questioned in terms of the norms of justice, and the question of legitimacy is always salient. The problematic of political science is placed firmly within this tradition. Another, Western, option is the positivist-nominalist conception of politics in terms of individual wills and their interactions. There is no *a priori* rationality in nature or community: the rules of the political game are created by agreement of the interacting individuals. Badie attributes this to specific religious ideas, Franciscan 'empiricism' (p. 36) and the ideas of the English Revolution (p. 66), which consider individual consciences to be in conformity with the divine will, and the pact or contract achieved by these individuals to be the only possible just order and the criterion of legitimacy.[4] The *de facto* consequences of these conceptions is to create a separation between the realms of religion and politics, with intellectual and moral autonomy of the political. This, for Badie, is one of the pillars of the distinction between

131

Western and Islamic political cultures.

In contrast, argues Badie, Islamic philosophy and theology developed a model of the ideal form of government based on divine revelation, in which the revealed law holds exclusive sway. But this ideal was only realised under the rule of the Prophet and his early companions. The dynastic governments which followed have, at best, incorporated some elements of the revealed law into otherwise worldly rule based on their interests and powers. But in so far as these governments protected the house of Islam and facilitated worship, they were to be obeyed and supported to avoid disorder and fragmentation of the community. Theirs was a rule of necessity, and the conditions of the ideal government could not be expected or applied. This duality of criteria exempted the 'government of necessity' from being judged in terms of systematic considerations of legitimacy and justice; these were reserved for the absent Utopia. This is well exemplified in the philosophy of Ibn Sina (Badie, 1986, p. 113): existential (human) being is precarious, it cannot provide its own *raison d'être*, only God can provide such reason. Power, being human, cannot, therefore, pretend legitimacy, it can only plead necessity. It can try, feebly, to approach the law of God. This distinction between human power/necessity and divine power/legitimacy is central to Islamic political culture. In this culture, challenges and qualifications to government cannot be conducted in terms of regular political discourses and processes, but only in terms of a radical and total challenge aiming to overturn the worldly government of necessity in favour of the City of God, a religious totalitarianism exemplified in the logic of some strands of reformed Christianity, notably Calvin's Geneva, but, it would seem, these tendencies are ultimately eroded by the dominant motifs of the political culture.[5] In the world of Islam, the political sphere, in so far as it is distinct from the religious, is not subject to challenges in terms of systematic discourses of legitimacy other than that which would abolish it. The regular political process of contest and opposition is, therefore, ruled out. That is why the riot is the most typical display of opposition or discontent. Whereas in the West a specific political space is created, within which contest and conflict are institutionalised, in Islam there is resistance to the idea of conflict in favour of enforced unity, the only opposition is at the limits of power, where oppression (*zulm*) becomes intolerable, hence the riot.

In Badie's account, this contrast between the West and Islam at the ideational level is reinforced at the institutional level. This is pursued in terms of the unique political history of the West – a familiar theme in Max Weber, later developed by Perry Anderson, among others – the 'triangular' structure of prince, barons and church, each with its own powers and jurisdictions. These are later incorporated into the absolutist state, and institutionalised in the form of the 'law state', with the bases of resistance to the 'patrimonial' tendencies of the monarch. The bourgeoisie and the cities have their own corporate forms which constitute another component of this pattern. Badie does go into the different patterns of development of different European states, such as England and Italy, but, somehow, these differences are minimised in favour of a common European political culture. There is a double germ contained in the Western state from its feudal birth: the law state, and the idea and practice of representation, both acting against patrimonial tendencies (Badie, 1986, p. 150). The modern European nation state and the political culture which goes with it are not the product, therefore, of some general process of economic development, generalisable to other parts of the world, but the product of a unique history, both ideational and institutional.

In contrast, the state in Islamic lands continued as a patrimonial state, centred on the ruler and his servants, with only feeble, if any, limits imposed by the *shari'a*. Its later development (Ottoman Empire and Iran in eighteenth and nineteenth centuries) was the opposite of Europe (Badie, 1986, pp. 165-74), towards fragmentation and the autonomy of local powers of *a'yan* and patrons. The *tanzimat* represented a kind of modernisation (under European influences and pressures) which was designed to bolster patrimonial power over the provinces and the regions, which largely misfired, making the *a'yan* into private proprietors. Intervention in the economy, unlike Colbertism in France, rather than serving to plan and strengthen the economy in terms of national needs, led merely to increased monopolies and corruption within the patrimonial system. European imported modernism, at both the ideational and institutional levels, appears, in Badie's account, to be a failure, leading to the formation of 'neo-patrimonial' states, whether revolutionary-nationalist or traditional-monarchic. The impediments to modernisation would appear to be Islamic political culture and mentality, at both the levels of state organisation and of political participation.

Let us take, for example, Badie's treatment of nationalism. Nationalism in the Islamic world is most successful as a mobilising force when it is against modernity, the main example being Iran in the nineteenth and early twentieth centuries (Badie, 1986, p. 181). Later (modernising) nationalists like Mossadeq, Nasser and Bourguiba did not fare so well in precarious nationalist mobilisation in a culture where the idea of the nation is accommodated with difficulty, especially when it excludes the country from the wider Islamic community. If successful (Nasser and Bourguiba) they create a new political order and a modern political elite, consolidating their powers with technological and international resources. But this 'political scene' (a key concept to which we shall return) remains alien and exterior to the 'social periphery' (which seems to include, for Badie, all the social groups and strata not directly associated with the state and its politics). This periphery continues in a dynamism of political reproduction in an activity of refusal and protest against this exterior political scene (Badie, 1986, p. 186) (one wonders what has happened to their traditional passivity). They denounce the subordination of political elites to foreigners in the name of authenticity and identity. The destabilisation of rural communities and the consequent rural–urban migrations create urban strata which contest modernity (Badie, 1986, p. 196). This type of statement, common in the contemporary literature, represents an attempt to read history backwards, ignoring or explaining away the heydays, not long ago, of popular nationalist and socialist agitations.

These apparently modern and modernising states and rulers are in fact 'neo-patrimonial', argues Badie. Nasserism, for instance, in contrast to monarchic regimes like Morocco, liberated state and society from traditional elites and discourses. It created a state elite, a state class and a military elite which dominated both. It controlled the economy, thus neutralising the financial and industrial bourgeoisie as possible rival forces. Through agrarian reforms it eliminated large landowners as a force. All this is conducted in the name of socialism, and a dominant mobilising political party is formed as the Arab Socialist Union. But both state and party, with a burgeoning bureaucracy in control, in spite of their modernist pretensions, operate in a 'neo-patrimonial' fashion. The state is controlled by a small clique of 'free officers' with family and marriage connections, which exercises overall hegemony over all aspects of politics and the economy. This political scene is feebly anchored to the periphery. The agrarian reforms, for instance, included the attempt to mobilise the rural population in support of the state, but ended up in various patronage relations and networks, to the bureaucracy and, most notably, to the local officials and

chiefs of the ASU. The political and economic difficulties of
Nasserism (necessary? inevitable?) aggravated these tendencies
and accentuated the contradictions between the idea of a
modernising national state and the realities of neo-patrimonialism
external and alien to the majority of people (Badie, 1986, p. 213).
Badie generalises this Nasserist model to other
revolutionary-nationalist military states like Iraq and Syria.

It follows, in Badie's terms, that political and social movements
in the Islamic world are radically different from their counterparts
in Western history. At first sight, it may appear that modern
movements in the Islamic world are analogous to Hobsbawm's
(1959) *Primitive Rebels* in Europe, popular movements of rebellion
and dissidence which he called 'pre-political' (Badie, 1986, p. 223
on). However, the Islamic movements cannot follow the same
course of development. The Western movements were eventually
integrated into a political and etatic system which can
accommodate opposition and conflict, guided by the models and
sometimes the leadership of bourgeois groups who preceded them
into the political system. They move from communalistic and
religious bases of solidarity and organisation to citizens'
organisations with universalist orientations. These institutions and
models have failed to develop in the Muslim countries. The
movements in question, therefore, remain external and alienated,
occasionally erupting into riot and total contestation. Furthermore,
the segmentary organisation traditional to Islamic societies and
cities – the divisions into quarters, lineages and clientalistic,
'vertical' solidarities – militate against national integration and
maintain the separateness and externality of social spaces to the
political scene. Modern and modernising processes of the division
of labour, urbanisation, etc. have failed to change this situation, and
to create 'horizontal' solidarities of class or party. The process,
already noted, of ruling elites and parties entering into patronage
relationships with elements of this segmented society reinforces the
segmentation and the failure of nation formation, as the very
leaders of modernity are compromised in traditional power
practices.

In Badie's argument, all these factors militate against the
success of nationalism as a programme of a state in power. As a
movement of opposition and protest nationalism may mobilise
popular support, but without the effect of integrating the various
segments into a truly national current. But once it advances from
protest to statehood with a modernising political programme it

gradually loses its mobilising potential. In this perspective, the current successes of Islamic political movements would appear to be a natural outcome of the particular history and the innate cultural features of Islamic societies and peoples. Modernism, which has failed in its European models, may succeed as Islamic modernism, with different forms of political organisation and mobilisation more consistent with the history and culture. The present, or a particular reading of it, is, then, the natural outcome of a particular history in which unique cultural essences are unfolding. This argument does not rest merely on the postulate of cultural-historical specificity: every country or culture or region are specific, and this would apply to England versus France as well as Turkey versus Iran. What we have here is a form of cultural *essentialism*, contrasting two histories/cultures with distinct essences underlying and unifying each course of development. The implantation of elements of one culture upon the other cannot work, as it does not conform to the essence of the host culture. General social processes of the type outlined above cannot alter the essential nature of that culture, but are somehow absorbed within it. On the other hand, this essence does unify apparently different histories such as those of Iran and Turkey, Egypt and Iraq. The differences then appear to be contingent variations, superficial to the uniform essence.

Badie organises this position in a sustained account of historical contrasts. Many other writers share these positions, but more as implicit or casual assumptions or speculations. These assumptions find their justifications in the apparent 'return' to Islam throughout the region. For instance, at the conclusion of a paper on religion and the state in Egypt, P.J. Vatikiotis offers the following observation:

It may be, of course, that a secular political order is the peculiar, nay singular, product of a particular political culture [Greek science and rationalism, Roman law, Renaissance, feudalism]...None of these foundations seem to exist in Muslim societies, including the Egyptian. Their antecedents rejected classical rationalism and humanism, and their more recent precursors simply superimposed a veneer of secularism on the state in an emulative way. (Vatikiotis, 1983, p. 70)

Another example: Olivier Carré arguing in favour of a specifically Islamic path to modernisation:

The return of a 'popular culture' or rather the reversion to it
and hence to Islamic representations is a normal thing and *a
priori* wholesome. Does that very fact amount to the rejection
of modernisation? Not necessarily; it may, in fact, be the
reverse. (Carré, 1983, p. 273)

Note the easy assumptions that this constitutes a 'return' to
something which has always been there, and that 'popular culture'
is synonymous with 'Islamic representations'. I shall return to these
questions below.

The arguments in terms of cultural essentialism derive their
plausibility from totalising and unifying contrasting entities of
culture/history. I shall argue that this totalising unity is not very
helpful in understanding the current situation which is made up of
a multiplicity of sometimes contradictory and unstable political and
ideological elements, and that modern political Islam is not the
product of a historical continuity with an essential Islam preserved
in the hearts and minds of the people as 'popular culture', but quite
the contrary, a modern ideological construction relating to current
conjunctures of nation state and international politics, and distinct
from the religious elements of 'popular culture'.

Historical specificity and historical continuity

Badie's argument, as we have seen, rests on the logic of historical
and cultural essentialism. Part of this logic is to suppose that the
events and configurations of the past determine or limit the
possibilities of further developments in future. This statement, by
itself, can be quite plausible at the empirical level without
essentialist assumptions. But at that level it is subject to empirical
qualifications. Particular historical conjunctures can reverse or
radically alter previous developments. Let us take, for instance,
Badie's characterisation of the Western state and its history. In
general terms it is true that the modern law state in the West is the
product of a course of evolution through a series of conjunctures
which give it its unique character, and that this course of evolution
is highly unlikely to be repeated elsewhere. This statement would
be true of any historical or cultural phenomenon. It is another thing,
however, to argue that further historical conjunctures could not
have outcomes which alter or reverse these characteristics. First,
the few Western European countries which shared common

historical elements leading to the law state developed different and distinct patterns of political formations depending on different conjunctures and outcomes.[6] Second, the law state was subject to breakdowns, the most recent and pertinent of which are the Nazi and Fascist episodes in Germany and Italy. These were not restored to democracy and legality spontaneously through their own internal processes restoring essential normality, but as the outcome of defeat in war, followed by massive American political and economic interventions. Both breakdown and restoration were related to international conjunctures and their outcomes. The law state in the Iberian Peninsula, presumably part of the West, was historically tentative, and recently in abeyance, to be restored also through world power alignments and pressures. These examples would indicate that historical continuity cannot be taken for granted, history proceeds in episodes of conflicts and struggles, each of which can have different possible outcomes. Such were the Russian revolution, the rise of Hitler, and the Iranian revolution. The success of each transformation was not inevitably written into the histories of these countries, the outcome of the struggles could very well have been different (we may reflect, for instance, on the possible outcome of the Iranian struggles if Reagan had been President of the United States instead of Carter). Equally, the historical continuity of the constitutional state cannot be taken for granted but has to be explained in terms of the conditions, socio-economic as well as political and cultural, which made it possible. Crucially, the continuity of forms of democracy and legality in Britain and France were made possible by the economic conditions of production or acquisition of wealth on a scale which allowed, for the most part, the containment or amelioration of threatening social conflicts. And this is a very important point to keep in mind when considering Third World polities today.

The assumption of historical or cultural continuity in Middle Eastern state and politics is even more problematic. The characterisation of historical Middle Eastern polities as 'patrimonial' is unexceptional in general terms, although many differences in the organisation of government and of ruler–ruled relationships can be distinguished at different times and places which limits the value of this general characterisation. The Ottoman and Iranian polities of the nineteenth century can be described as patrimonial, but this would hide important differences between them. The Qajar state did not even have a standing army, but had to rely on tribal levies for the disastrous wars with Russia.

It did not have a regular bureaucracy beyond the aristocratic court functionaries and their servants, while the Ottomans had highly developed and differentiated state organisation, with a number of different military establishments and forces. One of these latter, the Janissaries (before their abolition in one of the nineteenth-century reforms) developed over the years intimate links with the popular classes and the markets, which were very important in the relationship between ruler and ruled, and which played important parts in the conduct of popular politics and opposition in Istanbul and some other major cities. The relationship between the state and the religious institutions in the two polities were again different: almost a department of state in the Ottoman case, while institutionally, socially and financially independent of the state in Iran, a factor which had important political consequences at the time and subsequently (see Chapters 1 and 2 above). The impact of European penetration on the two entities accentuated these differences, with greater and deeper effects in the advanced parts of the Ottoman Empire: Turkey, Egypt and Greater Syria, leading to the development in these parts of important *modern* political fields of opposition and reform, as against the primarily *reactive* opposition in Iran led by the *mullahs*. All these differences would make the unification of the two entities under 'Islam' and 'patrimonialism' quite facile.

In terms of historical continuity, the modern states instituted in the old territories of the Ottoman Empire, after the First World War and a spell of more or less direct European rule, represented clear breaks with their predecessors, in the case of Turkey stridently and aggressively different. Iran proceeded to a modern state at a much slower pace and with many continuities of open patrimonialism. As I understand it, what Badie and others are arguing is that, after a period of 'pretend' democracy and constitutionalism these modern states reverted, in the course of struggles for power, to a 'neo-patrimonial' form restoring elements of the patrimonial state of historical Islam under modern conditions. The fact that Middle Eastern states manifest various degrees and forms of autocracy and arbitrary rule by rulers who assumed power for the most part by force of arms is not in dispute. However, it can very well be argued that this is a very general form of rule throughout the world and has little to do specifically with Islam or its cultural and historical continuities. It can be further argued, as it is indeed argued by 'dependency theory' among others to be considered below, that this form of polity is the product of modern socio-economic world conditions and relationships, which impede economic development and, consequently, political stability, and would therefore favour autocratic polities attempting to maintain their powers by force. Badie is clearly aware of the socio-economic conditions and relationships within each country which perpetuate autocracy. But for him all social and economic processes in the world of Islam seem to work towards the preservation or reproduction of these characteristic Islamic traits of society and government, as if constrained by the historico-cultural moulds which contain them.

Let us be clear as to what constitutes the failure of the modern nation state in the Islamic world according to Badie and others: failure of the law state in favour of arbitrary patrimonialism; consequently failure of democracy; failure of national formation, the majority being in 'peripheral social spaces' excluded from a 'political scene' dominated by the state and its associated intellectuals; opposition emanates from these peripheral spaces, is segmented into communities, is at its strongest when mobilised against modernity, and when expressed is totally negative, contesting the whole of the modern state and society; this is the character of contestatory Islamic politics and would explain Islamic resurgence. Some of these assertions are clearly, if partially, correct, such as that regarding the failures of legality and democracy. The characterisation of politics and the political field, however, are highly debatable and will be debated in what follows. It will be argued that a modern political field develops in all the countries in question in relation to the nation state but not tied to it; that the discourses, political models and forms of organisation of this field assume a nation and a national state, even when they are opposed to it in favour of some wider entity; that this field is the product of cultural and technical processes of modernity; and that most Islamic movements and ideologies are part of this field. The general tenor of the discussion is that historical continuities and essences suggested by terms like 'patrimonialism' and 'segmented communities' are superficial, and that the phenomena in question are easily explained in terms of current conditions which are not specific to the Middle East or Islam.

Dependency and the peripheral state

In the various forms of dependency theory, we have an approach which is, apparently, the opposite of the theme of historical continuity. Middle Eastern states are forms of the 'peripheral' state, which is shaped by dependence on a world market dominated by capital and the major capitalist powers of the 'centre'. The relationship of centre to periphery is governed by an economic calculus (derived in one form or another from Marxist theories of value) based on 'unequal exchange' and the transfer of value from the periphery to the centre. Dependency prevents the realisation of any 'genuine' economic development; this undercuts the legitimacy of the modernising state in that it fails to deliver what it promises; failure of development also exacerbates poverty, inequality, regional imbalances of development and distribution; these combine to produce social crises and contradictions which threaten authority and order; the state responds with more and more repressive measures, attempting to control, suppress or incorporate any autonomous centres or activities in the society it dominates; the state can only succeed in this enterprise with resources and technical means deriving from the centre on which it is increasingly dependent for this very reason; the other side of this dependence on the centre is increasing autonomy from the society which it rules. Thus the externalisation/alienation of state from society in the Third World, and the increasing oppressiveness of the state, are not historical extensions of 'Asiatic despotisms', but on the contrary, modern creations of the capitalist world market.

I should like now to consider a particular contribution within this framework of dependency theory but eccentric to it, that of Paul Vieille's (1984) essay entitled 'L'État périphérique et son heritage'. It reaches many conclusions parallel to Badie's regarding the failure of the nation state and its politics, and in favour of 'community', but from very different intellectual and value perspectives. Vieille's unit of specificity is not 'Islam' but the 'Mediterranean'. His definition of the Mediterranean is wide enough for his main examples to come from Iran, with occasional references to Saudi Arabia. He considers other examples, to illustrate some of his arguments, from Provence and the Languedoc. We shall see that the argument makes this wide definition of the region possible, and that it can also be applied to many other places which are much further away from the Mediterranean.

By the logic of dependency outlined above, the peripheral state in the Mediterranean (and presumably elsewhere) is necessarily oppressive. By the logic of its dependence on the world market, it disorganises the social formations which it governs and reorganises them according to its articulation to the world market. In the process it does not merely govern civil society but it negates it by attempting to assume all its functions; it does not tolerate any autonomous organisation or function in civil society: the economy, community, religion, education and even the family are penetrated by the state and its cumbersome bureaucracies. The state attempts to absorb civil society into itself. It derives its powers primarily from its association and dependence on the central powers, and not so much from internal power bases. These latter are in fact built up by the state rather than preceding it (the state makes the nation). The state is economically oriented to extracting surplus value from its internal economy and sharing it (as the minor partner) with the centre (its conflicts with the centre revolve around the proportions).

Ideologically, this is first done under the banner of modernisation and development, and when development fails the failure is blamed on the backwardness of the people (Iran under the Pahlavis), and the people are forcibly modernised (e.g. compulsory deveiling of women under Reza Shah). When the strategy of modernisation is discredited, the state may turn to the ideology of authenticity and fidelity to the true national traditions, then blaming the people for their infidelity, and forcibly directing them on to the true path (compulsory veiling of women under the *mullahs*). In either case the state has an ideological pretext for oppression and the invasion of the most intimate corners of civil society, ruling out free choice and personal autonomy.

Here we come to the historical continuities. The peripheral state is another form of the 'pillage state' of old, built upon the logic of appropriating the wealth and revenues from the social formations it governs. Only, under contemporary conditions its relations to society are changed. Whereas the old pillage state was content to leave society alone for the most part, so long as the revenues were forthcoming, the peripheral state, as we have seen, must disorganise, reorganise, penetrate and dominate society. The traditional Islamic city maintained a (permeable) boundary between the public and the private: the first the domain of politics and affairs, and as such exclusively male; the second the domestic domain veiled and obscured, where the primary considerations were those of honour, and where honour rested on the comportment and isolation of women. A man's capacity as an actor in the first field depended on his security in the second. In the struggle for advantage in public life, considerations of a man's honour in the private sphere can be subtly brought into play, to injure or to sustain. The modern peripheral state, by invading this private sphere (and the main example is the unveiling of women), dishonoured the men, emasculated them in the public sphere and undermined their political capacity.

The second, more important and (explicitly argued) historical continuity for Vieille, is that of the anti-etatism of the people of the Mediterranean region. The Mediterranean is a region where the formation of states is of great antiquity. At the same time it is a region in which people have always manifested a distrust and an opposition towards the state, an anti-etatism. To explain this Vieille draws on elements from Marx's *Grundrisse* on pre-capitalist economic formations. The self-subsistent agricultural commune (of the Asiatic type, although Vieille does not use this designation) is the predominant type of community. The fringes of the region spawned pastoral peoples, militarily organised for raid and pillage, who are the bases of the formation of the state. As such this 'pillage state' has always been oppressive and external and engendered this anti-etatism. Examples drawn from various parts of the region (mainly Iran and Provence) illustrate this ingrained feeling of 'them' versus 'us' characteristic of these communities. The processes of modernity, especially de-peasantisation, have the effect of breaking down the communities. In the Iranian example this process has been dramatic and violent, especially following the agrarian reforms of the early 1960s. But these processes did not create the 'Jacobin' nation implicit in the idea of the nation state, but bodies of disorganised and disorientated individuals, retaining the sentiments of anti-etatism, now strengthened by the intrusions of the capitalist state (in Provence) and of the peripheral state (in Iran). Islamic agitation in Iran found a ready echo partly because it recreated the 'imaginaire' of community *contra* the state (the old opposition of *mellet* versus *dowlat*). The state was toppled by throngs of people ready for martyrdom (Iranian history and culture) including ranks of veiled women taunting the men into action: the private triumphant, invading the very locus of the state which invaded and suppressed it.

The above exposition presents the bare logical bones of the argument. In fairness it should be added that Vieille advances many of its elements cautiously and with qualifications, insisting, for instance, on historical and conjunctural specificities within these general processes. The argument is very interesting at a number of levels, not least the manifestation of Mediterranean regionalist populist sentiments which considers the ferments and struggles of the Islamic side of the Mediterranean as exemplars of a regional phenomenon, which, presumably, has implications for Provence, Corsica, Catalonia, etc. It is a kind of modern Narodnik argument for the oppressed communes of the Mediterranean, and the political implications are towards a Utopian populist anarchism. It points out the failure of the nation state model in the region. What is envisaged, or rather hinted at, by Vieille is a kind of populist-community state.[7] The quest for community in the resulting situation then explains the attraction of Islamic radical ideas, postulating an Islamic community or *umma*, a new form of solidarity replacing the old, and filling the gaps which the modern state creates but cannot fill. In its generality, this proposition is true, but much more generally than the 'Mediterranean', hence the preoccupation with similar problems in 'classic' sociological theory, dealing with the processes of the transformations of Western European societies. At the same time, by being so general, it ignores many of the important developments of associations and solidarities, some of a 'national' kind in many countries in the region in the course of this century. I shall pursue this line in the context of a wider argument.

The concept of a world market producing systematic inequalities of exchange and consequently dependence between 'centre' and 'periphery', is a controversial one which has been widely debated in the literature.[8] In the case of the oil states, which Vieille clearly has in mind as his major example, it is only possible to speak of 'unequal exchange' (or for that matter equal exchange) by means of some arbitrary definition of value. But we do not need dependency theory with its tortuous economic acrobatics to arrive at the conclusion that many Third World states, and certainly the oil states of the Middle East, are highly dependent on resources, financial, technical and military, from the advanced countries, primarily the United States. In this respect, Vieille's conclusions about the autonomy of these states from the social formations they govern, and their destructiveness and oppressiveness with regard to these social formations, may stand, but without the assumptions of dependency theory. The effect of these assumptions, however, do have important consequences for the argument; they suppose that this state of affairs is *necessary* by virtue of some economic logic. The only escape from this necessity is by some impossible condition of 'self-sufficiency', tied up in turn to some Utopian state of communal autonomy. Further, the relation between state and society has been in the process of evolution over the last century, and this evolution has resulted in a number of different conjunctures at different moments of this history. Vieille's argument recognises this evolution in that it supposes that the condition of alienation/oppression of state versus society is the product of successive failures of modernisation/development (failures which are necessary outcomes in terms of dependency theory). But the course of this history, and the conditions of previous conjunctures, are ignored in favour of these recent conditions. It is only by ignoring this history that it becomes possible to present the problem as a confrontation between the 'community' and the state, without taking account of the important socio-political developments of a 'national' kind which have marked previous decades of this century. There is also the question of different courses and patterns of development in the different countries. Vieille, as I have indicated, recognises the specificities, and indeed points out the very unique configuration of Saudi Arabia, but the necessary oppressiveness of the peripheral state seems to cut across these specificities.

There seems to be a convergence, therefore, from radically different theoretical standpoints, on the characterisation of the modern Middle Eastern state as autocratic, as the instrument of self-interested cliques, featuring heavy-handed bureaucracies which are oppressive and intrusive into the lives of people to whom the state is external and alien. These conclusions may be justifiable in very general terms, but the difference such a generalisation hides are as important, at least, as the similarities. As I indicated earlier, Iraq and Egypt are very different political entities, the product of different histories and social structures; the incumbent Ba'thist regime is similar to the Nasserite state in Egypt only in very general terms. Perhaps these differences will become more apparent in the course of the discussions to follow.

The formation of the modern political field

It is quite clear that the implantation of Western models of the modern nation state in the Middle East, as well as in many other parts of the world, have led to very different patterns of formation, different from the West and from each other. These are for the most part modern states, in terms of forms of organisation, administration and rule, but they are not modern Western states. Alongside these state forms there developed a whole complex of political models, vocabularies, organisations and techniques which have established and animated what I call a *political field* of organisation, mobilisation, agitation and struggle. The vocabularies of this field are those of nation, nationality and nationalism, of popular sovereignty, democracy, liberty, legality and represent-ation, of political parties and parliamentary institutions, as well as various ideological pursuits of nationalism, Islam and socialism. These ideas are underpinned by structural and institutional transformations: urbanisation and the dissolution or weakening of many primary communities, urban and rural, the emergence and widening of an individualised (but not always universalised or impersonal) labour market in which the state is a major if not the major employer, and crucially the spread of education and literacy, aided by technical means of printed communication, of what Benedict Anderson (1983) called 'print capitalism'.

In each country, this political field developed with the modernist as well as the reactive struggles against patrimonial states and the threats of foreign incursion and domination (Iran at the turn of the century presents an interesting example of the convergence of the modernist and the reactive forces). These are perpetuated in the ongoing struggles for national independence, as well as in the contest between the different forces and ideologies. These contests are sharpened in relation to the national state and within it, with constant attempts by those in power to impede, suppress or divert oppositions and challenges. In many countries the ultimate triumph of a particular group or current culminated in the monopolisation and the suppression of the whole political field in favour of organisation and mobilisation managed by the government to the exclusion of all other forces, at which point the oppositional forces have to operate underground, in exile and in different forms of dissimulation. This is the situation which has become familiar in most countries in recent decades, part of the oppressive, autocratic regimes which have dominated the region.

Closely involved in the constitution and the functioning of the political field is what Benedict Anderson (1983) has called 'the possibility of imagining the nation' (p.40) as a community, and the conditions of that possibility. Anderson contrasts the nation as an 'imagined community' with another form which preceded it, the religious community and the dynastic state. The religious community, such as that of Christianity or Islam, is imagined world-wide. It is conceived by its adherents as 'cosmically central, through the medium of a sacred language linked to a superterrestial order of power' (p.20). Each actual small (face to face) community, imagined a multitude of replicas of itself who enacted the same rituals in a sacred language they did not understand, but whose ideographs were part of the cosmic order. Accompanying this conception of community is 'a conception of temporality in which cosmology and history were indistinguishable, the origins of the world and of men essentially identical' (p.40). History does not move in empty calendrical time in chains of cause and effect and without end; time is marked by divine interventions and sacred episodes, one prefiguring or shadowing another. Events are connected by their significance in a sacred order rather than by chains of cause and effect.

The nation, for Anderson, is a different type of imagined community, imagined in different conceptions of time and space. 'It is imagined because the members of even the smallest nation will never know most of their fellow-members, meet them, or even hear of them, yet in the mind of each lives the image of their communion' (Anderson, 1983, p.15). As against the hierarchical model of the dynastic realm, in which the apex of power is in the realm of the sacred and the taboo, the nation is imagined as a horizontal solidarity and comradeship between the citizens. The community is imagined in terms of a sociological space with different occupations and positions, institutions and locations, which constitute part of the stock of common knowledge which each member has about the community. And this sociological organism moves along in homogeneous calendrical time. History is conceived in linear time, in which the constructed history of the nation acquires antiquity and ancestry. Two modern literary forms illustrate the national imagination: the novel and the newspaper. The old-fashioned novel shares a world with its readers, in which different characters, not necessarily known to one another, move simultaneously or in clocked, calendrical time, in social locations and spaces familiar or imaginable to the readers:

> The idea of a sociological organism moving calendrically through homogeneous, empty time is a precise analogue of the idea of the nation, which also is conceived as a solid community moving steadily down (or up) history. (Anderson, 1983, p.31)

The newspaper is equally dependent on the conception of empty, homogeneous time, and on the assumed community of interests and knowledges of its readers. What unifies the diversity of items on any front page is the date at the top of the page. The knowledge of each reader that the same page is being read by a large number of compatriots reinforces the imagination of community.

Printing and the rapid spread of the printed word, in parts of the Middle East from the second half of the nineteenth century, is a crucial factor in facilitating the conception of the nation. It is the factor which underlies and makes possible all others. It also facilitates the development of a print language, such as modern standard Arabic, distinct from the language of the sacred texts and the historical classics as well as from the multitude of spoken Arabics. This print language creates a unified field of exchange and communication, which is one of the conditions for the emerging political field. The book, then the newspaper and the magazine, are infinitely reproducible commodities, which by the logic of 'print-capitalism' are pushed to every possible market, and indeed create new markets through expanded literacy.

Anderson's formulation of the factors and conditions involved in the conception of the nation as imagined community is clearly highly relevant to our discussions. The units postulated as nations in the Middle East, as elsewhere, were highly variable: Turkey, Egypt and Iran could be held to constitute historic and cultural unities, reinforced by the new processes of the conception of the nation. But the division within Greater Syria and the entity of Iraq had no such logic, nor the exclusion of Armenia or Kurdistan from nation statehood. However, the debates and struggles over these divisions and units were themselves part of the developing political field(s), underlaid by the new cultural and technical processes. Once the new states are established, their very existence promotes the genesis of new 'imaginaires' of the nation: common education systems incorporating the symbols of etatic power as nation; education feeding into employment markets for the most part dominated by the state; national networks of communication and transport; military conscription facilitating the interaction of youths, mostly from the poorer rural classes, with widely different regional and cultural backgrounds. These and many other factors facilitate the conception, not necessarily self-consciously political, of the nation within the boundaries, however initially arbitrary, of the new states. It should be emphasised that this idea of the conception or imagination of the nation does not necessarily entail political commitment to this entity: pan-Arab, pan-Islamic as well as narrow ethnic commitments are clearly beyond that of the nation state, but the *conception* of the nation becomes the field and the model in terms of which to think of these other commitments and loyalties. The factors and processes outlined above facilitate the conception or imagination of the nation whatever unit of nationhood emerges from historical backgrounds or current conjunctures.

The conception of the nation and the processes which facilitated it were clearly not universally diffused throughout the postulated national unit, the participation in these conceptions and practices being differential, and the urban intelligentsia dominating the field. It may also be objected that many of the participants in the emergent political fields were but thinly disguised representatives of primary solidarities of tribe, ethnic/religious or regional groups, that is to say factional solidarities pre-existing the nation, but seeking to obtain power, influence and resources within the new political entities, using the language of nationality and of political ideologies to that end. This contention has a *prima facie* plausibility which hides a multitude of different political processes. Iraq would, perhaps, present a good illustration for an argument on these issues because of its particularly fragmented social structure. It has been shown in this regard (see Chapter 4 pp. 90–4 above) that the Iraqi Shi'a, for instance, never constituted a unitary political force, but that Shi'i interests and outlooks contributed significant inputs to various political movements and forces at different points in time. The Shi'i landlords and shaykhs of southern Iraq played particular political roles in qualified support for the monarchy and the British until the 1950s, while their co-religionists in the intelligentsia and the working classes contributed significantly to a number of radical forces, most notably the Iraqi Communist Party. Neither of these could be said to be straightforwardly engaged in communalist politics, but in the promotion of economic or ideological interests. Being Shi'i may play an important part in the constitution or conception of these interests, as, for instance, in the fact that Shi'is were not notable for their support for pan-Arabism, possibly because this would align Iraq with a predominantly Sunni Arab world. But if these sentiments did exist they were not expressed in political organisation based on communal solidarity, but in a variety of affinities to forces which could not themselves be explained in terms of these sentiments. In other words, communalist sentiments enter into the political field, but the form they take is shaped and sometimes transformed by the forces and conjunctures of that field. Similarly, the by now well known domination of the Iraqi Ba'th party and government by a clique based on particular clans from the country towns of the northwest, especially Takrit, would also serve as an illustration of this point. The situation is the end product of conspiratorial and factional politics with the logic of the progressive elimination of rivals, thus encouraging the reliance on kin loyalties, which are in turn progressively narrowed by the same process. But this process, in itself, cannot explain the formation and development of the Ba'th party, its assumption of government power, or its policies and politics. Under the conditions of the political field of the nation state, communal and ethnic divisions are constructed and conceived in terms of that field and its topology; in Anderson's terms they become part of the imagined community. It should also be emphasised that these divisions are not unique to 'Islamic', or even to Third World politics, but are common to many parts of the 'West', notably Italy, Spain and the United States. I shall return to this theme in a later section on the question of patronage networks and the 'neo-patrimonial' state.

Let us now turn to the question of the range of participation in the national political field by different groups in the population. The cultural and technical processes noted as underlying the formation of the field are located primarily in the cities and related to literacy. As such the participation in them by rural populations and recent rural migrants into cities is likely to be limited.[9] It may even be argued that this political field and its conceptions of the nation are largely confined to the intelligentsia to the exclusion of the popular strata, rural or urban. This view would reinforce the notion that the popular strata are politically animated, if at all, by an Islamic and not a national identity. Here we enter the realm of reified and essentialised identities. I favour a much more fluid picture, postulating the coexistence of different political and cultural discourses and practices, elements of which are brought into play in relation to particular conjunctures and struggles. For instance, Shi'i politics in Iran are not the product of some essential, historically given body of beliefs and practices preserved in the lives and minds of the people, but of particular constructions of religious discourses in relation to current situations, constructions which incorporate the vocabularies and models of the national political field (see Chapters 1, 2 and 3 above). This political field, in the process of its evolution, has constituted the arena in which many struggles were fought, many with popular participation. It is, of course, difficult to ascertain the ideas and images which popular participants bring into the field, but in the process of participation the vocabularies and concepts of this field become parts of their ideological stock, which may coexist with and possibly transform previous cognitive models. In this respect we should note the difference between participation in the sense of occasional mobilisation in demonstrations, strikes or riots, around particular issues and slogans, and more sustained and continuous political organisation. While the integration of the 'people' into political activities is an explicit political objective for practically all nationalist and socialist ideologies, in practice it has been the parties of the left, notably the communist parties, and the populist Islamic parties, notably the Muslim Brotherhood in Egypt, which have actually made systematic efforts in this direction, with various degrees of success. The other parties have related to the masses either through agitations on particular issues or through networks of patronage and clientelism.

Egypt is the country in which the modern political field has had the longest history of evolution, and in which the popular masses have been involved in various forms. It would be interesting to follow Gabriel Baer's (1983) account of the development of political forms from the Urabi revolt in 1882 to the revolt of 1919 around Saad Zaghlul and the Wafd. In the earlier parts of the nineteenth century, popular movements in Egypt, both urban and rural, took fairly traditional forms. Urban riots and revolts marked the turbulent years at the turn of the eighteenth/nineteenth centuries of the French invasion followed by the power struggles which ultimately brought Muhammad Ali to power (Marsot, 1984). These were variously led by high ranking ulama, lesser religious shaykhs, or local *futtuwa* (tough guys) of the quarters. The issues related predominantly to excessive taxation and other forms of oppression, and Islamic slogans featured as part of the rhetoric, especially when the adversaries were the French. Rural movements also related to fiscal oppression, but were led by heterodox charismatics, one, later in the nineteenth century, claiming *mahdiship* (Baer, 1983, p.38). These rural movements continued into the century along similar patterns. By the time of the Urabi revolt of the 1880s, Islamic slogans and leadership continued to play an important role, but then it had become secondary (Baer, 1983, p.39). Urabi thought of himself as an Egyptian nationalist fighting against the control over the army and state by Turko-Circassian officers, as well as against British domination. Many of his supporters, however, were religious shaykhs who spoke in terms of the defence of Islam and even of a *jihad*. Clearly, this religious appeal played an important part in mobilising popular support, but this time for a specifically nationalist cause which also featured the support of Coptic elements. Accompanying Urabi's revolt, but not part of its programme, were attacks in various parts of the country on Copts, Greeks and Jews, who were apparently identified as money-lenders. This 'communalist' element of popular sentiments at times of turmoil was to recur till the present time. I shall return to this question presently. While the leaders of popular agitations in this instance included many shaykhs and religious students (the higher ulama generally siding with the Khedive against Urabi) 'the motivation and purpose of the different social groups of which the movement was composed were . . .other than Islamic' (Baer, 1983, p.40), such as targeting the money-lenders. It would seem then that although the Urabi movement itself was 'modern' in the sense of being nationalist, many of the forms of agitation and action involved in it followed 'traditional' patterns. The 1919 agitations led by Saad Zaghlul and the Wafd (later to give its name to a political party), were much more explicitly secular and featured much more widespread participation by Copts. The higher ulama were marginally involved (as signatories to the appeal for calm at one point), but did not belong to the leadership of the movement. At the popular level, leadership had passed from the Azhar students and local *imams* of previous years to students and teachers of the modern secular schools and the newly opened university (Baer, 1983, p.44). The secular intelligentsia, then, emerge as the leaders of popular movements, no longer tied to Islamic models and slogans, but receptive to slogans and agitations in modern nationalist terms. This is not, however, by any means the end of Islamic appeal, which as we shall see emerges in new forms, nor necessarily of previous cognitive models of politics and society.

Islam and the political field

The significance of Islam in the modern political fields is various: there are many forms of Islamic political ideas, and many different ways in which they are articulated to political attitudes and movements. I should, at the start, distinguish one particular form, specially relevant to popular attitudes, which is 'communalist' ideas and sentiments. This is Islam as an 'ethnic marker' marking the boundaries of a community (or 'imagined community') as against others identified in terms of different religions. This form of communal identification, we may add, is quite common throughout the world, historical and modern. Communalist sentiments are often competitive, and under suitable conditions break out into open conflicts and struggles. These are quite common in the history of the Middle East, sharpened and aggravated by European penetration, which generally promoted the religious minorities and gave them protected status, later to be incorporated into Ottoman legal reforms giving minorities equal citizenship, to the chagrin of the discontented Muslim majorities, for whom the *dhimmis* could be protected as long as they kept to their (inferior) places in the social hierarchy of religions. The violent attacks on Christians in Syria in the 1860s were notable examples of this accentuation of communalist conflict. One result of this process is that Christian and Jewish communities became identified, in the popular mind, with European Christian powers, and sentiments against these powers were sometimes directed against local religious minorities. This promoted a communalist model of international relations: the world as blocks of solidary religious communities antagonistic to one another. The formation of the state of Israel and its military dominance has no doubt reinforced this model. We should note that communalist sentiments and models do not presuppose any specific Islamic political ideas, other than those of the necessary separateness and inferiority of other religions. As such they are quite distinct, at the level of ideas and political programmes, from modern political Islam. However, they can be important mobilising sentiments in favour of any movement calling for the restoration of Islamic superiority. That is to say, popular ideas and sentiments which are not specifically 'Islamic' in the doctrinal or political sense can and do act as important stimuli for support of Islamic political movements. The attacks on Copts, Greeks and Jews in parts of Egypt at the time of the Urabi revolt and subsequently on the occasions of anti-British agitations can be seen in this light. Recent communal conflicts between Muslims and Copts in Egypt show the persistence of these ideas and sentiments. These occurrences are often disapproved by leaders of the national or even Islamic movements, but this is not always the case. Communalist appeals often play a part, openly or covertly, in demagogic political appeals, as in the case of King Fuad attempting to discredit the Wafd by pointing to the prominence of Coptic leaders in its ranks (Baer, 1983, p.46). We should keep this form of Islamic politics in mind when we later

153

discuss the question of popular support for modern Islamic movements.

Official Islam, or the official utilisation of Islam in the struggle for legitimation, is another form. Most Middle Eastern states (not Turkey or Tunisia) subscribe to Islam in some formula or another as the state religion, while at the same time providing for equal citizenship for all regardless of religion, and for secular forms of government, law and education (with some qualifications, especially with regard to personal status law and procedure). It may be argued that these provisions have, until recently, been purely symbolic. But alongside this symbolic commitment, Islam has been brought into play on frequent occasions in political battles. Hereditary rulers have often played the Islamic card against their democratic or radical challengers. The example of Fuad's attack on the Wafd cited above is part of a much wider strategy involving the king's attempt to assume the title of the defunct caliphate, frustrated by the Wafd leadership as well as rival claims elsewhere (Baer, 1983, pp.44-6). His son Faruq continued to flirt with Islamic ideas and movements in his battles against the national movement and elected governments, and to that end patronised Hassan al-Banna and the Muslim Brotherhood for a brief period. Conservative governments throughout the region, however secular and ungodly in their rule, have always attempted to play the Islamic card against the radicals and the left, and more recently to pre-empt the Islamic radicals by emphasising their own commitments to orthodoxy. The late President Sadat of Egypt promoted the Muslim Brotherhood in the 1970s as a bulwark against the left and the Nasserites. Saudi Arabia has always promoted political Islam in *other* countries as a counter against nationalism and radicalism. But this official utilisation of Islam is by no means confined to the monarchist and conservative regimes. Nasser, more than any other leader, subordinated Islamic institutions and practices, like other spheres of social life, to his bureaucratic state. He appropriated Islam and felt free to resort to its slogans and rhetoric in his speeches, and to use it as part of state propaganda in the school curricula (Carré, 1983). At the same time his use of Islam was in no way systematic or central, pan-Arab nationalism and socialism being the central pillars of Nasserite ideology. Islam in this capacity, as a resource for official legitimation, drawn upon by conservative and radical governments for different ends, drawing different conclusions according to need, has always constituted an important part of the political field.

The most important Islamic element in the modern political field is that of the organised populist Islamic movement or party, most notably the Muslim Brotherhood in Egypt. In terms of ideology and organisation it represents a radical departure from historical forms of Islamic political agitations and actions. It is primarily urban and orthodox, distinct from the rural heterodox movements led by charismatics and often featuring messianic expectations. It is also distinct from urban movements in previous centuries. These were sporadic, led by ulama or lesser shaykhs in response to aggravations of oppression, mostly fiscal – prices of bread or other commodities – in the support of one or other princely faction in situations of open conflict and civil war. Basically they were movements to redress perceived injustice in the name of religious norms. They were not usually calls for the institution of an Islamic state and society, these being assumed to be extant under the prevailing sultan or caliph. Historically, calls for the institution of a legitimate state as against an allegedly ungodly one were always made in the name of an alternative prince, usually designated in terms of lineage, notably the Alid, or of a messianic Mahdi. The Brotherhood is distinguished from these past patterns in being a modern political party, with a systematic organisation and recruitment, and a political programme imbued with the assumptions of the modern national political field:

> Like popular Islamic revolts in Egypt at the turn of the eighteenth century, the Muslim Brothers enjoyed the support of a considerable part of the urban masses, but unlike these earlier eruptions the Muslim Brotherhood was a well organised body with an operational scheme of a leader, councils, assemblies, secretaries, committees, sections, branches and so forth. (Baer, 1983, p.47)

The objectives of this organisation were the displacement of the existing order with one based on Islamic law and principles of social justice. This was to be done through popular organisation and mobilisation; the 'people' mobilised in relation to abstract political principles, not in the cause of a more legitimate prince or charismatic. The desirable future order is postulated in terms of an organic unity between community and government, mediated by institutions of representation (through elections), legislation (but within the limits of *shari'a*), economic and social policies and plans. That is to say, an Islamic form of the nation state, assuming modern political forms and processes. The general antagonism to

155

the idea of multiple political parties is no different to many secular nationalists, nor to right-wing European ideologies of the organic state (to which progressive Arab thinkers likened the Brotherhood). Another aspect of the 'modernism' of the Muslim Brotherhood is that it is one of the few political organisations which did not rely heavily on patronage and clientelism for its popular support, but on ideological persuasion and commitment, accompanied at times by aid and welfare programmes. However, this pattern is currently being transformed, at least in some sectors of the Islamic movement, by the introduction of Islamic banking and investment (largely from Saudi and Gulfi sources), into new forms of power and patronage. This does not, however, alter the earlier history of the Brotherhood.

We thus see that Islam, in one form or another (the above account being by no means an exhaustive enumeration) has always constituted part of the modern political field. We also see that hardly any of these forms represent historical continuities in terms of ideas, institutions, or forms of political organisation, but relate, for the most part, to modern political fields. Islamic communalism is perhaps the form which exhibits the most continuity with past models of social organisation. In this regard two points can be made: one is that it does not involve specific Islamic political ideas or doctrines apart from the assumption of Islamic exclusiveness and superiority in relation to other religions; and second that this form of thinking as a stimulus to political action is by no means confined to Islamic contexts but can be found in many societies in many parts of the world historically and at present.

In relation to the foregoing account of Islam in the political field we may raise questions regarding the issues raised by Badie and others. Do Islamic politics represent popular rejection of modernity? Are they the products of social spaces external to the space of authority and politics, to the 'national political scene' (Badie, 1986, p.245)? Do they represent a total contestation of the political order, seeking to replace it with the city of God? To answer these questions we have to break up totalities and look at different currents and strands.

First of all let us examine the concepts in use. Badie uses 'political scene' interchangeably with 'official' politics of the state and perhaps legal or approved political organisations. He contrasts this space to 'external social spaces' where oppositions and rejections are fomented, often of a segmentary and communalistic nature, thus militating against the formation of a national political community with orderly institutionalised opposition. The concept of the 'political field' which I have been using is significantly different. While it is historically tied to the formation of modern states and the socio-economic and cultural processes they engender, it does not remain tied to the state and the official political scene. The monopolisation of the political field by totalitarian regimes has driven many political organisations and forces underground to operate more or less secretly depending on the degree of repression and surveillance. Nasserite repression did not eliminate Islamic politics from the political field, nor Pahlavi repression the forces of the Iranian left. While we may agree with Badie that there are social spaces outside the political field, but which nevertheless can make inputs into it, we cannot relegate the whole of non-official politics to these spaces. The question then arises of the relationship of these spaces to the field, which is not the same as their relation to the state.

The Muslim Brotherhood has, since its foundation in the 1920s, clearly constituted an important force in the Egyptian political field. I have argued that its forms of political organisation and ideology make it a modern political force. Its rejection of European cultural forms does not necessarily represent a rejection of modernity *per se*, but can be seen as a reconstruction of modernity according to Islamic models and motifs (Carré, 1983). It did not always engage in total contestation of the political order, but has often engaged in the institutionalised politics of opposition, pressure and compromise: first under the monarchical regime in the 1930s and 1940s, then in the early days of the Free Officers regime and before they fell foul of Nasser. Under Nasser's repression they came nearest to total rejection of the political order, but even then, the moderate leadership of Hudaibi was ambiguous. It was at this stage that the most important splits occurred with new radical strands to which we shall return. The mainstream of the organisation returned to the open scene under Sadat and resumed participation in institutionalised politics, to the point of the formation of the tactical electoral alliance with the Neo-Wafd (a secular party with a strong Coptic element) in 1984. At the time of writing they constitute a regular opposition party in parliament. Here is one important instance in which Islamic politics and opposition are not ones of 'total contestation'. That is not to say that such politics do not exist in Egypt.

The total rejection of the political order and the nation state in favour of a Utopian, even messianic model of the city of God, crystallised in one tendency of Islamic political thought under Nasser's repression, that most notably theorised by Sayyid Qutb (Carré, 1984; Kepel, 1985; chapter 2 above). Qutb characterised contemporary societies, including those which were nominally Muslim, as a *jahiliyya*, a realm of barbarism and ignorance, suffering the rule of man over man, where God and his law are absent. He proposed the re-enactment of Muhammad's fight against the *jahiliyya* of his time, through the formation of a vanguard of true Muslims, who would build up their spiritual and physical powers, in spiritual and emotional isolation from the errant society and its rulers, to confront and overcome this *jahiliyya* when the time comes, and to establish the sovereignty of God and His revealed law. These ideas were taken up and acted upon by the radical Islamic groups which split off from the Muslim brotherhood in the 1970s, such as *Jamma'at al-Muslimin*, dubbed by the media *al-takfir wal hijra*, and the *Jihad* group involved in the assassination of Sadat. Socially, these groups are recruited predominantly from the intelligentsia, mostly students, but also including teachers, functionaries, technicians, craftsmen and junior officers. They are, that is, among the mainstream participants in the political field, and not representatives of 'external social spaces'. Between the mainstream Muslim Brotherhood and these groups there are many intermediate positions, such as those of the Islamic groups in the universities, and of the radical preachers. The question remains: how do these various groups relate to the 'people'?

As we have seen, the 'people' are a very important category in the explanation of modern Islamic political phenomena, for both observers and participants. It is assumed that Islamic ideas and identities are preserved in the popular mind and in popular culture, masked for the best part of a century by foreign grafts of the secular nation state and the political and cultural ideas and practices which go with it. But these forms are but superficial accretions which pertain to the intelligentsia but do not penetrate the popular realms. The arrival of the popular classes on the political stage (presumably through the socio-economic processes of modernity) puts Islam back firmly on the political agenda. Albert Hourani, for instance, in the 'Preface to the 1983 reissue' of his *Arabic Thought in the Liberal Age 1798-1939*, states that when he first wrote the book he was mainly concerned to note the breaks with the past, and was later troubled by this tendency and wondered whether he should not have traced the continuities with the past:

In the present century they [traditional Islamic leaders] have lost much of their domination, or so it seemed at the point in time when I was writing my book: it is clearer now than it was then, at least to me, that the extension of the area of political consciousness and activity, the coming of 'mass politics', would bring into the political process men and women who are still liable to be swayed by what the Azhar said and wrote, and what the shaykhs of a brotherhood might teach. (Hourani, 1983, p. ix)

What 'masses' are being referred to here? The most active, as we have seen, are the new intelligentsia, the products of modern educational systems facing grim prospects of employment and career in a society and state which cannot absorb the mass of intellectual proletariat which they produce and where the prizes go to those who have access to wealth and patronage (Davis, 1984). The counterparts of these groups in earlier decades provided the cadres of nationalist and leftist as well as Islamic agitations. These groups are not new to the political scene, except, perhaps that their situation now is more transparently desperate, and they have emerged on to a new political conjuncture of repeated failures of leaders and ideologies, and, crucially, of the triumph of the Islamic revolution in Iran. They do not follow the teachings of al-Azhar or of the shaykhs of brotherhoods, but treat them with indifference and sometimes contempt. Their ideas are not extensions of traditional loyalties and cultures, but modern creations, constructed in relation to current politics. The specific forms of these politics cannot be explained in terms of the popular sentiments which may attach to them because of religious piety, except that this piety can only attach to modern Islamic politics precisely because it has been detached from its traditional anchoring in village, mosque and brotherhood.

Again, what of the 'people'? This is far too wide and diffuse a category, let us narrow it down. First of all we are talking about urban populations in the major cities, but in the Egyptian case, also in some specific country towns in Upper Egypt. These populations include the old inhabitants of the central urban quarters, plus layers of rural or provincial migrants who arrived at various stages, mostly over the last few decades, first into the old quarters then further out into the sprawling suburbs and the shanty towns. Many of the older inhabitants are not new to politics, they have witnessed or even participated in the various nationalist agitations and mobilisations over the past decades. Some, necessarily a minority, will have been involved in organised politics of the left (sectors of the industrial workers) or of the Muslim Brotherhood. Some will have been clients to political notables or bureaucrats. The analogy to Hobsbawm's 'primitive rebels' drawn by Badie (see p.135 above) would not seem to be appropriate for these populations: many of them may be outside organised politics, but they are not 'pre-political'. We may speculate as to the contents of urban popular culture. Islam will certainly play a part in it but in different ways: daily observances for some, religious festivals for many, *rites de passage* for most. In terms of religious thought and practice, popular religion is not noted for its orthodoxy: many strands of mysticism, syncretism and magic are present in popular culture (see Chapter 5 above), not always distinguished (in the popular mind) from religion as such. Religious reformers, Wahhabis and Salafis, have for generations fought against popular heterodoxy, only successfully where they could impose their reforms directly, as in parts of Arabia. The modern political Islamists are the heirs of the Salafiyya in this respect, and are no more tolerant of heterodoxy and syncretism, but this is not an issue at present. Most important in the present context is the communalist, solidaristic aspect of religious identity which we have already noted (see Chapter 5, pp.106–8, and pp.152–4 above), and which can be elicited in popular reactions, especially in situations of discontent and frustration: Islam as a communal identity against outsiders and foreigners. It is interesting to note in this respect that the towns of Upper Egypt, such as Assiut and al-Munya, which are the homes of considerable Coptic minorities, are also the centres of the most militant Islamic popular agitations and confrontations with the authorities and the Copts.

In addition to these religious components, we may expect many other layers of popular culture and consciousness, including Badie's segmentarity in terms of kinship or neighbourhood, and Vieille's dichotomic communal attitudes of 'us' versus 'them'. We may add another important dimension of popular culture: international mass culture diffused through the media and consumerist pressures, and which is such a worry for the Islamists, the nationalists and the left. The enticing symbols and gratifications of Coca Cola, Marlboro and blue jeans, of cowboys and Dallas (Amr Ibrahim, 1987) are feared by all would-be guardians of the people as corrupting drugs, especially for the young, the insidious machinations of cultural imperialism. This is at once the realm of dreams which lead away from political or moral commitments of any kind, and the field of anomic frustrations at the inability to achieve further consumerist pleasures and statuses, and as such a further alienation and a stimulus to dissidence and opposition. All these, and many others, are components of popular culture. Various combinations and patterns of these components can be brought into action in relation to various situations and stimuli.

How does this heterogeneous field of popular culture relate, then, to the political field, and in particular to Islamic politics? The answer to this question would depend on place and time. Assuming the current situation in most Middle Eastern countries of mounting economic deprivations and political repression, then the urban populations are ripe for political agitations and mobilisation. This coincides with a situation in which the political field is heavily restricted by watchful governments and their security services, especially when it comes to popular agitations and organisation. Under these conditions the religious opposition has much greater opportunities of access to the popular locations, through religious venues and channels, notably the mosques. This was particularly important in Iran, where the secular opposition had been successfully suppressed after the Mossadeq episode in the early 1950s, while the channels of religious organisation stood a better chance of evading SAVAK vigilance in their covert activities through the mosques and the religious institutions. In Egypt, Sadat's selective liberalisation in the 1970s favoured the religious forces as a counter to Nasserism and the left. This differential and more favourable access to popular locations constitutes at least one factor in the explanation of the recent success of Islamic politics. Clearly this is not the only factor; another notable factor is the demoralisation and sense of failure of the nationalists and the left in many countries, and the historical association of some of their ideas and symbols with the very oppressive regimes generating the problems in question. A crucial factor is the demonstration effect of the Iranian revolution, and its spectacular profile on the world stage as the prime combatant against Western might in the name of Islam. These explanations do not suppose any special affinities of the people to Islamic ideas. Even the popular potential for solidaristic and communalist identifications noted above can be equally drawn upon by nationalist causes: the phenomenology of nationalist appeal does not necessarily correspond to nationalist ideology. Badie's contention that nationalist movements are only successful in popular mobilisation when in opposition and lose their potential when in power (a point he makes to reinforce his characterisation of Islamic political cultures as only capable of generating contestatory opposition of total rejection) is not self-evidently plausible. Nasser and Nasserism were unknown in opposition, but had a spectacular popular impact in government. We may conclude by saying that the 'people' have no essential or intrinsic attachment to political Islam, which is, in any case, quite distinct from their usual religious ideas and practices. The popular success of Islamic politics, where it occurs, is the product of particular situations and conjunctures, as I have argued throughout these essays.

The state: external and patrimonial?

As we have seen, a regular theme in the characterisation of the state in the Middle East is in terms of its 'externality' to society. This externality has been posed in terms of historical continuity of the 'patrimonial' (or 'Asiatic despotism') state under modern conditions as the 'neo-patrimonial' state, or in terms of the dependence of the 'peripheral' state on the world order which maintains it as an agent and an intermediary in relation to the social formations over which it governs. 'Externality', however, means something quite different in relation to historical states of the so-called 'Asiatic' or segmentary types than it can mean in relation to modern states in the Middle East or elsewhere. As we have seen, the historical states are said to be external in the sense of being outside the social relations and institutions of the social formation: it does not have the interest or the resources to penetrate society beyond the most superficial level in regions accessible to the centres of power. This cannot be said of the modern states, some of which are highly intrusive and directive in many spheres of social and even domestic life. They are said to be 'external' in the sense of deriving their powers and resources, in good measure, from sources external to the social formations which they govern. The prototype for this situation is the 'petrolic' state, whose powers and resources are highly dependent on the so-called 'rent'. Many other states in the Middle East, however, have benefited directly or indirectly from petroleum revenues without themselves disposing of oil resources. Egypt, Jordan and Syria have enjoyed Saudi and Gulfi handouts in various forms, as well as the remittances from migrant workers in the oil states. This is a 'pillage' state (in

Vieille's terms) in a peculiar sense: unlike its historical predecessor it is not pillaging so much the wealth and the labour of the people, as a resource which happens to be there and whose production consumes a very small part of the national energies (for which those lucky enough to be working in that sector are usually well remunerated). Quite the contrary, this state is a provider, which distributes the petrolic wealth, not according to some economic or ethical rationality of investment or need, but predominantly in accordance with a political rationality of acquiring and maintaining clients and loyal supporters. This distributive function also applies to bureaucratic 'socialist' states, with petroleum (Algeria) or without (Nasser's Egypt, Syria), which take control of the major and most strategic components of the economy, and are thus able to command resources and revenues. But in so far as those resources are procured from the internal functioning of the economy, the sense in which the state is 'external' becomes attenuated. It can then be said to be external in Vieille's sense of the 'peripheral' state deriving its powers from dependence on world powers and the world system. We may recognise a certain plausibility in this contention without necessarily subscribing to the full rigours of 'dependency theory' in terms of economic 'laws' relating to the extraction of surplus value and unequal exchange. Financial, military and technical aid, from the petrolic states or from the world powers (especially the USA) constitute important externally derived resources for countries like Egypt. Consequently, the ebb and flow of these resources, like the fluctuations of oil revenues, become very important factors in the political fortunes and ultimate stability of these states.

Badie calls this form of the state 'neo-patrimonial', presumably to mark its continuity with or resemblance to the historical patrimonial state. Two characteristics which make this classification plausible are: personal or clique rule, and the extensive use of patronage and clientelism in maintaining support and control. Identification of the state with the power and leadership of a particular person, family and/or clique is not confined to the traditional monarchies such as Saudi Arabia and Morocco, but is also common in the 'revolutionary' states such as Iraq and Syria. When we add Nasser's Egypt and revolutionary Iran to this list, the unity of this characterisation becomes stretched. True, Nasser was the dominant figure in the state, and there was a clique of Free Officers around him enjoying great power; Khomeini is the supreme arbiter of the revolutionary state. But there the comparison ends: each of the states in question presents a complex web of power relationships, including conflicts and struggles, and quite different from one another. And they are both very different from Saddam Hussain's personal rule in Iraq, with a much greater degree of direct control over the state and the party, with far less scope for conflict or dissidence within the state apparatuses and cliques. We may add that in the more sophisticated political culture of Egypt, when Anwar Sadat attempted to assume the mantle of Nasser, he was the subject of considerable, sometimes open ridicule. He could never appropriate the legitimacy and the charisma earned by Nasser. Nothing could illustrate the contrast more than their respective funerals: a truly emotional, traumatic mass event for Nasser; a cortège of foreign dignitaries for Sadat. This is not merely an every-case-is-different type of objection, but an attempt to point out different conditions and consequences of personal power in a state structure. After all de Gaulle or, for that matter, Mrs Thatcher were, in a sense, personal rulers.

Let us turn to the question of patronage. We should first note that 'patronage' is a widespread phenomenon existing in many societies and situations, in the Third World as well as in the West. It occurs at many levels, from small-town politics and business to national political parties and institutions (as in Italy and the USA). As such it is not a sociologically homogeneous phenomenon, in fact quite different in the various and heterogeneous contexts in which something called 'patronage-clientelism' is identified. What is being called patronage in relation to the Middle Eastern states is a system of distribution of national resources following a political calculus of powers and loyalties and the pre-emption of threatening conflicts. This goes hand in hand with elaborate military and security apparatuses of repression, which, in turn, consume a major, if not the major, share of state revenues, and are themselves the avenues for extensive networks of patronage. The state and its agencies are major, if not the major, employers, and have control over the most desirable jobs and careers, this being one of the most important avenues of patronage. There is a tendency to concentrate career privileges in particular families and cliques. Other forms of patronage involve the regional and sectorial directions of investment and project resources, the award of contracts and of trading licences.

The question of state patronage relates directly to that of 'class' and 'class analysis', which has preoccupied the Marxist and neo-Marxist literature (Alavi, 1982; Turner, 1984; Leca, 1987). In the classic Marxist scheme, classes are formed in their relationships to the means of production, and on the bases of interests formed at that level enter the political field through mediations and representations as political forces waging the class struggle on the political arena. In this scheme the state represents, in one way or another, the interests of the economically dominant class. In many Third World states this scheme does not seem to work, because the state controls so much of the economy, production and distribution, that relationship to the state and its agencies determines access to economic opportunities. The state does not entirely determine the class system, such as ownership or non-ownership of land, of businesses and of other property, but within these limits it can radically affect the life chances of individuals, families and groups defined in terms of ethnicity, religion or region. The state is clearly not the instrument or representative of a dominant class but, through its domination of resources, determines the relative advantages and powers of social groups and sectors. The contention that the 'revolutionary' states represent the 'petty bourgeoisie' confuses social background with systematic class interests.[10] Another contention is that the state, while not representing a particular class, mediates between the 'dominant classes'. But the etatisation of the economy in Nasser's Egypt and in Ba'thist Iraq and Syria, had precisely the effect of radically curtailing, if not destroying, the interests and powers of the dominant classes such as landlords, industrialists, and large-scale traders. The subsequent *infitah* in Sadat's Egypt, and similar restorations of the private sector in Algeria, Iraq and Syria in recent years, did not restore independent capitalist classes, but mostly created new business classes largely parasitic on the state and its resources, and as such dependent upon it, often in symbiotic relationships with powerful state personnel acting as sponsors if not partners.

This system militates against the emergence of class solidarities, or of political forces based on class interests (which is not to say that Western capitalist systems necessarily feature such class-determined politics). The groups which derive benefits from the state do not do so on the bases of class affiliation, but as individuals, families, particular communities, villages or regions. Each one of these units has to negotiate its own terms with the state and its agencies and personnel, often in rivalry rather than in solidarity. The support enjoyed by any particular state, then, is dependent on the volume of resources it can command and the range its distributive system covers, and is as such highly vulnerable to the fluctuations of revenues from oil or other resources depending on world markets and other international conjunctures. Even on the best performance, this system leaves out large sectors of the population from the higher advantages of the distribution of resources. A crucial factor in this respect is the problem of the young educated sectors of the population and the exclusion of the great majority of this population from career prospects to which they are led to aspire. The firm linkage between education and career in the popular mind arouses the expectations. Practically all countries in the region have a policy of absorbing as many as possible of high-school and university graduates into the public sector, mostly into state bureaucracies. Egypt since Nasser has had a policy of guaranteeing a job for every university graduate. The vast expansion of the young population practically everywhere places a great strain on this policy. One of its byproducts is the continuous growth and gross overmanning of the state bureaucracies, making them ever more cumbersome and slow. The level of pay of these graduates is generally low in relation to the cost of living, making it necessary for many to take second jobs, and facilitating bribery and corruption in the few positions which may offer opportunities in that direction. Career and promotion prospects for the majority are very limited, while desirable career options are increasingly reserved for the children of those who already enjoy high positions or a favourable place in the distributive system. It is no wonder, therefore, that this constitutes the sector of the population most open to the agitations against the prevailing order, which at the present time is dominated by the Islamic currents.[11] The fragility of support for these regimes, and the growing bases for dissent and conflict make dependence on force and repressive apparatuses all the more necessary. The only way, in this perspective, to promote political stability on a firmer and more permanent basis is to find a path to secure a productive economic development, a course which seems to be ever illusive for most Third World countries, and certainly the Middle Eastern states.

Infitah, the opening up of the economy to private enterprise as well as foreign investment, was a policy inaugurated by Sadat in the aftermath of the 1973 war and the escalation of oil prices and revenues. It was a departure from Nasser's state socialism and tight control of the economy, designed, ostensibly, to attract investments from the vast stock of accumulating oil wealth of Saudi Arabia and others. It inaugurated a private sector which accumulated immense riches mainly through enterprises in construction, trade (mostly imports) and tourism. The most notable 'productive' element in these investments were new projects in the production or assembly of arms and military hardware, initially a joint enterprise with Saudi investment, but that remained within the state sector. The later 1970s and 1980s have seen one form or another of *infitah*, in the sense of expansion of the private sector at the expense of the public, in other Arab states, Algeria, Syria and Iraq (Leca, 1987; Springborg, 1985). While Sadat's *infitah* was an attempt to cash in on expanding oil revenues, the later phenomena in the other countries are, at least in part, a result of the exigencies of the decline in these revenues,

> the result of the state strategy attempting to transfer on to the 'private sector' the responsibility for meeting demands, creating employment, mobilising potential savings when its financial difficulties (be it debt, a fall in the oil income) no longer allow it to do without a bourgeoisie. (Leca, 1987, p.6).[12]

The distributive strategy of the state is limited by the extent of its revenues in relation to spending commitments, of which military expenditure takes a considerable share. The resort to the private sector can then be seen as an attempt to shift some of the burdens and the responsibilities. But, as Leca points out, this is a risky political strategy. It creates a much more visible disparity in wealth, accentuating discontents and resentments of the excluded masses, and weakens the socialistic claims to legitimacy of the state for its own supporters. These are class sentiments (not in the classical Marxist sense, perhaps, but ones of poor against rich), which, because of political repression, have no regular channels of expression, so they take the form of sporadic riots. They also feed into organised, if outlawed, oppositional movements, the most prominent of which in most countries in recent years is the Islamic.

The case of Syria may be a good illustration of the configuration of factors discussed. Syria has a well established urban bourgeoisie of merchants and landlords, predominantly Sunni Muslim, who formed the social base for the various regimes between independence and the union with Egypt in 1958 (followed by the Ba'thist coup d'etat in 1963). The Ba'thist regime undermined the interests and powers of these groups, with the etatisation of the economy and the land reforms. It dispossessed some sectors, and heavily restricted the prospects for business and trade for others. The rural background of the personnel of the new regime, and its promotion of peasant interests, further antagonised the urban classes. Hafiz al-Assad's assumption of power in 1970 and his close identification with the Alawi sect (predominantly rural and peasant from the north), and the increasing dominance of members of this sect in the inner circles of power in the army and the bureaucracy, added another dimension to the antagonism, the sectarian. This factor gave the Muslim Brotherhood in Syria a particular stamp, for it represented, among other grievances, the opposition of a Sunni bourgeoisie to a government associated with a sectarian minority from a peasant background.[13] Assad, partly in an effort to broaden his base of support, or at least to restrict the base of opposition, embarked on the policy of 'rectification' in the 1970s, which broadened out the economy to allow business opportunities for the urban bourgeoisie, but without foregoing state control of the strategic heights of the economy, or diluting the promotion of rural interests. This involved a balancing act of great complexity, especially in relation to the very heavy military expenditure commitments dictated by the position of Syria as a front-line state to Israel, and its commitments in the Lebanon. A considerable, but fluctuating, portion of the revenues necessary for the maintenance of these policies has been provided by grants and aid from Saudi Arabia, the Gulf states, Libya and Iran, making Syria an oil state by proxy. The opening up of the economy, accelerated in the late 1970s and 1980s, would certainly explain the weakening of support for the Islamic opposition in Syria. This would illustrate the conjunctural determinants of communalist politics. The dominance of Alawi personnel in the higher echelons of power does not make the state and its policies 'sectarian': the balancing act of state distribution has included wide sectors of Syrian society, so far quite successfully. State bureaucracies and enterprises provide jobs which absorb considerable numbers of the working population. These employees are then beholden for their jobs and prospects to patrons and institutions within the power structure. Their membership of official trade unions tied to the state is another mechanism of consolidation. As we have seen earlier, state enterprises and bureaucracies do not follow the norms of economic rationality but one of a political calculus of distribution and the consolidation of allegiances. Development policy in agriculture follows the same logic, providing production facilities (especially water) and credit on the bases of patronage and allegiances, and following tribal and lineage networks of clientelism. The basic requirement of this policy is that it can evade economic exigencies of productivity and surplus production through the flow of revenues (from the oil states) which do not arise from internal resources, and is, as such, highly dependent on continued flows, and vulnerable to its fluctuations. The necessary limits on the extent of resources deployed for political purposes by the state can be said to generate a 'class struggle', but one between 'classes' determined in their relation to state distribution: between public and private sectors, between urban and rural interests, and between the different spheres and levels of the public sector. The regime can sometimes use these conflicts in its own interests, as when trade unions are allowed to criticise management for parasitism or inefficiency:

> in criticizing managers for their corrupt, anti-national practices, trade unionists had no intention of holding private bosses up as an example. Rather, faced by a crisis, those in power stage-manage a scenario, they highlight the 'class struggle' between workers and managers, the latter then become scapegoats from whom they dissociate themselves and to whom they issue a warning by way of the Union mouthpiece. ... This 'lower'-'upper' opposition allows at one and the same time symbolic or real 'causes' to be found for the economic irrationality of public sector management when it is no longer possible to handle it by increasing salaries. (Leca, 1987, p.37)

The question remains: for how long can this strategy be maintained with the decline of oil revenues and by the fluctuations in the conjunctures of international and regional relations? And will the class struggles become more real and less controlled under these conditions?

Modern Syria, then, is a very good example of what is called a 'neo-patrimonial' state. Its 'patrimonialism' is clearly a very different one from that of the historical state, and yet again different from systems of patronage to be found in the electoral political systems. In line with the general segmentation of society and polity, patronage in the historical state was also segmented in different localities and corners; it did not constitute a system of interdependence between different groups and networks at a macro-social level. This is precisely what it is in Syria and in many other Middle Eastern states: the state distributive system reinforces the sense of interdependence within the territorial unit of the nation, each group and section is orientated to what others are doing. The 'imagined community' of the territorial state extends ever further into the deepest rural and desert areas, where the people are ever more conscious of their dependence on the territorial polity. This does not necessarily imply solidarity or loyalty to the state, but a heightened consciousness of the national dimension of their livelihood and their relations to politics, which is crucial in both loyalty and opposition.

Where in this situation can we discern historical continuities? Personal and autocratic rule is not so unique historically for the assertion of its specificity or continuity in any country or region to be sustained. Patrimonial models and mentalities are equally widespread, and, in themselves, cannot account for a specific political system; they can be found in a variety of systems including sectors of the United States electoral politics. We are left with the conclusion that the Syrian system is not the product of some historical or mental essences, but of a specific political sociology, which can only be constructed in terms of general social processes and conjunctures. Sure enough, as we have seen, segmented communal interests do play a central part in this system. However, they are not fixed communal units given to the system from time immemorial, but shifting groups whose boundaries at any given point in time are determined by political conjunctures, as in the example of the ebb and flow of Sunni solidarity against the Alawite-dominated state in relation to shifting state economic and distributive strategies.

It would also be difficult to find support for the assertion, made by Badie and many others, that the territorial state, distinct from the Islamic *umma,* is an alien concept for Muslims. It would seem that the conditions discussed above have produced mutual interests in the territorial state, and that it is at least the working concept for all the actors on the economic and political stages. The challenges to the territorial state, pan-Arab or pan-Islamic, have come primarily from elaborate modern ideologies worked out by intellectuals, but who have in practice pursued their politics within the territorial state. The major exception to this rule is the Lebanon, whose war-torn polity has been a stage for forces and allegiances of other regional states and ideologies. But then that is a very special situation beyond the scope of the present argument.

The military-inaugurated 'revolutionary-socialist' regimes in the region, starting with Nasser's Egypt, represent the monopolisation of the political field by the state and the leading party. The political and ideological battles of the field are displaced or driven underground (which is not necessarily to say eliminated). Then the politics of the distributive system, of patronage networks and rivalries, become dominant. These are ostensibly non-ideological, or rather do not overtly pose ideological challenges to the regime. But, as we have seen, few regimes are rich enough to avoid more or less numerous sectors of the 'excluded', especially among the young educated, a group highly susceptible to ideological challenges. The vulnerability of the distributive system, and its dependence on international forces beyond the controls of the regime, raise questions as to its continued ability to deliver to all the sectors with expectations from the system. The current accumulation of problems for the Syrian regime, with extended military and security commitments but declining resources, is a case in point. This may very well lead to the ideologisation and the politicisation of ever-wider circles of discontent, some, perhaps, into the Islamic camp(s), some within the factions of the Ba'th party, some with revived versions of the left or the nationalist forces now hegemonised by the Ba'th party. All will be calling for democratisation and liberalisation. This may or may not come; we already have examples of limited democracy in Egypt. But will such a development lead to the formation of a stable political field within which conflicts and struggles become institutionalised and orderly, or will it resume the vicious circles of disruptive contestations followed by intensified repression? Without the amelioration of the basic problems of limited and halting economic development in relation to increasing demands on resources from growing populations and from the vast military budgets, it is difficult to see the growth of stable democratic fields. Explanations in terms of a specific political culture of total contestation would appear to be superfluous in relation to the overwhelming factors arising from the political economy of the region.

Finally, a note on the specificity of Egypt. In the course of the discussion in this section, I have tended to switch the argument from one example to another as if they are interchangeable. Of course, they are not. While the processes under discussion are fairly general, their particular socio-political manifestations are very different in the different countries. As we have seen (pp. 151–2), Egypt has a long history in the formation of the modern state and the interaction of state/society/economy, much of it long before the era of oil revenues. We can, perhaps, venture a tentative conclusion that this history has had the effect of a qualitatively different political field and of political institutions, more elaborated and differentiated than in the neighbouring states. The Nasser era, at least in some of its episodes, suppressed and monopolised this political field under an ever more monolithic state bureaucracy. But some of the pluralism of that field was reproduced within the regime, carrying out political manoeuvres and struggles. Even at its most severe, this regime never attained the heights of bloody repression and disregard for basic rights and liberties manifested in the other military 'revolutionary' states, such as Iraq and Syria. At present, Egypt is the only (formerly) revolutionary state in which a certain measure of democracy and political pluralism are restored. Whether these can survive under the threat of further economic deterioration and the daunting weight of an ever-growing population is another matter. I have argued above that historical continuities can only be maintained under favourable conditions, and, at the time of writing, the prospects for Egypt do not appear very bright.

The Islamic state and the nation state

If the nation state and its trappings is an imported model unsuitable for Islamic cultural and social conditions, then does the Islamic state escape these imported models in favour of a more authentic and harmonious form? Of the extant Islamic states, Iran is the most appropriate model to consider. Saudi Arabia emerged out of archaic tribal polities, and is sustained in its present form by vast oil revenues; it raises interesting questions, but outside the scope of this paper. In Pakistan, like in Numeiry's Sudan, Islam was imposed by a military dictatorship, against widespread opposition, in an effort to engender some legitimacy and reinforce control. Iran is the only example of an Islamic state installed through a popular revolution, which raises all the questions under discussion. I have discussed explanations of the Iranian revolution elsewhere (see chapters 1, 2 and 3) and argued that the hegemony of the clergy over the revolutionary state were the product of particular conjunctures, in which the nature and history of the religious institutions in Iran played an important part, and that as such, it was not in some way the inevitable product of the will of an Islamic people who understand or accept no other form of ideology or government. What I want to discuss here is the sense in which the revolutionary state is Islamic and how it differs from the imported models of the nation state.

There is a dualism in the Iranian state of nation-state models intermingled with Islamic forms. These Islamic forms are not revivals or continuities with historical instances, but quite novel creations (see Chapter 1). The duality is indicated in the very title of Islamic *Republic (jamhouri)*, 'republic' held in common with the discursive products of the French revolution and of all the revolutions of this century in the region and outside, which have toppled a monarchy. It has a written constitution, drafted, after wide-ranging and heated debates, by an elected Assembly of Experts[14] (on the model of a constitutional assembly), an elected president, a parliament *(majlis,* the same term used for parliament in the defunct monarchial regime, as well as in most countries in the region). A contradictory duality of sovereignties is written into the constitution: the sovereignty of the popular will (article 6), in line with democratic nation-state constitutions, and the principle of *velayat-e-faqih,* giving sweeping, almost arbitrary powers to the ruling *faqih* (see Chapter 1 and below). Popular sovereignty is embodied in parliament, but the legislative powers of this parliament is subject to the approval of the ruling *faqih.* The *faqih* and the 'Council of Guardians' (half the membership appointed by Khomeini and half by the *majlis)* watch over the compatibility of legislation with Islamic law and general principles. In theory, the ruling *faqih* has wide discretion in interpreting the Islamic sources and their applicability. In practice, so far, the *majlis,* itself composed of the revolutionary elite, has enjoyed considerable legislative powers, and has only been restricted by the Council of Guardians on particular issues, namely, land reform and the nationalisation of foreign trade, which were judged to be incompatible with Islamic safeguards of private property.

The Islamic Republic has a cabinet system with the familiar divisions into functional ministries and departments, with bureaucratic rules and procedures. Its legal system is, up to the time of writing, quite diffuse and sometimes chaotic. According to the Constitution, the Islamic *shari'a* is the basis for all law and legislation. However, many of the codes of civil law survive from the previous regime, and are administered by civil *(madani)* courts, distinguished from *shari'a* courts (a distinction also made in many of the other countries in the region). The judges include secular personnel, some from the previous regime, but it is stipulated that they should all be competent in Islamic law. In addition there are 'revolutionary courts' which deal with offences against the revolution (often arbitrarily defined by the prosecuting authorities of *komitehs* and revolutionary guards), much in line with revolutionary practice elsewhere. It is generally recognised that this state of affairs is unsatisfactory, and there are calls for the codification of Islamic law into a unified system which would cover all spheres of legal transactions and processes. But nothing has been done so far, partly, it is thought, because such codification would infringe the traditional autonomy of *mujtahids,* each of whom can (theoretically) reach a different but equally valid judgment on the same case. On the other hand, this autonomy is being increasingly infringed in favour of central state controls, with the Islamic state asserting itself as the higher authority. Elements of this centralisation are the appeal system which goes all the way up to Tehran, and can therefore overrule the judgment of individual clerics, and the centralised administration of justice in the appointment of a state prosecutor with overall responsibility. In the meantime, the most publicised aspects of the workings of the legal system are the applications of the Quranic penal code of amputations and executions, some by stoning. The legal system in revolutionary Iran well illustrates the mixture of modern bureaucratic and Islamic elements. It would be interesting to see, if and when a unified system of Islamic law is introduced, how this will cope with matters so far covered by civil law.

Of the Islamic elements in the revolutionary state, the most central is the principle of *velayat-e-faqih,* which, as we have seen, is enshrined in the Constitution. This idea, quite novel in relation to politics and government (see Chapter 1), gives the ruling *faqih* (in this case Khomeini) or his collective equivalent (there is provision for a council of *fuqaha*) supreme authority in the interpretation of the sacred texts and the Prophetic and Imamite traditions, and as such to intervene and direct legislation on any matter of general policy to which he judges his authority and expertise to be relevant, and to arbitrate in any conflict or dispute.

Other Islamic elements in revolutionary Iran are the multitude of revolutionary organisations at all levels of government, society and the armed forces. Some of these parallel state organisations and intervene in their operations as revolutionary monitors and censors, if not rivals. The most important of these are the Pasdaran or revolutionary guards, first started as a revolutionary militia with police and internal defence functions. The war added general military functions parallel to the regular armed forces, partly to keep these forces in check. Eventually the Pasdaran became major rivals to the regular forces, complex and well equipped in all three services and with a special ministry to administer their affairs. Of the revolutionary organisations, the Pasdaran are unique in performing parallel functions to their regular equivalents. Revolutionary committees in government departments and public enterprises do not perform parallel functions but watch over the revolutionary purity of the organisations (interpreted in relation to current political factions and struggles, with occasional purges of supporters of one side in favour of another). They also watch over the Islamic morals and comportment of the employees, in terms of the observation of rituals (prayers and fasting), or the correct forms of dress, particularly for women. More important, in factories and other enterprises employing workers, they maintain industrial and ideological discipline, and counter subversive radical but non-Islamic notions of trade unionism. Other Islamic committees and organisations control urban quarters performing police and security functions, yet others administer charitable distributions to the poor (building up patronage networks in the process).

This proliferation of revolutionary committees and councils are highly reminiscent of the situations following other populist revolutions, such as the French or the Russian, citizens' or workers' committees watching over the revolutionary purity of government and society, and in the process engaging in factional struggles. Their Iranian equivalents are different in the contents of their ideology, and, crucially, in the fact that they are not elected but appointed from above. The 'routinisation' of revolutions includes the suppression or incorporation of the zealous censors. There are indications that this step is part of the hidden agenda of the 'moderates' in the revolutionary establishment.

It would seem, then, that constitutionally, the most important Islamic elements in the state is the principle of *velayat-e-faqih*, and the application of the notable features of the *shari'a*. There are no systematic Islamic principles, such as constitutional or public law to apply to the system of administration or to the organisation of government departments. Islam does not significantly alter the constitution or the administration of the state as such. An interesting aspect of state functions is the question of taxation. In Shi'i practice a religious tax, called the *khoms* (one fifth of specified items of wealth) is paid by the believer to his chosen *mujtahid* who, at his discretion, uses it for religious administration

175

and charities. The question arises: now that an Islamic state is in power, are the dues of the believer to that state or to his chosen *mujtahid*? The official ruling is quite emphatic on the duty to pay state taxes, quite distinct from the *khoms* which remains a matter between the believer and his chosen *mujtahid*. State requirements are not compromised or subordinated to religious practice, in spite of the ruling of some conservative clerics to the contrary. The supremacy of the Islamic state in religious matters has been further enhanced in a recent declaration by Khomeini that a truly Islamic state has discretion over the most basic rules of Islamic worship such as prayer and *hajj* (pilgrimage).

The most Islamic element of the Islamic republic is not so much in the administration, as in the political field and its personnel. Religious institutions and personnel are in the ascendance; after defeating, banishing or subordinating their opponents and rivals, the Islamic republic became basically a government by clergy. (Not all the clergy. Many of the conservative senior clerics remain quietly opposed to *velayat-e-faqih* and the direct involvement of religion in government.) They occupy most of the senior positions in government, parliament, the revolutionary organisations, and the institutions of recruitment and mobilisation of cadres, supporters and soldiers. Religious functions and ceremonies which they lead have now acquired political and mobilisatory significance. Most notable are the Friday prayers and sermon (*khotba*), now a major political institution in each city, the *imam jom'a* or preacher being an official appointment, enjoying considerable power in the city or region. Many of the major mobilisatory initiatives of the regime started at the Tehran Friday prayers, attended by vast throngs in open public spaces.

The open political field has been entirely Islamised, Islamic justification and rhetoric being the final criterion of legitimacy of a political position. Antagonists berate one another in terms of non-authenticity of their advocacy. Factions of radicals and conservatives, left and right have emerged within this Islamic field (Vali and Zubaida, 1985): sanctity of private property or primacy of social justice? This is a central question debated in terms of Islamic sources and historical precedents. The different factions are made possible by the existence of rival power centres within the state and the clergy organisations, each with networks of supporters and clients. Particular identifiable political groups and factions may be dissolved or suppressed if they lose out or become an embarrassment to the regime, as in the case of the conservative Hujjatiyeh Society (Vali and Zubaida, 1985), but then their positions re-emerge with different organisations and personnel.

This political field is clearly different from those of neighbouring countries in that its discourses of legitimacy and contest are entirely Islamic. It is also a surprisingly more open and diverse political field than that of most other countries in the region. These differences, if anything, bring it closer to the model of the modern national political field than the others, with ideologically based organisations contesting 'class' issues among others. The pan-Islamic commitment of the revolution is at one significant level to do with the question of the export of the revolution, itself an issue of contest. But this does not alter the fact that the field is primarily concerned with national issues within the well identified and unquestioned entity of the Iranian nation state. The identification of Iran with Shi'ism marks it off, in religious terms from the surrounding countries, and reinforces its separate national identity, which is ever more emphasised by the war with Iraq, and in effect, with most of the Arab world. It should be emphasised, however, that this separate Shi'i identity is underplayed and mostly unspoken in public, the emphasis being on the unity of Islam.

What of the relation of the revolutionary state to society? Following Vieille (above pp.141–3), we can say that it is highly intrusive into all aspects of social and domestic life, which follows from its attempt to create an Islamic nation in its image. It may be argued, however, that the Islamic state is not as 'external' to the social fabric as its predecessor; the religious personnel and institutions, now in government, are involved in various social networks, especially in the bazaars and the old urban quarters. But do these relations and networks continue when their apexes are now in the very different positions of state power? Or are they transformed into the patronage networks of the distributive state? Let us not forget that Iran is an oil state, and that oil revenues are at the basis of the power of the Islamic republic as much as it was for the ancien regime, and the primary resource for the conduct of its long war with Iraq.

The revolutionary state does indeed function as a distributive state, but with different sets of clients and priorities than its predecessor. Since 1980 the most pressing priorities have been those of war, an issue beyond the present discussion. The populist emphasis of the revolution, and its championing of the *mustazefin*, the weak and the oppressed, was translated in the early days of the

177

revolution into handouts and various forms of assistance with, for instance, housing to selected groups of the urban poor. Radical measures for systematic welfare policies, and for the rights of workers and peasants, have been for the most part blocked or subverted by conservative groups headed by the leading conservative clergy, some in the Council of Guardians. The selective handouts then established networks of patronage and support tied to particular institutions and personnel. The recruitment of bands of militant young men for Hizbollah and other vigilante organisations is, in part, aided by this process. Resources are also channelled to the families of the war dead and wounded. At higher class levels, networks of patronage and allegiance connect the state clergy to bazaar merchants. Disadvantaged under the Shah in relation to other 'modern' businessmen and financiers, some of the bazaar merchants played an important part in the support for the revolution (see Chapter 3). These same supporters were later worried by the radical rhetoric of the revolution and the proposals for land reform and the nationalisation of foreign trade. They shared these fears with their patrons in the conservative factions of the clergy who have been largely successful in blocking these measures, as well as reversing or subverting policies on workers' and tenants' rights (Vali and Zubaida, 1985). These are general 'class' gains. In addition, particular groups of merchants have benefited from business opportunities gained through preferential considerations for import and export licences, which they owe to particular patrons among the state clergy. This leaves many sectors of the bazaar still discontented, especially with the restrictions on business opportunities resulting from the interminable war, and in this too they have support from sections of the political clergy, some of whom advocate an early settlement. It would seem, then, that the clergy and their networks are adapting very well to the logic of the distributive state which we have noted for their Arab neighbours.

The multiplicity of factions and their rivalry would also appear to have its (limited) parallels in the earlier history of some of the Arab states, as in the early days in the 1960s of the Ba'th regimes in Iraq and Syria, for instance. These were ultimately ended by the emergence of one dominant clique by the process of progressive elimination or subordination of the others. This is not an unlikely scenario for the future of the Islamic republic. So far, the war situation as well as Khomeini's restraining influence and authoritative arbitration of intra-regime disputes have prevented serious fights from reaching fatal conclusions. Under different conditions, and after Khomeini, factional fights might very well develop differently, to favour the emergence of a dominant clique which would control and suppress the others, much like the outcomes of similar struggles in the neighbouring states.

These structural similarities should not detract attention from the striking contrast which the Islamic republic presents to all other countries in the region. The institutional differences, government by clergy, the spectacles of popular manifestations, the factional struggles with ramifications into government as well as religious institutions and personnel, the political discourses of disputation, with exotic mixtures of class rhetoric and religious scholasticism; all these and many more elements mark revolutionary Iran as a quite unique phenomenon. But at their own level the structural similarities are important, especially in determining future developments.

Does Islam in revolutionary Iran negate the nation-state model? The indications from the foregoing account are that the Islamic elements of the republic fit in very well with the nation-state model both in terms of state organisation and of the structure of the political field and its discourses. The one Islamic strand that does not fit in is that of the power and the autonomy of the conservative *mujtahids*, notably in the instances of law and taxation cited above. But these powers are at odds with the Islamic republic, and may very well constitute the issues for future confrontations and struggles in the religious institutions and in government.

Conclusions

The foregoing analyses have been conducted in terms of a general political sociology, and the contention throughout has been an advocacy of the value of this form of analysis as against cultural and historical essentialism. I have argued that cultural-historical *specificity* is not compromised by such an approach. Socio-economic and political processes take place within historically and culturally given contexts, but these historical givens exist or are reproduced under particular socio-economic conditions, which do not necessarily guarantee their continuity. The example of the Iranian revolution and the subsequent revolutionary state discussed above are pertinent illustrations. Specifically Iranian-Shi'i cultural elements have played crucial parts in the symbols and events of the revolution, as they have done in previous political conjunctures of modern times. But at each one of these conjunctures they had been constructed anew in accordance with the objectives and strategies of the political forces involved and the situations in relation to which the struggles were waged. In the events surrounding the Tobacco Regie of 1891, religious authority and leadership headed a protest against foreign economic intrusion through the machinations of an unjust prince. These were conditions under which religious forces and leadership had a near monopoly of the political field, and to which secular nationalists could only be minor and subordinate followers. In the Constitutional Revolution of 1906, the religious opposition was speaking a different language, in which religious authority enunciated ideas congruent with the objectives of the modernist intelligentsia for a constitutional state. At that time religious authority shared the leadership of the political field with the secular nationalists. In the struggles of the early 1950s, secular forces dominated the stage, leaving little room for religious ideas and symbols, which were at best marginal to that episode. The Khomeinist opposition, which emerged on the political stage in the agitations of the early 1960s, itself underwent a radical transformation in the years leading up to the revolution of 1979, from forthright opposition to the Shah in the name of religious authority, to the idea of the Islamic Republic and *velayat-e-faqih* displacing princely rule and taking over government power, a complete innovation in Shi'i thought. At each one of these conjunctures, Shi'i ideas and symbols were constructed differently. As we have seen, the conditions generated by the modern state and the modern political field have entered into these constructions in crucial, if sometimes implicit, respects. More important, the salience, then triumph of clerical Islam (by no means the only Islamic contender in the field), is itself the product of political struggles under conditions generated by an autocratic and repressive state, which eliminated organised political forces of opposition, giving religious-clerical institutions and networks a considerable advantage over their rivals under the conditions which favoured revolutionary transformations. We may conclude that this particular element of cultural-historical specificity, Iranian Shi'ism, is subject to radical transformations in relation to prevailing conditions and discourses, and that it is given political significances by the evolution of these conditions and discourses. Its salience and eventual triumph are not the inevitable results of the evolution of some Islamic or Iranian essence, but the product of particular conjunctures, in a situation in which alternative conjunctures and outcomes are easily conceivable. The explanations of these conditions and conjunctures are to be found in social and political analyses following concepts and processes which are common to a general political sociology, applying to 'Islam' as much as to the 'West'.

A momentous event such as that of the Iranian revolution of 1979 comes to occupy a prominent part on the world stage and in the political discourses of that world. The idea, almost axiomatic in recent decades, that progress and modernisation lead inexorably to secularisation, was shattered. The opposite notion, that specific cultural-religious essences persist and ultimately triumph over superficial, imported modernity, came to hold sway. This notion, as we have seen, is active in the thought of some Western observers, but most importantly in the ideologies of the Islamic movements in the region. The ideological significance of the Iranian revolution comes to occupy a central part in the political fields and struggles of the neighbouring countries. Within this framework, the political history of the region is being read backwards, both by the Islamic participants and by many of the Western students and observers of the region. The Islamic forces and episodes of that history are highlighted. Islamic involvement in the formative episodes of that history, however marginal (as in the Mossadeq episode in Iran), are underlined and given great significance. The great political struggles of this century, fought for the most part by non-religious forces, operating with the 'imported' ideologies of nationalism and socialism, are being marginalised as the games of intellectuals unconnected with the popular masses, whose ideas and sentiments have always remained faithful to Islam. The foregoing arguments have examined the validity and significance of these notions, and attempted to unravel the various dimensions of their assumptions. In so doing I have attempted to place Islamic politics in their proper historical and political context.

Notes

1 Whether the feudal state is 'external' to society depends partly on where the state-society boundaries are drawn, in particular, whether the feudal lords are considered to be constituents of that state or subordinate to it. A consideration of these conceptual intricacies and debates on the feudal state are outside the scope of this paper. See Hindess and Hirst, 1975.

2 For an account of Muhammad Ali's rule and modernisation projects, see Marsot, 1984.

3 These themes are scattered in Weber's works. For the most systematic general statement see the Introduction to *The Protestant Ethic and the Spirit of Capitalism*, 1930.

4 This statement of Badie's is interestingly contradicted by Max Weber's characterisation of the Protestant Ethic which places the believer in a state of constant struggle against a world dominated by sin, and attributes the creativity of that ethic to this fact.

5 In fact, Lutheran pronouncements on government show striking similarity to conventional Islamic political thought. Consider this passage from Melancthon, Luther's theological lieutenant, written in 1521:

> The magistrate's administration of the sword [that is the maintenance of secular order] is consonant with piety....If princes command anything contrary to God, this is not to be obeyed....If they command anything arising out of the public interest this must be obeyed....If any of their commands are tyrannical, here too the magistrate is to be suffered for charity's sake in all cases where change is impossible without public commotion and sedition. (Quoted in Elton, 1963, p. 62)

Badie, as we have seen, realises that some of the Reformation ideas go against his general characterisation but in the overall unity and continuity of Western history they do not seem to have any lasting effects.

6 For an interesting example of the analysis of these differences, see Barrington Moore, 1967.

7 This idea, of a regionally based community-state (as against the Jacobin model of the nation state), seems to be quite prevalent in some intellectual quarters in France, especially in the context of regionalist (Mediterranean, Provençal or Occitan) culturo-political sentiments.

8 See, for instance, Kitching, 1982, and Roxborough, 1979.

9 This generalisation must be qualified. In some countries and regions, the boundaries between some cities and nearby country areas are fluid. A notable example is Palestine, where the close proximity of many villages to urban centres has involved them in the politics of those centres. Similar examples can be found in parts of Egypt.

10 For a discussion of the 'petit bourgeoisie', see Chapter 3.

11 See Gallissot, 1986 for an interesting discussion of this process in relation to the Maghreb, and the resulting *ressentiment* as a stimulus for the Islamic appeal to the young.

12 I draw on Jean Leca's (1987) article for some of the arguments and many of the examples in this section.

13 This example should underline the different bases for Islamic politics in the various countries where they occur.

14 For an account of the institutions and politics of revolutionary Iran, see Bakhash, 1985.

References

Abrahamian, E. (1982), *Iran Between Two Revolutions*, Princeton, Princeton University Press.

al-Ansari, H. (1984), 'The Islamic militants in the politics of Egypt', *International Journal of Middle East Studies*, vol. 16, no. 1, pp. 123-44.

Alavi, H. (1982), 'State and class under peripheral capitalism', in H. Alavi and T. Shanin (eds), *Introduction to the Sociology of Developing Societies*, London, Macmillan.

al-Banna, H. (n.d.), *Islah al-Nafs wal Mujtama'* (The Reform of Self and of Society) (Arabic), Cairo.

al-Daywachi, S. (1975), *Taqalid al-zawaj fil Mosul* (Marriage Ceremonies in Mosul) (Arabic), Iraq, Mosul.

Algar, H. (1972), 'The oppositional role of the ulama in twentieth-century Iran' in Nikki K. Keddie (ed.), *Scholars, Saints and Sufis*, Berkeley, California University Press, pp. 231-56.

Algar, H. (1980), *Religion and State in Iran, 1785-1906*, Berkeley, California University Press.

al-Ghazzali, M. (1948), *Min Huna Na'lam* (From Here We Learn), Cairo, Dar al-Kutub al-Haditha.

al-Ghazzali, M. (1951), *al-Islam Wal Manahij al-Ishtirakiyya* (Islam and Socialist Programmes), Cairo, Dar al-Kutub al-Haditha.

Anderson, B. (1983), *Imagined Communities: Reflections of the Origins and Spread of Nationalism*, London, Verso.

Anderson, P. (1974a), *Passages from Antiquity to Feudalism*, London, NLB.

Anderson P. (1974b), *Lineages of the Absolutist State*, London, NLB.

Arberry, A.J. (1964), *The Koran Interpreted*, London, Oxford University Press.

Arjomand, S. A. (1979), 'Religion, political action and legitimate domination in Shi'ite Iran: Fourteenth to eighteenth centuries AD', *Archives Européennes de Sociologie*, vol. 20, no. 1.

Arjomand, S. A. (ed.), (1984), *From Nationalism to Revolutionary Islam*, London, Macmillan.

Badie, B. (1986), *Les deux états: pouvoir et société en occident et en terre d'Islam*, Paris, Fayard.

Baer, Gabriel (1983), 'Islamic political activity in modern Egyptian history: a comparative analysis', in G.R. Warburg, and V.M. Kupferschmidt (eds), *Islam, Nationalism and Radicalism in Egypt and the Sudan*, New York, Praeger.

Bakhash, S. (1985), *The Reign of the Ayatollahs: Iran and the Islamic Revolution*, London, Tauris.

Batatu, Hanna (1978), *The Old Social Classes and the Revolutionary Movements of Iraq*, New Jersey, Princeton University Press.

Beetham, D. (1985), *Max Weber and the Theory of Modern Politics*, Cambridge, Polity Press.

References

Carré, O. (1983), 'The impact of the Muslim Brotherhood's political Islam since the 1950's', In G.R. Warburg and U. M. Kupferschmidt (eds), *Islam, Nationalism and Radicalism in Egypt and the Sudan*, New York, Praeger, pp. 262–80.

Carré, O. (1984), *Mystique et politique*, Paris, Cerf.

Cockcroft, J. D. (1980), 'On the ideological and class character of Iran's anti-imperialist revolution', in Georg Stauth (ed.), *Iran: Pre-Capitalism, Capitalism and Revolution*, Saarbrucken, Verlag Breiterbach.

Davis, E. (1984), 'Ideology, social class and Islamic radicalism in modern Egypt', in S. A. Arjomand (ed.), *From Nationalism to Revolutionary Islam*, London, Macmillan.

Digard, J. P. (1982), 'Shi'ism et État en Iran', in Oliver Carré (ed.), *L'Islam et l'etat*, Paris, Presses Universitaires de France.

Eliash, J. R. (1979), 'Misconceptions regarding the juridical status of the Iranian ulama', *International Journal of Middle East Studies*, vol. 10, 1979, pp. 9–25

Elton, G. R. (1963), *Reformation Europe 1517–1559*, London, Fontana.

Enayat, H. (1982), *Modern Islamic Political Thought*, London, Macmillan.

Encyclopaedia of Islam, New Edition, volume 1, 1960; volume 4, 1978; Leiden and London, Brill.

Farouk-Sluglett, M. and Sluglett, P. (1985), 'From Gang to Elite: the Iraqi Ba'th Party Consolidation of Power, 1968–1975', presented at the World Congress of Political Science, Paris, July.

Fischer, M. M. J. (1980), *Iran: From Religious Dispute to Revolution*, London, Harvard University Press.

Fischer, M. M. J. (1982), 'Islam and the revolt of the petite bourgeoisie', *Daedalus*, vol. 111, no. 1, pp. 101–25.

Floor, W. M. (1980), 'The revolutionary character of the Iranian ulama: wishful thinking or reality?', *International Journal of Middle East Studies*, vol. 12, pp. 501–24.

Gallissot, R. (1986), 'Les limites de la culture nationale: Enjeux culturels et avènement étatique au Maghreb', in J.-R. Henry (ed.), *Nouveau Enjeux Culturels au Maghreb*, Paris, CNRS, pp. 47–56.

Gellner, E. (1983), *Muslim Society*, Cambridge, Cambridge University Press.

Gibb, H. A. R. and Bowen, H. (1950), *Islamic Society and the West*, London, Oxford University Press.

Goitein, S. D. (1967), *A Mediterranean Society: The Jewish Communities of the Arab World as portrayed in the Documents of the Cairo Geniza*, 4 vols, Berkeley and Los Angeles, University of California Press.

von Grunebaum, G. (ed.) (1955), *Unity and Variety in Muslim Civilisation*, Chicago, University of Chicago Press.

von Grunebaum, G. (1970), 'The sources of Islamic civilisation', *The Cambridge History of Islam*, vol. 2, Cambridge, Cambridge University Press.

Habib, J. S. (1978), *Ibn Sa'ud's Warriors of Islam: the Ikhwan of Najd and their Role in the Creation of the Sa'udi Kingdom, 1910–1930*, Leiden, Brill.

References

Hindess, B. (1980), 'Classes and politics in Marxist theory', in G. Littlejohn *et al.* (eds), *Power and the State*, London, Croom Helm.

Hindess, B. and Hirst, P. (1975), *Pre-Capitalist Modes of Production*, London, Routledge & Kegan Paul.

Hobsbawm, E. (1959), *Primitive Rebels*, Manchester, Manchester University Press.

Hourani, A. (1962), *Arabic Thought in the Liberal Age 1798–1939*, Oxford, Oxford University Press.

Hourani, A. (1983), *Arabic Thought in the Liberal Age 1798–1939*, Cambridge, Cambridge University Press.

Ibrahim, A. (1987), 'Consommation et décalages culturels en Egypte', in G. Stauth and S. Zubaida (eds), *Mass Culture, Popular Culture and Social Life in the Middle East*, Frankfurt, Campus Verlag and Boulder, Colorado, Westview Press, pp. 85–136.

Ibrahim, S. E. (1980), 'Anatomy of Egypt's militant Islamic groups: methodological notes and preliminary findings', *International Journal of Middle East Studies*, vol. 12, no. 4, pp. 423–53.

Keddie, N. R. (1966), *Religion and Rebellion in Iran: The Iranian Tobacco Protest of 1891–1892*, London, Cass.

Keddie, N. R. (1972), 'The roots of the ulama's power in modern Iran', in N. R. Keddie (ed.), *Scholars, Saints and Sufis*, Berkeley, Los Angeles and London, University of Chicago Press.

Kepel, G. (1985), *The Prophet and Pharaoh: Muslim Extremism in Egypt*, London, al-Saqi.

Khomeini, Ayatollah (n. d.), *Al-Hukumah Al-Islamiyya: Wilayat Al-Faqih* (Islamic Government) (Arabic), Beirut, Dar al-Tali'ah.

Khoury, P. S. (1983), *Urban Notables and Arab Nationalism: The Politics of Damascus 1860–1920*, Cambridge, Cambridge University Press.

Khoury, P. S. (1984), 'Syrian urban politics in transition: the quarters of Damascus during the French Mandate', *International Journal of Middle East Studies*, vol. 16, no. 4, pp. 507–40.

Kitching. G. (1982), *Development and Underdevelopment in Historical Perspective*, London, Methuen.

Lane, E. W. (1895), *Manners and Customs of the Modern Egyptians* (written in Egypt during the years 1833–1835), The Hague and London, East–West Publications.

Leca, J. (1987), 'Social Structure and Political Stability: Comparative Evidence from the Algerian, Syrian and Iraqi Cases', Paper presented at the Annual Conference of the British Society for Middle East Studies, Exeter.

Lévi-Strauss, C. (1966), *The Savage Mind*, London, Weidenfeld & Nicolson.

Lewis, B. (1984), *The Jews of Islam*, London, Routledge & Kegan Paul.

Lewis, B. (1985), 'The Shi'a', *New York Review of Books*, vol. 32, pp. 7–10.

Maghniyya, M. J. (1979), *Al Khomeini wal Dawla Al-Islamiyya* (Khomeini and the Islamic State) (Arabic), Beirut, Dar al-Ilm li'l Malayin.

Marsot, A. L. (1984), *Egypt in the Reign of Muhammed Ali*, Cambridge, Cambridge University Press.

References

Marx, K. (1958), 'The Eighteenth Brumaire of Louis Napoleon Bonaparte', in Karl Marx and Frederick Engels, *Selected Works*, vol. I, Moscow, Foreign Languages Publishing House, pp. 2343–4.

Mauss, M. (1972), *A General Theory of Magic*, London, Routledge & Kegan Paul.

Mitchell, R. P. (1969), *The Society of Muslim Brothers*, Oxford, Oxford University Press.

Moore, B. (1967), *The Social Origins of Democracy and Dictatorship*, London, Allen Lane.

Patton, W. M. (1897), *Ahmad Ibn Hanbal and the Mihna*, Leiden, Brill.

Plant, R. (1983), *Hegel: An Introduction*, Oxford, Blackwell.

Qutb, S. (1980), *Ma'alim fil Tariq* (Landmarks along the Path), Cairo, Dar al-shuruq.

Rex, J. (1973), *Race, Colonialism and the City*, London, Routledge & Kegan Paul.

Roxborough, I. (1979), *Theories of Underdevelopment*, London, Macmillan.

St John Philby, H. (1968), *Sa'udi Arabia,* Librarie de Liban, Beirut.

Sassoon, D. S. (1949), *A History of the Jews of Baghdad*, Letchworth, Sassoon.

Shari'ati, A. (1974), *Ummat va Imamat* (Persian), n.p.

Shari'ati, A. (1979a), *Red Shi'ism* (translated by Habib Shirazi), Tehran.

Shari'ati, A. (1979b), *On the Sociology of Islam* (translated by Hamid Algar), Mizan Press, Berkeley.

Shari'ati, A. (1980) *Marxism and Other Western Fallacies* (translated by R. Campbell, edited by H. Algar), Mizan Press, Berkeley.

Springborg, R. (1985),*''Infitah*, Agrarian Transformation, and Elite Consolidation in Iraq', paper presented at the World Congress of Political Science, Paris, July.

Stauth, G. and Zubaida, S. (eds.) (1987), *Mass Culture, Popular Culture and Social Life in the Middle East*, Frankfurt, Campus Verlag and Boulder, Colorado, Westview Press

Taymiyya, Ibn (n. d.), *al-Siyasa Al-Shar'iyya* (Arabic), Dar al-Ma'arif, n. p.

Turner, B.S. (1984)*Capitalism and Social Change in the Middle East: Theories of Social Change and Economic Development*, London, Heinemann.

Vali, A. and Zubaida, S. (1985), 'Factionalism and political discourse in the Islamic Republic of Iran: the case of the Hujjatiyeh Society', *Economy and Society*, vol. 14, no. 2, pp. 139–73.

Vatikiotis, P. J. (1983), 'Religion and the State', in G. R. Warburg and U. M. Kupferschmidt (eds), *Islam, Nationalism and Radicalism in Egypt and the Sudan*, New York, Praeger.

Vieille, P. (1984), 'L'état périphérique et son heritagé, *Peuples Mediterranéen*, France.

Warburg, G. R. and Kupferschmidt, U. M. (eds) (1983), *Islam, Nationalism and Radicalism in Egypt and the Sudan*, New York, Praeger.

Watt, W. M. (1973), *The Formative Period of Islamic Thought*, Edinburgh University Press, Edinburgh.

References

Weber, M. (1930), *The Protestant Ethic and the Spirit of Capitalism*, London, Unwin.

Weber, M. (1965), *The Sociology of Religion*, London, Methuen.

Zubaida, S. (1986), 'The city as the location of political thought and action', in K. Brown *et al.* (eds), *Middle Eastern Cities in Comparative Perspective*, London, Ithaca Press. pp. 327–40.

Index